PENGUIN BOOKS

Airhead

Emily Maitlis presents the BBC flagship nightly current affairs show *Newsnight* and specializes in election coverage in the UK and the USA. The Canadian-born, Sheffield-raised, British television presenter and journalist began her career in Hong Kong. She lives in London with one husband, two boys, and a large whippet.

'Revelatory, riveting and frequently hilarious. A joy from beginning to end' – James O'Brien

'A remarkable journey through the jungle of newsmaking. It combines razor-sharp analysis with compelling narrative drive and wit. A must-read' – Matthew D'Ancona

'Smart, funny and brilliantly told stories about what goes on behind the scenes of television news. A joy' – Elizabeth Day

'*Airhead* is, like its author, funny, wise, self-deprecating and insightful' – *You Magazine*

'Smart and *Broadcast News*-funny, *Airhead* is peppered with insider anecdotes you could only pick up working on the big kind of news stories that the journalist has covered for decades – *Daily Telegraph*

'I'm just very disappointed there's only one chapter about me' – Piers Morgan

Airhead

The Imperfect Art of Making News

EMILY MAITLIS

PENGUIN BOOKS

PENGUIN BOOKS

UK | USA | Canada | Ireland | Australia
India | New Zealand | South Africa

Penguin Books is part of the Penguin Random House group of companies
whose addresses can be found at global.penguinrandomhouse.com

First published by Michael Joseph, 2019
This edition published by Penguin Books, 2019

008

Copyright © Emily Maitlis, 2019

The moral right of the author has been asserted

Set in 12.69/15.1 pt Garamond MT Std
Typeset by Jouve (UK), Milton Keynes
Printed and bound in Great Britain by Clays Ltd, Elcograf S.p.A.

A CIP catalogue record for this book is available from the British Library

ISBN: 978-1-405-93834-1

www.greenpenguin.co.uk

For my boys, Milo and Max, who have inspired me
and laughed at me in equal measure.

And for Mark, who agreed to marry me,
and who continues to make every day of my life
better. It was the best question I ever asked.

The first and greatest sin of the deception
of television is that it simplifies; it diminishes
great, complex ideas, stretches of time; whole
careers become reduced to
a single snapshot.

James Reston Jr, *Frost/Nixon*

Contents

CONTENTS

CONTENTS

Introduction: The 2 a.m. Call

My phone is on silent. But it's still managed to wake me up. The yellow flashing glare perhaps or a sort of fuzzing of atoms. It's 2 a.m. and I see on the screen it's my *Newsnight* editor, Ian Katz.

No thanks, I think, and hide it under a book about psychological warfare. It's the heaviest one next to the bed.

Ian has a way of wanting to talk about things at odd hours. He normally catches up on his texts around one in the morning – which is lovely for him, but slightly confusing for everyone else. This time, I'm not in the mood. It's a Friday night in November 2015. I have just stepped off a plane from Washington, after two weeks on the road, reporting. My body doesn't know what continent I'm in or what day it is. I've had a vodka shot and a blue sleeping pill and, frankly, I'm out for the count.

But five hours later, my phone is still ringing from the depths of psychological warfare where it's been buried. And this time it's my deputy editor, Rachel Jupp – her voice sounds both apologetic and pleading. 'We need you to go to Paris.'

I am still asleep, my eyes won't open, my mouth is gluey and stuck. But my mind has raced ahead to the sense of what she's saying, and from nowhere I hear myself weighing up her request, asking the worst question a journalist can ask:

'How many?'

And she tells me more than a hundred are dead – many inside the Bataclan theatre – and several gunmen are still on the loose.

Two hours later, I'm on the Eurostar. My usual grab bag – packed for emergency travel – had just been emptied into the wash, so I've scrabbled together just enough to see me through the next forty-eight hours. Something dignified for on-air reporting. Something warm for all the waiting around. Something waterproof for when the heavens open. A zillion chargers, adapters, cables and three slabs of dark chocolate – for skipped-meal replenishment.

There is a familiarity to this journey. Just ten months earlier I had taken the same Eurostar to cover the *Charlie Hebdo* massacre. Subliminally, I have begun to associate the City of Light with darkness and fear. The Gare du Nord still makes me shake.

This time, scrolling through emails on the train, I find a generic BBC one sent to all those heading to Paris. It tells us to avoid a black licence-plate-free Renault if we see it. They believe it's being used by the terrorists and is packed full of explosives. The email is meant to be helpful, but it makes me burst into tears. I haven't seen my kids for two weeks, I haven't slept more than a few hours in two days, I haven't eaten since the plane, and now I'm being told to avoid black cars. What am I even doing?

Paris isn't really working when I arrive: you can't get a cab, police barricades are up all over, the streets are eerily empty in parts and rammed full in other places where spontaneous vigils have sprung up. We broadcast for an hour – a BBC Two Saturday-afternoon special from outside the Bataclan; we are asking people to give us eyewitness accounts of events they haven't even processed. I find the band U2 leaving flowers beside our live point, their own commemoration of young lives lost in the simple act of attending a concert.

The terrorists have struck when Europe is already feeling fragile; the migrant crisis has brought thousands from the Middle East and Africa – some seeking asylum, others better employment – marching across the continent and making EU politicians assess their own political response to the outsider. That night, as we try and piece together the scale of the tragedy, all sorts of conflicting narratives begin to emerge: that the terrorists were home-grown, or Syrian, or from neighbouring Belgium. That they were ISIS fighting jihad in France, or they were disenfranchised young men betrayed by their treatment as Muslim French citizens. It is too early to know why it's happened. We barely understand what has happened.

Over the weekend, we see the raw Gothic beauty of Notre-Dame reflected in the flickering of a hundred tiny candles of remembrance on the ground. In Place de la République, a shrine has evolved – photos of loved ones, white roses, a lone violinist playing of the pain which has only started to seep into this grieving city. As I cross the square, a French reporter recognizes me and asks if we, the English, are sympathetic. It is such an extraordinary thing to ask I feel my eyes welling up again. Surely we are beyond the Hundred Years' War, the neighbourly rivalry of World Cup penalties. I can't even find the words to tell him that yes, God knows, we are.

By Monday night we – *Newsnight* – are back on air. I have already fronted a *Panorama* report for BBC One and I have interviewed (in French) Rachida Dati, the former French Justice Minister with special focus on migration and counter-terrorism, who blames Angela Merkel for the 'error of judgement' in letting so many people cross into Germany. Now I am standing in front of the camera, microphone on, facing one of the most complicated live shows we will ever attempt. We have seven live guests, three different reports, Gabriel Gatehouse will be live in Greece with those crossing the border and our investigations editor will be live in London with news of what they've learnt. It is ambitious and complicated and we are about two minutes into the live forty-five-minute programme when everything starts to go wrong.

It goes wrong when I suddenly shout 'MIGRANTS!' down the barrel of the camera, without realizing my microphone is faded up. The word comes as such a shock to our investigations editor he yanks his head up and his earpiece pops out. I am standing there looking like a swivel-eyed xenophobe stuck in the middle of

Paris, but I am broadcasting to millions live on telly. And the reason I have just yelled 'Migrants!' out loud, as if seeing a crowd of thousands descend on Place de la République, is because I am trying to warn my producer, Vara, which sequence is coming up next so she can ready the guests and bring them in. I have to be the conduit between the London studio and her as I am the only one who can hear the programme go out. I do not realize at this point my microphone has accidentally been left on. I do not realize my exclamation has come out of nowhere; I do not realize that in homes across the land viewers trying to piece together the horror, grief and pain that has left more than 130 dead in our neighbouring capital will simply see a deranged anchorwoman in the throes of verbal spasm.

But as soon as I do, I also realize that it will almost certainly be the only thing anyone remembers from our fateful broadcast in Paris.

Working in television has thrown up some extraordinary chances. I've been lucky enough to interview two US presidents, the last five UK prime ministers, the world's fastest sprinter, Nobel Prize-winning writers, footballers, billionaires and prisoners. I have covered UK elections that shook the political firmament and presidential elections, announcing the moment Barack Obama and Donald Trump could claim the path to power; I revealed the moment in the Brexit referendum when it became 'highly likely' we had chosen to leave the EU, and I have covered more incidents of terrorism and mass murder than I care to recall. The news cycle these past few years has been relentless. There's been little time to stop and make sense of it all. Each time I appear on screen or interview one of the key players, it leaves a defining moment in my head. But each time, I'm left with the impression that that is all it has been — a moment; because of the pressure and time constraints of live television, much of the context is never fully relayed.

What follows is my attempt to put that right.

Sometimes I'm asked about a particular tone used in an interview, or a question I put in or left out. Sometimes it's about why I dressed in a particular colour or even stood a certain way. And of course there is never the space to explain the background to any of these things. I am, above all, flattered people read so much intention into things that have usually emerged as the result of chaos, mechanical failure, a last-minute let-down, or finger trouble. In other words, for all those looking for conspiracy, it's nearly always cock-up. When people asked why I blurted out 'MIGRANTS!' that day, I didn't really know where to begin.

When I interviewed President Clinton I was allowed to do so only on condition of an extraordinary deal we had made with his team that morning. You'll understand why when you read that chapter. I never expected to have to provide Donald Trump with my home address, I never expected to have just ten minutes' notice before interviewing the British prime minister, I never expected to end up in a room full of male strippers talking about the Me Too movement, I never expected to be drinking red wine at Steve Bannon's kitchen table, I never expected to spend a bank-holiday Monday stuck in a lift with Alan Partridge or to meet the Dalai Lama at the Prestige Suite of an airport hotel, I never expected to feel empathy for a white woman who thought she was black, and I certainly never expected to be surrounded by twenty thousand Hong Kong students chanting, '*Thank you, BBC*' in unison when we turned up to cover the umbrella democracy protests one long, humid summer (we had to shush them before our filming was ruined).

In other words, there was much that was never conveyed through the interviews we showed on tape. Unlike print there is no room for annotation or commentary as you go along. What appears on the screen is what people see. Everything else is just interpretation.

When I chose the title of this book – *Airhead* – I did so with some trepidation. It is not my intention to reduce what I do to the cliché of a TV broadcaster with an empty brain; it is my attempt to invert it. To explore the broadcaster's state of mind in those moments before, during and after the cameras roll: what happens when things don't go according to plan but your mouth has to keep on moving; what happens when your reputation stands or falls on how you phrase your very next question. What happens when the camera stops rolling and the shouting in the room starts. What happens when you wake up in the dead of night, shouting, '*No, no, no!*', reliving a cringeworthy TV exchange of your own making.

This, then – *Airhead* – is my attempt to explain what goes on in those moments of utter panic: living, breathing, hyperventilating and overthinking the seconds when you're about to go live on air – and you don't have a clue how it will turn out.

Donald Trump and Miss USA

Six years before he became President of the United States, Donald Trump agreed to make a documentary with me for the BBC. I interviewed him four or five times, as well as each of his grown-up children (Don Jr, Ivanka and Eric) and his wife, Melania. I met Donald Trump on his home turf, in Trump Towers New York and Las Vegas, and on his golf course in Aberdeen, and what strikes me when I see him now is how little he has changed since those days. The girth is broader, the words come slower but the character was already set in stone. The question I never asked him at the time was whether he would ever run for president, a journalistic omission that has given me (as you can imagine) many a pause for thought. But, in truth, my bigger regret is that I never called him out on the lies he told. I shrugged, let them pass, put them down to an exuberant personality. 'Celebrity exaggeration'. I wonder now how I could have been so relaxed about the truth. That, in all honesty, should be the cause of more of my sleepless nights.

For our first-ever meeting I am summoned to the twenty-sixth floor of Trump Tower. I take the golden escalator – passing the queues of visitors who've come to marvel at the gushing fountains in his rose marble atrium – then the lift, until I am in the more clinical business part of the building. I wait, flipping through magazines, until our appointed time, and I hear him before I see him. He grabs my hand, a proper macho handshake, and when I comment on his reported 'germophobia' he explains it with a casual flap of the wrist: 'Oh, I'll shake hands with you – you're fine. It's *them* I worry about.' Them being the general public. Or, as we will come to know them, the voters.

Our first meeting is about his business, New York real estate, and his deals. It is the meeting in which he tells me he has 'the biggest ballroom in New York'. It is an odd boast, and one that will not make the slightest bit of difference to the documentary. But I check it out anyway and discover it's wrong. There are other hotels with larger ballrooms. And I have a choice: I can correct him, sound fussy over something that is in any case quite esoteric, or I can make a mental note and move on, assuming it is just a manner of speech – like a stutter. At the time, it seems unimportant. Journalistic pedantry. I do not want to mess with billionaire ballroom machismo. My producer and I make the decision to leave him uncorrected; the line itself will never make the final cut anyway.

But the verbal sleight of hand continues. He can 'dictate' the number of floors in his skyscrapers by merely numbering them however he chooses. There is no illegality in this. It is a mere trick of speech. If you choose to call your first floor your sixteenth floor, you create the impression of many more storeys. I am not familiar enough with architectural exaggeration to know whether this is 'a thing'.

I now realize, of course, it had nothing whatsoever to do with architecture and everything to do with Trump.

We get what we want that afternoon: an introduction to this larger-than-life man, in his office, surrounded by photos of, well, himself. And as the interview wraps up we get what we *really* want.

'You must come to Vegas,' he throws out, an invitation that will be impossible to resist. I am invited to join him at the finals of the beauty pageant he owns: Miss USA. It will be my second and perhaps most curious encounter with the man who will go on to become America's forty-fifth president.

The finals are held in Planet Hollywood, Las Vegas, two months later, and we will attend the dress rehearsal the day before to get a feel for what to film and an interview with Trump, *in situ*, who this year will not be officially judging but will still be in charge. As we watch him arrive, by limo, an old line from a Simon Le Bon interview creeps into my head. When asked once why pop stars always seemed to end up marrying models he had referenced the joke about why dogs lick their balls: 'It's because they can.' It seems to explain so much about Donald Trump. The fortune, the skyscrapers, the hotels, the golf courses, the private jet and the third model wife.

Why would he choose to buy a beauty pageant? Because he can. It is vintage 1980s gold-tap, fluffy-loo-seat Trump.

We arrive at the auditorium in time for the warm-up – the opening dance routine of the show. The finalists are learning their steps to Kelly Rowland's song 'Commander'. Who could have imagined the celestial irony of that moment: scantily clad women dancing under the watchful gaze of Donald Trump as lyrics warn them that he'll be their 'commander' and he'll supply the 'answer'.

There are fifty-one contestants in the beauty pageant, one for each state, plus the District of Columbia, all vying for individual recognition whilst synchronized in step. We can only wonder how seminal this moment is to Trump's understanding of the Electoral College system.

One of them, Miss Michigan, has a quote emblazoned on her chest: 'It's beauty that captures your attention, personality that captures your heart.' She's had the motto printed on a stack of T-shirts which she's now handing out free to fans.

A bold guess tells me they probably didn't come for her personality. But the curious thing is that, for all my scepticism, she is actually the one to leave an impression on me straightaway.

It is not her beauty that captures me, or even her merchandise. It is the fact that during the rehearsal she strides up to the microphone, in the centre of the stage, and addresses Donald Trump directly as he sits in the first row of the auditorium.

'Hello, boss,' she purrs, eyeballing him. 'Hire me!'

As an opening gambit to a man best known (at that point) for the TV reality show *The Apprentice*, it is hardly ground-breaking. But the bustle of a two-thousand-seater stadium suddenly goes quiet; Miss Michigan has done the unthinkable: she is the only contestant to break the rules by addressing the businessman directly.

Later that afternoon, I get my time alone with Donald Trump and I make a mental note to ask him about her. It is the first time I have been on my own with him since our interview in Trump Tower, New York. We have vanished backstage to a green room with mirrors surrounded by light bulbs on every wall. Donald Trump catches sight of his reflection, tugs at the architectural enigma that is his hair, and demands hairspray.

There is a flurry of movement from three assistants. They each head off in a different direction in search of shiny gold Elnett cans. Each will return minutes later, triumphant, and he will reach out, gratified, for the priapic container.

He begins by asking *me* which one of 'the girls' I am most impressed with, which momentarily floors me. Actually, I do have a soft spot for Miss Maine, because she reminds me of my first Pippa doll and I have the urge to scissor her legs into the splits and then pop her on a plastic horse and make clicking noises whilst I gallop her off, but I don't tell him that. Instead, I say Miss Michigan – she of the 'Hello, boss' – because she is actually the only other one I remember. He nods immediately with recognition. So hats off to the guy for remembering their names. I mean states.

'She was *very* aggressive,' he begins. 'It'll be interesting to see whether that aggression works. Will people like that kind of aggression – because she's a very aggressive girl – or will they not?'

Really? I think to myself. *That* aggressive? Because I don't remember her head-butting anyone. I just remember her saying hello. Perhaps in Trump language 'aggressive' is a compliment. Anyway, it's irrelevant, he insists. He will not be judging. This year, the task falls to Melania. She will be one of the celebrity judges to decide which contestant gets to live for twelve months in Trump Tower – yes, a mere lift ride away from the Trump family themselves. It is hard to know whether a year from now the winner will be running the UN or bringing the next can of hairspray.

This pageant is such unfamiliar territory I begin to look into the rules that govern it. The contestants must not be married, or have had a marriage annulled, or have ever given birth to a child. The title-holders are asked to remain single throughout their reign. They are demanded, in other words, to walk the line somewhere between virginal baby and sassy chick – a sort of fairy that sits at the top of the Christmas tree but can never be touched. I can't even work out if they're allowed to have sex – an observation I put to Trump.

There is a rare flicker of a smile as he responds with

tender deliberation and tells me he's never been asked the question quite like that.

'They are very high-quality people – very high-quality women. As to whether or not they sleep around, I can't tell you.'

It is a line that will return to haunt me years later when, weeks before his election, a tape emerges that reveals him talking about fame enabling him to grope women and – the now notorious line – grab them 'by the pussy'. 'It's like a magnet,' the voice on the tape goes on. 'When you're a star they let you do it. You can do anything.' This from the man who freely admitted to walking into beauty-pageant changing rooms without knocking.

For the record (lawyers!) I saw no malfeasance from him then. But I may have come close to understanding the mindset that tells you you are master of all you survey. A bikini fiefdom, with King Donald. 'You can do anything' could be a California bumper sticker. Or an admission of boundary-free behaviour.

When I put to him that the beauty-pageant model feels like a washed-up anachronism from the 1970s (I remember watching them in the front room with my nan, boiled sweets at the ready for a fine night in) he tells me, 'It's the most watched show anywhere in the world on TV.'

We're back into ballroom territory again. I am almost a hundred per cent certain that this is not correct. There are World Cup finals, general elections, Super Bowls and space travel. But I have no proof it's not true. Maybe Southeast Asian markets love it. Maybe it's default Saturday-night viewing for Indonesia. So I leave it, recognizing there is in fact nothing to stop him repeating it if he likes.

'Beautiful women attract eyeballs,' he tells me. I think he might be talking about ratings again but it sounds a bit creepy so I leave it there.

I ask him what made him want to own the beauty pageant.

'When I bought the business,' he explains, 'it was a sick puppy. It was almost off the air – and now we're doing better than ever.' He is so matter of fact talking the mechanics of company profit, yet I sense he relishes this kind of commander control – holding beautiful women's fortunes in his palm.

After our encounter I leave the Planet Hollywood casino darkness for the thick bright light of a late-summer evening. It is my first time in Vegas – a land of excess and self-invention. It is dotted with places trying to look like other places: Paris, Venice, London. A bright blue sky that is actually a ceiling. Appearances, it says, can become reality if you convince enough people.

And then twenty-four hours later we are back in the betting-parlour gloom: the auditorium of Planet Hollywood. It's time for the finale – and our backstage encounter with the boss and his winners.

We take our seats a couple of rows behind Donald Trump. And prepare for a night of shininess.

The lights go down at 4 p.m. prompt; the show will be beamed live across two time zones in America, hitting the East Coast at prime time.

First up on stage is Trump himself. 'This is the most talked-about event of the week!' he claims, superlatives at the ready. It is the same week which has seen outrage at the large-scale environmental catastrophe in the Gulf of Mexico caused by the BP oil spill. But to enter into the spirit, I am prepared to believe, for the next two hours only, this show is more important.

After he sits down, the women are introduced alphabetically – that is, by state. Misses Alabama, Alaska, Arizona and Arkansas are up first.

A shimmy of gold and silver lamé enters the stage. They look highly confident and highly flammable. When all fifty-one are assembled they begin their routine. As they dance, an American TV voiceover tells us little-known facts about them.

'MISS A A A A A Alabama! Audrey Moore is a talented air guitarist! She'll rrrrrock your socks off.'

'Miss Alaska is an AU PAIR! She makes grrrreat peanut butter and jelly sandwiches!'

(I wonder which parent did that job interview.)

'Miss Tennessee says she may be thin, but she LOVES M&Ms. She once ate THREE POUNDS in ONE SITTING!'

There is also a moment when the contestants themselves tell us what they're wearing and describe the colour of their evening gowns as they parade around the stage. I can only assume this is for the small minority that prefer their beauty pageants on the radio. The political minx in me wonders if this will yield the mixed outcome of a Nixon/Kennedy presidential debate ('Those watching TV called it for Miss Wyoming, but those gathered around the wireless were utterly convinced by Miss Hawaii . . .').

The fifty-one are whittled down to a list of fifteen and, eventually, five. But this is where it gets complicated. To prove the contest is not merely cosmetic, each contestant will answer one question from five judges. The place falls silent as five bits of paper are thrown into a goldfish bowl. It is meant to represent the lack of privacy the winner will face for the next year. And this is the moment, I have to admit, when all my beauty-pageant preconceptions are hurled five floors out of the window. The first question is from the comedy actor Oscar Nunez, aimed at Miss Oklahoma.

'Arizona's new immigration statute authorizes law-enforcement agencies to check the immigration status of anyone they believe may be in the country illegally. Critics say this may amount to racial profiling. Do you think this should be mandated by the state or federal government?'

Hang on? What happened there? Did I just walk back into *Newsnight*? Or the Supreme Court? Is Miss Oklahoma secretly a district prosecutor? I am trembling for her as I imagine the worst. But this beauty queen doesn't miss a beat. She begins by praising the power of the state over federal government (loud cheers), acknowledges the twin difficulties of illegal immigration and racial profiling. And then she shuts up. Which is possibly the cleverest bit of all.

The other questions aren't much easier. Miss Virginia is asked if BP should pay for the total damages caused by the oil spill even if it costs American jobs; Miss Michigan is asked whether the pill should be paid for by health insurance – a question that has been keeping conservative America awake since Carl Djerassi first walked into his chemistry lab and invented oral contraception. Without so much as a pause or a glance, she declares it should. And then goes on to win the competition.

After the glitter has descended from the ceiling and the balloons have floated upwards to meet it, I am invited up on stage with the winners. I am roundly embraced by Donald Trump, although I'm not sure why. Miss Michigan is now Miss USA 2010 and she is given a tiara and holds a spontaneous news conference, admitting the first thing she's going to do with her new-found title is eat pizza.

As the cameras flash around us I remind her of her 'Hello, boss' line and whether she thinks that sealed the deal. What I get back is far more than I had imagined. She tells me the entire reason she went into her business major at college was because of Donald Trump. How she sold her car to pay for her registration to the pageant. How she grew up in New York and read about him every day and teared up when she saw him on stage, how it would have been unthinkable for her not to have approached her 'god'. I decide not to mention he had virtually described her as Rambo's twin sister.

The contest now at an end, we emerge, blinking, into the sunlight after three hours of neon darkness.

There is a new Miss USA. She is Lebanese-American. She is gracious and beautiful and articulate. She will be feted for a year and given the Trump Tower apartment. The woman who sacrificed her old banger will now be flown everywhere first class. The American dream has come true. I will look back on her words years later when Trump is on the cusp of power and realize that she epitomized the kind of people who were buying his vision even then. She is the first-ever Muslim winner of the competition. And just a few years later, she will change her religion to Christianity. A curious omen, perhaps, of how Trump will change America.

It is another two months before I will meet Trump again. This time we are invited to Scotland, where he is trying to construct a golf course on the Menie dunes, high above Aberdeen. It is a billion-pound investment encompassing two courses, a luxury hotel, a clubhouse and smart new houses. For residents who see the project in terms of cash and jobs, Trump has become something of a hero. And a highly visible one too – his helicopter lands to the sound of two Scots pipers wearing bright red kilts. These will be his outriders for the visit.

But there are some locals who want to meet Donald Trump for a whole host of different reasons. Michael Forbes is one.

'If I thought he was coming down here,' he tells us, 'I'd buy a shotgun and he'd get a load of buckshot up his arse.' Michael Forbes owns a house on the dunes and has lived there for decades. If Donald Trump gets his way, Forbes will be moved on – so the place can be developed without obstruction. There is no love lost between these two. Indeed, it's got intensely personal of late. Trump – never one to take the diplomatic route in areas of confrontation – tells me he's doing them all a favour.

'His property is a SLUM. In the United States we would call it a slum. When you have tractors rotting and rusting into this beautiful sand, oil tanks that are leaking . . . I think someone should do something about it.'

Suddenly the billionaire developer is painting himself as the environmentalist who's come to save Scotland. It is, in its own way, a touch of genius. And it is pure Donald Trump.

It is in this context, up on the dunes of Menie, the putative golf course, that I have my third encounter. It is a windy Aberdeen day – I remember fearing for his hair on camera – Mother Nature curating a perfect storm from which even three hairspray-wielding assistants would struggle to deliver him. And we have set up the shot overlooking the sea, high on the crest of a hill. I am trying to understand how popular the proposed golf course is amongst locals and he keeps quoting a survey at me that shows more than 70 per cent approve of it. He may be right – and I am prepared to believe he is – but I ask him to show me the survey he keeps referencing. He can't. He quotes it without seeming to have any idea where it comes from, and when I ask who commissioned it, or where I can see it, how I can better understand it, he gets annoyed. Finally, he throws off his lapel mic and stomps off ('We're done here'). I am left awkwardly at the top of the hill, watching his back as he descends, realizing this will be the last I see of him before the documentary airs.

A week after it does, I receive a call from his office demanding my home address. 'DON'T GIVE IT TO THEM!' screams my husband. 'IT'S PROBABLY A WRIT. HE'S SUING.' But within a month a parcel has arrived on my desk. It is a photograph of him and me together; he's signed it. Effusively. In gold Sharpie pen. The bad mood, it seems, has been forgotten. One grudge he has been able to leave behind.

It will be another five years until we meet again, this time on the US presidential campaign trail. It's Veterans Day, 2015, and we are in the key swing state of New Hampshire. Veterans are his most loyal constituency. And they have paid and queued to come to breakfast at the Radisson Hotel in Manchester, New Hampshire.

I remember wearing a military-style coat that day (navy, double-breasted, gold buttons) and I can't work out if I was trying to fit in or stand out. Either way, he catches my eye as he enters the room (a *ballroom*, as luck would have it). I get from him a broad smile of recognition and a shoulder squeeze (the Trump handshake has not yet entered the realms of the viral meme), and I elicit the promise of a question or two with him after the speeches. When our time comes I decide the best chance of a serious answer is to ask a question that takes him seriously. Given that we are exactly a year away from the presidential election, I ask him what he intends to do on his first day in the White House. At this point, it seems a fantastical proposition – at least to the professional commentariat. No one will believe Donald Trump can *actually* become the next president until his victory socks us in the jaw twelve months later.

He turns his full attention to me as he answers: 'So many things you won't believe it,' he says. He doesn't enumerate at that stage. But then he goes on to explain how popular he is and how good his TV ratings are. 'So is it policy or poll numbers that you care about?' I ask. 'It's both!' he shouts. And disappears to sign books and red 'Make America Great Again' baseball caps.

This is a man who believes his key weapon is being DJT. His art form – euphemistically called 'the power of positive thinking' – is, when reduced to the sum of its parts, to make things true by saying them.

I will replay his responses that day many times – both in my head and on television when he wins a year later. He has lied to me about the ballroom. Confused me with the height of his skyscrapers. Fudged his own environmental statistics. In Trump's world everything is a bit bigger, taller, shinier than it really is. This, then, was my first encounter with Donald Trump's hazy relationship with the truth. It was all there before me in black and white. And I had chosen to laugh it off.

How I Got into Television by Not Speaking Chinese

There are lots of long explanations as to why or how I became a journalist, but the simplest and shortest is perhaps this one. I went for two jobs on the same day whilst I was living in Hong Kong.

My first interview was for a PR job. The gent who interviewed me was American, expansive, square-jawed and oddly formal in that way American gents are. His name might even have been Hank.

I had put on my CV that I was learning Mandarin. He opened with the greeting *'Ni hao!'* ('Hello!') – the simplest phrase there is. Literally the words a Chinese Dora the Explorer would use to encourage four-year-olds. I returned a blank stare. I guess in my class we had started with characters and grammar structure rather than conversation. As a result, he didn't believe another word I said and I didn't get the job.

The second job I went for was in radio news bulletins. I didn't mention the Chinese and they didn't ask. I got that one.

Simon Cowell: The Vampire Hour

Let me start with an admission: I am predisposed to like Simon Cowell before I even enter his office. He has arranged the interview for late afternoon because he keeps what he calls 'vampire hours'. When I hear this, I cheer silently. No orange-juicy breakfast meeting in a boardroom then, no fake early-morning jollity followed by a snap departure. This is a man who goes to bed at five thirty in the morning and only starts the serious work of the day around 3 p.m. We will be fine.

The last time I met Simon Cowell was at a *GQ* dinner in the Dorchester some years previously. He sat opposite me and asked me to explain the then current parliamentary issue of the day: the row over the forty-two-day detention period of terror suspects. I was a few drinks in and, to my eternal shame, I took him at his word, and I did. In some depth. The bluestocking bore with a celebrity hostage. He listened intently and asked polite questions and I – riveted by my own voice – held this media mogul in a conversational hijack. I learnt something very interesting about Cowell that night too. He is excellent at making other people feel important.

This time, I find him in the west London office of his company, Syco. It looks more like a Four Seasons spa resort. Soft suedes and chic leathers in the kind of colours that interior designers call taupe, ecru, mink and stone. When I enter the room he comes to greet me with a peck on the cheek. At least I think he does, but maybe it was I who initiated the kiss. It is a thought that leaves a cringing burn between my eyes and will haunt me through at least the first ten minutes of the interview.

He is shorter in real life: a trim figure in unremarkable clothes. His skin is smooth and his voice is cool. He is not particularly handsome but he is attentive, with what I will come to understand as his trademark impeccable politeness.

He lights up almost immediately. I do a double take as I suddenly realize I have not seen anyone smoke indoors (outside Russia) for about five years. He offers me one – a menthol Kool – and his aura of power is such that I *almost* say yes before remembering I do not smoke.

There are a lot of things to ask Simon Cowell. I want to hear about the latest series of *Britain's Got Talent* and *The X Factor*, I want to know about Cheryl and Dannii and Sharon and Britney. I want to know what he really thought of his recently published biography. Instead, I blurt out, 'I read you were looking for a wife. You're not, are you?'

His reply is cautious. 'I am not actively looking for a wife, no.'

And so we talk about what Facebook might call his relationship status and his approach to the women he has dated.

'I'm happy single, and when I'm in relationships as well. I tend to be in a relationship more than being single. Terri lasted six years, Mezhgan lasted two years, and that was in a nine-year block so I was only single for about a year out of those nine years . . . but I'm very good on my own (*a*) because I never get bored and (*b*) because there is always something I need to catch up on – or actually just think.' He has answered the question by seamlessly moving it on to a more comfortable topic. And he is clearly much happier talking about his work. Well, aren't we all?

I ask him why he is still so close to his exes. It is one of the things I find most unusual about the Simon Cowell I have read about. He remains attached or indebted to the women he has, well, fired.

'They do seem to get on well. Yes, Sinitta and Mezhgan were on holiday with me this year. They have never spent much time together but they got really close.'

'Don't you think that's odd?' I press. 'I mean, it's unusual, isn't it?'

But he tells me it's the reverse. He rarely ends acrimoniously – by his own admission, he is a good 'breaker-upper'. Indeed, he is renowned as a rather generous jilter, sometimes throwing a house into the equation as well.

His business head is harder, of course. When we meet, the first few shows of *Food Glorious Food* have just got the TV critics going – the tabloid word here might be 'panned'. I ask him what he thought of the viewing figures.

'Disappointing,' he says. 'We would have liked another million. What's frustrating – and it's both a blessing and a curse – is that if you are well known, your shows get publicized, which is great. But if the figures aren't quite what people are expecting, I get slaughtered.'

He points out that the show still got 2.6 million viewers, a number many prime-time shows could only dream of, and sounds annoyed that so much is made of his ratings in the press. 'Seriously, I've had times where numbers have gone down by one per cent and the headline is "*X Factor* Figures Down".' I point out that if he didn't want to be judged on ratings, surely he wouldn't leap into America predicting what they would be on his shows. But since we are now on to *The X Factor* and since he has brought it up, I ask him what went wrong last season. And he is beautifully and bluntly candid.

'The format is ten years old and any format that has lasted that long, if you want the figures to have a chance of going up, you have to change the format – because the inevitable result is, if you don't, they will go down.'

What's changing? He can't say. The environment is 'too competitive out there'. He tells me the basic formula will stay intact, but he will change 'every aspect of the show in some particular way. It will look like a slightly different show to one you have seen before.'

Is that, I ask, because he recognizes it's getting boring? And, again, it's an impressively no-holds-barred response: 'When the numbers go down, regardless of the excuses people come up with – time shifting or whatever – for me it's that they don't like the show as much as they did. My job is to try and make the show better than it was two or three years ago.' The mathematics of his statement are eyewateringly simple.

He admits there has been too much emphasis on the judges and not enough on the contestants. And I cannot stop the jaded cynic inside me wondering what kind of backstories is he looking for now – how vulnerable or screwed up or unhappy will the next kids have to be?

'Er . . .' He pauses. 'I wouldn't put it quite that way. I would say that you have got to find contestants who are interesting people, that's for sure.' He denies that it is the troubled contestants people want to watch and insists it's the Stacey Solomons and the Leona Lewises – people who don't take themselves too seriously – that we root for.

'Does it ever get to you,' I ask, 'that level of discomfort where you think you're playing with people's lives here?'

He sighs. And I'm not quite sure whether it's because the question troubles him or frustrates him.

'It happens on every show you make. There is a moment where you feel uncomfortable but then you look at things with perspective, and the truth is, over the years, the show has benefited a lot of people's lives who wouldn't have had an opportunity.' It's a good spiel. And I can tell that he is uncomfortable in a pseudo Mother Teresa role. He makes no bones about his commercial interests – the reason he makes the shows. And he will be the first to admit he's not driven by a messianic yearning for the betterment of mankind.

'When you pick your judges,' I ask, 'are they basically women you fancy?'

He gives his first real laugh. 'A lot of them, yes, I'm not going to lie.' Was he madly in love with Cheryl? 'I think my entire production staff – including a lot of gay people who were working on the show – were madly in love with Cheryl Cole.' It is a prime-time Cowell response: an answer to a slightly different question.

So does it bother him when people say he's gay – or ask when he's going to come out?

'If I was living two hundred years ago in a coal mine, maybe, but I work in possibly the gayest industry in the world. Music and TV. It would make absolutely no difference to my life or my career if I was. A lot of my friends are gay but I don't even think that way any more.' (Wait – has he just fed me the 'some of my best friends are gay' line? I think he has, but I get what he means.)

He describes the falling-out with Cheryl Cole over the American show as a time when he became 'public enemy number one – she didn't like me very much' – but says they have made it up now and, 'It's almost back to where we were.'

Cowell divides his time these days between London and Los Angeles and says he feels at home in both. His fitness regime certainly sounds as if it owes more to

Hollywood than Hammersmith. I've read, I tell him, that he does five hundred press-ups a day, has vitamin jabs, colonic irrigation, Botox . . .

'It's all true,' he confirms. 'I mean, not five hundred push-ups, but I work out three or four times a week, I have Botox, take tons of vitamins and vitamin infusions – if you believe that these things work, you will feel better.' It's an interesting admission of quackery for such a hard-nosed businessman. His luxuries – he's happy to admit – are fast cars and lemon bath milk. But does he know what he's worth?

'Yes.' A one-word reply. So I hazard a guess: three hundred million. (OK, not a pure guess; I've read it somewhere.)

'Well, I wouldn't actually like to put a figure on it. I mean . . . It's quite a lot.'

Is that because it fundamentally embarrasses him still? I am trying to work out if the boy from London is still more English at heart than American.

'I'm not embarrassed about it, I think it's – I don't feel comfortable saying what I've got. It's not something I would ever have that conversation about.'

So yes, embarrassed then.

I ask him what hits him when he returns to the UK. What does he think is going wrong here in terms of getting the country to work? And he launches unapologetically into a diatribe about the importance of training apprenticeships, 'one hundred per cent apprenticeships – I don't think we do that enough.'

A curious response, I point out, for someone like him to talk about the benefits of patience, of learning a trade, whilst creating shows based on instant fame and gratification.

'Well, yes, I think there is a certain irony to it – I agree with you. The juxtaposition to that is someone like Susan Boyle who, without *Britain's Got Talent*, would still be sitting in that house having people throw stones at her door.'

Ha! I *knew* he wouldn't be able to get through a whole interview without mentioning Susan Boyle. We don't dwell on her mental health. But I ask about his.

There was a time last year when he famously switched off his phone for two months. So was he a nervous wreck?

'It was BLISS. I went through a phase – I can't remember what actually happened – it was probably just one unpleasant text message too many but I thought, This is going off for a day. And then it got to two days, then a week . . .' He talks like a recovering alcoholic. And lets slip he has two phones, not one. But he is a man who has learnt to shut himself off when he needs to, as he would put it, just think.

And then the interview is over. We have photos taken and I am still wondering if I have tried hard enough to guess who his next celebrity judge on the show will be. When I start asking if it's Pudsey the dancing dog I think we all realize it is time for me to go.

This time, he comes towards me. A farewell kiss on

the cheek that frees me of my earlier pain – nothing if
not impeccably polite. As I leave the building I glance at
my watch: 6 p.m.; the rush-hour traffic is building. His
vampire day is just beginning.

Two Days with President Clinton

The first time I see the president in the flesh, the thing I notice is how little flesh there now is. He is wearing a primrose-yellow polo shirt, beige 'sightseeing' pants and soft sports shoes. From the back, he could be a regular, slightly frail American tourist. Then he turns around, and I get the Bill Clinton pierce: the blue eyes and the fixed gaze that I have heard so much about.

I used to assume it was hype. Now I know it's not.

We are in a bakery and it is, without doubt, the hottest place I have ever been. The kind of heat that is unbreathable.

It is Jaipur, India; it is mid-July. It feels like an oven. And then I see that's because it actually is an oven. A giant machine is spouting forth freshly made chapatis with comedic regularity.

If he's feeling the heat, he isn't showing it. He's getting the guided tour from the monk who runs the project – part of the Clinton Global Initiative on health and education. This project provides free school lunches to Indian school kids to encourage them to attend. We – my cameraman Tony, producer Vara and I – have been invited to spend two days watching its work around

Rajasthan with the promise of a sit-down interview at the end if we behave.

The president has a garland of jasmine around his neck and looks genuinely delighted to find himself in the hottest place on earth. And I start to believe what I have heard so often: that he is at his happiest when out mingling, campaigning, meeting people on the street.

He looks older these days – because of a triple heart bypass – and is thinner too. Much of that is down to his daughter who, I've heard, persuaded him on to a radical diet around the time of her wedding.

'What's with the vegan thing – is it true?' I ask his minder. Or perhaps he's my minder – we've yet to establish. And the guy laughs.

'Damned if you do, damned if you don't,' he replies. He explains he doesn't know how to answer that: 'President Clinton is mostly vegan but eats a bit of fish. If we describe him as vegan, then he looks hypocritical when he strays, but if we don't, then the vegans jump up and down asking why we're not promoting the most powerful role model they could dream of.'

It is a description of the president I am mulling over in my mind. A description of a man who has not held political office for nearly two decades, but whose standing with the American people is, when we meet in 2014, higher than that of any other living president: a 'favourability rating' of 63 per cent.

He is passionate about his not-for-profit work but, as

I am to see later, the time he really lights up is when he's talking pure geopolitics – and America's future.

That evening, after the bakery, and the school kids and the rows of waving local faces lining the streets to watch the presidential convoy pass, I am invited to have dinner with Bill Clinton. We are to visit the Amer Fort of Jaipur as the sun is setting. It is exquisite, romantic – a maharaja's pink palace set high on a hill within a walled citadel. The convoy feels like something out of an E. M. Forster novel. Our small party rattles around in the silence – we have the place entirely to ourselves.

We are taken to see the maharani's bedroom – tiny convex mirrors on every curved wall. The president is enchanted and leans over to me, showing me the patterns a single candle can make dancing on the ceiling as it catches the light. Inside, I can feel the bubbling of a giggle. I am suddenly aware of Bill Clinton showing me the mirrors on the ceiling of a princess's boudoir. It is more elegant, more erudite, than that, of course, but my brain has momentarily reduced it to that perfect tabloid headline.

Out in the open, we discuss the Mogul, Mongol and Ottoman empires. As you do. He begins an animated defence of Genghis Khan, explaining to me – and here I can finally admit I know nothing of dear Genghis – that his foreign policy was extraordinary.

'He conquered their lands but left people in peace, didn't make them fight for him and didn't over-tax them.'

I wonder if I'm meant to be reading a blueprint for

US foreign policy in there somewhere. But it seems a little ambitious.

As the sun sets, we dine in the palace. There are around twenty-five of us: Team Clinton, Team BBC (the three of us) and then some fundraisers, donors, doctors and locals, who have all played a part in bringing Clinton here. I barely remember the food, but I recall it being good, Indian vegetarian. No alcohol is served.

We head back to the hotel – we have barely slept for reasons that will shortly become clear – and decide to grab a nightcap in the bar. It is next to a rather plush gift shop and, although I feel uneasy perusing high-end luxury items during a guided tour of India's most impoverished, a rather beautiful cashmere pashmina has, unfortunately, caught my eye. I am trying on the offending item when who should walk into the gift shop but the president himself. I am so mortified to be caught shopping that I wrap the thing entirely around my head so I am unrecognizable. Then I watch. He, of course, does not go for the cashmere. Nor the knick-knacks. No Taj Mahal lighter for him. No, Bill Clinton goes straight for the book section. My embarrassment deepens as I assume *his* foray into the gift shop will yield a new understanding of Mogul India, or Fortress Jaipur. But I am wrong.

As I glance down at the book in his hand – heavily decorated, beautifully illustrated and somehow familiar – I realize it is, in fact, the *Kama Sutra*.

It is time for a discreet exit.

*

The next day, we are on his private jet first thing, leaving Jaipur for Lucknow, then heading deep into rural India to hear him spread the word on clean water and HIV/AIDS, and on the rights of women here. It is a scene of colourful chaos. Goats and water buffalo sweep alongside the presidential motorcade, the villages are mud, the children climb trees to sneak a look at the president. Large banners welcome him at every corner, as if he's standing for election to be the local mayor.

It is here, amongst the flies, the mud, the technicoloured saris and the wild-growing cannabis that supports a sign reading 'Welcome, Mr President', that we are to have our formal on-camera interview. I have waited two days for this. Or perhaps it's fairer to say I've waited twenty years and two days for this. It will be one of the most extraordinary encounters any journalist could ask for.

In the planning of this interview – back and forth with my *Newsnight* producers and editors – one thought has dominated. Will I ask him about Monica Lewinsky? Now, it would almost seem remiss not to ask it. But this was a time before the Me Too movement would assess and reinterpret that affair. A time when the sexual peccadilloes of an older statesman were not being thought of in terms of the damage done to the women around him; a time when his own impeachment would be written off as merely the bloodthirsty work of his political opponents.

Our recalibration, in other words, of this president through the lens of the Time's Up movement was still three years away.

But it is in my mind because, after nearly two decades of silence, Lewinsky has penned a rather brilliant piece for *Vanity Fair*. Two months earlier she had described with honesty, humour and extraordinary self-awareness the effect that liaison with Bill Clinton would have on the rest of her life.

She tells of job interviews that ended in refusal (because of her 'history' she was never 'quite right' for the position). She recounts how one potential employer said he would have to check with the Clintons first in case Hillary became the next president. She claims full responsibility for her actions ('it was a consensual relationship') but ruefully notes that when men err they are welcomed back into the fold with almost immediate effect; 'The women in these imbroglios return to lives that are not so easily repaired.'

She also exposes – with bold and brilliant wit – the irony and indeed the horror of some of America's most esteemed feminists writing of her with disparagement and venom. 'They joined', she observes wryly, 'the humiliation derby.' It is a piece that has struck a chord with me. I was in my teens at the time Lewinsky hit the headlines. I spent many years wondering why she had been so mauled by the press and why we – young women, feminists – had turned a blind eye to it for so long.

So that, to complete the diversion, is why she was so much on my mind as I prepared to encounter Bill Clinton.

Here he was, offering to talk about women's rights in

India. And here I was, wondering if he fancied exploring them a little closer to home. Would he agree with Monica Lewinsky's assessment that 'the women in these imbroglios return to lives not so easily repaired' or, more accurately in her case, shattered?

The *Newsnight* office had been divided. My deputy editors, Rob Burley and Neil Breakwell, had been very much in favour of me pressing the nuclear button with a Lewinsky question. They wanted drama from the interview and thought it was an important question of accountability. Others had been more circumspect. What was the point, they asked, of riling him in the one BBC interview we had, shortly before his wife would become one of the most central figures in US electoral politics. (Ironically, I now see, the very argument the potential employer had used against Lewinsky in her piece.)

These workplace conversations are not unusual. They are what my job is about. A chance to thrash out the pros and cons of any interview strategy and try and find a way through. My own position was clear: I wanted to ask the question. I felt, bizarrely, I owed it to Lewinsky to somehow make up for the decades of catty, misogynist coverage she had endured internationally. Yet I was terrified. Absolutely terrified. What if they stopped the interview then and there? What if they seized the tape? What if I had to return to my boss and my team empty-handed from an encounter with Bill Clinton?

The two nights before my interview had been sleepless ones. I had played out each scenario – how could the question be asked without it sounding prurient? How could I tie it back to his work with the Clinton Foundation? Would I sound tabloid? Was that good or bad? Would it rupture future relations between the Democratic Party and the BBC?

I called a couple more wise counsels. They were very much 'no's. And then I realized I could keep on asking more and more people for advice but, ultimately, it was all down to me. I would ask the question if I could. If the scene was set; if he seemed amenable. If, broadly, it felt right. *If.*

There was nothing more to decide until the time actually came.

That morning, then, made the Jaipur bakery feel like a climate-controlled Ferrari. The goat farm was miles from anywhere. I had started the day in a khaki cotton shirt dress but ten minutes after getting out of the van there were rivulets of sweat down the front. My hair was seconds from a full-frontal frizz and my pothole-jolted make-up looked crayoned on by a three-year-old. I changed my clothes in a barn, my bag gingerly placed on the stone floor between three offerings of goat poo.

When I emerge I find the Foundation media team trying to show us a room – which is a hut no cooler than the outside – to set up our shot. My cameraman, Tony, shakes his head. We can't, he says, come four thousand miles to one of the most colourful countries on earth and then film President Clinton against a slab of grey concrete.

In the end, we decide to do it outdoors, two chairs stuck into the farm mud and baby pot plants of actual pot, with a row of beautifully saried women kneeling in the background.

We ready the two cameras and wait. Then we wait some more. The wilting process begins all over again. It is now 43 degrees beneath the midday sun.

Finally, the presidential aide, Matt McKenna, emerges and invites my cameraman, my producer and me into a huddle.

It is his curious turn of phrase I remember most clearly: 'Between us girls,' he says, 'I have to tell you that the president had a funny turn this morning.'

My heart stops. He is trying to say the interview is off. I can't tell whether I am about to burst into tears or be quietly relieved I don't have to choose what to do with the Lewinsky questions. Then he continues.

'I don't know if this can go ahead. He isn't well and I don't want him sitting through this awful heat.'

I explain that we have no other chance to do it. We have waited two days and our flight is the next day.

He tells us frankly that if we hadn't come four thousand miles and if the interview weren't for BBC *Newsnight*, they would pull the whole thing. As it is, they are prepared to let us go ahead – with conditions. If 'anything happens' during the interview, the tape is pulled. No questions asked.

My brain is racing. Is he trying to tell us that if the president faints, or throws up, or – worse – if the president dies on camera, we don't report it?

All the ethics questions of every journalism course seem to lead to this moment. And I can tell you one thing I learnt in that split second: the belief that you have any control is mythical. Like those children's books where you choose your own adventure but ultimately end up at the same place whatever you do.

Here, then, is the choice: agree to the presidential aide's terms (jump to page 46).

Or refuse them and go home.

Except we can't even go home because we have come here without our own transport as part of the presidential convoy and it is, as I might have mentioned, a goat farm in the middle of the Uttar Pradesh countryside three hours from Lucknow.

Is it becoming clearer now?

And thus all my agony of indecision disappears.

If I ask a statesman who we've just been warned might die on camera about a twenty-year-old affair with his intern, I will be the one who ends up looking like the bad guy.

And even if I did ask, the likelihood is they would simply take the tape away and leave us to hitchhike home.

And so begins a massive internal rethink of the interview as the president himself emerges into the midday sun.

We have been told to ask about the work of the Clinton Foundation – it is a year or so before the funding of the Foundation itself will be mired in controversy – and we start the interview there, talking sanitation and clean water.

But it is not until I steer the conversation on to geo-politics that the steely blue gaze suddenly lights up.

He wants to discuss America and its place in the world and he agrees the country is showing very little leadership right now. He tells me Iran can be part of the solution to Iraq – he is gently combative, his eyes fiery with humour and curiosity as he probes me to define my statements.

I had noticed over the previous two days that when-ever the president is discussed by his people it is always 'he' for Bill and 'she' for Hillary. Their names are never actually said out loud. Like a weird superstition – *Macbeth* in a theatre – or perhaps it's a way of creating an anonym-ity that the couple so lack in real life.

American presidents keep their title for life. And so I ask him if he can imagine two President Clintons inhabiting the White House. I am expecting him to clam up at any mention of his wife's plans. She has, at that stage, yet to formally declare if she will run. But he is extraordinarily candid. He tells me something I have never heard before – the fifty-two-year deal he made with Hillary.

She supported him through a political life twenty-six years long – from Arkansas governor through two-terms as US president. And now, he says, it's her turn. She can do what she wants and he will do what she tells him. The big beast, it seems, is happy to be tamed. But, he laughs, he'll be eighty by the time their deal is up.

She's never asked me whether she should run for president, he says. I snort and tell him I don't believe him. It's true – he chuckles – absolutely not. Presumably in their life together there will have been many things she's never actually asked him.

'It's her time, she gets to decide, and if I can help I will.'

Of course it will be her decision – and the choice of the American people. But looking into his face right then I couldn't imagine anyone who would want it more. He believes in the office of president – still thinks it can change the world. I ask him if he accepts he was a 'lucky' president. Bush faced 9/11; Obama faced the economic crisis. Could he have done more to avoid either? And it is the only time he bristles. He puts on his reading glasses and glares me out. I am slightly unnerved. He tells me it's an odd way of looking at things. He had bombs, he had terrorists, he faced them down. And caught them.

And then he uses a curious phrase: he is talking about the polarized politics of America's Congress: the stalemate that blocks anything getting done.

'We're going to have to govern with a level of cooperation we're not used to,' he says. *We.*

Of course, by 'we' he means America, or the Democrats. Or mediators in general. But for a second I am struck by his words. And I wonder if he actually means Hillary – with a little help from her sidekick, Bill.

In the event, of course, with the sepia tint of hindsight, none of it comes to be: history takes care of that fantasy in the way it does all blind assumptions.

Bill Clinton will not end his life in front of a BBC camera on a goat farm in rural Uttar Pradesh. He will prove himself a formidable force on his wife's 2016 campaign trail, albeit accompanied by the lingering ghosts of his sexual past. But Hillary will not win. The Clintons will not move back to the White House, and their fifty-two-year deal will remain incomplete.

And what of Monica Lewinsky? I think of her frequently and will never know. Perhaps she would be mortified by the very idea of anyone feeling they had to run to her defence – shining armour glinting in the media glare. What could be more patronizing?

Or perhaps that very question – that attempt to reframe how we see powerful men and the women who work for them – would have started a whole new global conversation, if only it had been asked, against the odds.

The Umbrella Movement, Hong Kong

The first unspoken rule of live late-night television reporting is this: you always want to fly west, never east.

Reporting from Washington is a (relative) doddle. On air at 5.30 p.m., off air at 6.30 p.m., and suddenly one of those rare beasts for the *Newsnight* team: a free evening. Anything involving China is, by contrast, a killer. To be live for *Newsnight* in the Far East means working through the night until 5 a.m. and then going on air as dawn is breaking. The second unspoken rule is, of course, that none of that matters when the story is good enough. And this time it was.

Hong Kong has been a sort of spiritual home for me for decades. It was the place I fled to after university, in the middle of a recession, looking for work. It was the place I made some of my closest friends, found my husband and discovered a career that would keep me interested. It was a place that allowed me to make all my journalistic mistakes with relative anonymity, the place I experimented with gold lamé in gay clubs and the teachings of the Buddha on retreats with saffron-robed monks. It is somewhere I have always felt I owed – a place that allowed me to do the growing up I hadn't quite finished doing at university.

I went out there in 1992. Chris Patten had just arrived as Hong Kong's last governor and was anxious to put in place democratic strongholds that would help it stand up to China when the territory was handed back in 1997. I saw those structures tested two decades later, when I flew out to Hong Kong to report on the student democracy movement that brought thousands of teenagers out on to the streets for weeks on end: the movement we would come to call the Umbrella Protests, for rather sinister reasons.

October 2014. We have had half an eye on the student protests over the weekend, but it's the middle of the political conference season and much of *Newsnight* has been sent off to Birmingham to report from there. The office is empty, as are the coffers, and Rob Burley, deputy editor, suddenly realizes we are in the wrong place. It's all kicking off some six thousand miles east. He is keen to get me on a plane to Hong Kong that morning. He knows I lived there and has a more generous belief in my ability to speak Chinese than anyone who's actually heard me. It is one of the quickest decisions we ever make. I will head out with a producer, Warwick Harrington, who also knows the Far East well. We will arrive without our cameraman but locate him once we're there.

The Hong Kong I had left behind in 1998 was a place of efficiency and movement. No city I've ever visited had the ability to make things happen faster. A contract for a flat rental could be drawn up in a lunch break, business cards printed within the hour. Even a blow-dry was done double speed: two hairdressers, two brushes, one client. At times, that speed was too much. We felt like skaters on a pop-up ice rink, slippery and slightly out of control, the ex-pats clinging for dear life to the barriers around the edges. It was a place that refused to slow down, to let you off.

This time, however, there is an air of stillness when I arrive. The main arteries of Hong Kong Island, the roads going into Central (the business district), are all sealed off. There are no cars, just protestors. They are unlike any demonstrators I've ever seen. Scrupulously polite, and very, very young. I see a group of boys with huge plastic bin bags and litter-pickers. They are running around collecting rubbish from the ground. This will be a tidy protest. Neat posters cover the ground. Their mothers would be proud. Another couple of volunteers are handing out water bottles to make sure all those settling in for the evening are well hydrated.

They are protesting for one very simple reason. Beijing, which promised universal suffrage to the people of Hong Kong after the British left, has gone back on its word. The mandarins have decided that they will vet the suitability of Hong Kong's next chief executive (governor, as was) and China has narrowed the field of candidates down to those who are pro-Beijing. In other words, Hong Kong people have been locked out of any real decision-making. And the young, brought up on this new detox diet of democracy, care enough to show it on the streets.

We make our way through the gathering crowds. The girls are in gingham skirts, white blouses, grey socks. It strikes me as an odd uniform for anarchy until I realize that it is in fact a school uniform. It quietly breaks my heart. Not just that I have understood their true age but that I have seen how, in a part of the world that prioritizes academic excellence and endeavour above all else, they are still prepared to come down here after the school day has ended and fight for their rights as citizens. The posters on the ground, I see now more clearly, are actually exercise books. They have brought their homework to do on the front line so not a moment is wasted.

A sunset in Hong Kong, sitting so close to the equator, is the stuff of minutes: like a light switched off, or a tea towel over a parrot's cage. Night descends and with it – suddenly – the heavens open. The next two hours are chaos. The streets are now thick with people, the air is heavy with rain, the underground is rammed and it takes fifteen minutes to cross a single street. I drag Warwick to the Legislative Council building to try and find politicians to interview, but the LegCo has moved from where it was twenty years ago, and all I find is reclaimed land. Even the seafront is not where I last left it. It's disorientating. It makes me feel like a foreigner in a place I once called home. It would be funny had it not just taken us forty minutes to walk three hundred yards. We still have no cameraman, we have no interviews, and the mobile signal is intermittent because there are too many people in a tiny space. They are expecting a piece from us by the next morning and we have nothing filmed, no means to film and no guests set up.

We head towards Admiralty, one stop east from Central on the Mass Transit Railway, and I am freshly struck by the way these protests have changed the balance of the urban space. Hong Kong pedestrians are usually found deep underground or on the web of mid-air walkways that link skyscraper to skyscraper. Ground level is left to the heavy traffic. This time, however, we emerge from the subway on to a dual carriageway now thick with bodies, banners and human energy. A huge covered footbridge straddles the five lanes, with escalators leading up and down: a nod to the insufferable tropical heat that envelops the island four months of the year. I've now lost Warwick, but from the viewpoint in the middle of the bridge I start trying to scout faces in the crowd as if I will miraculously find him.

At that moment, for a matter of seconds, my mobile signal comes back and I see the phone ringing. It's Luke, whom I've never worked with before. He's our designated cameraman and he tells me to head to the nearest McDonald's. It is a farcical request in a city with fast-food joints on every street corner. But I describe the bridge I'm on and tell him there is a McDonald's at the bottom of it and, painfully, in the rain and the humidity and the noise of chanting and the mass of sweating bodies, I descend and shuffle along, until I hear my name being called. I assume Luke recognizes me 'from the telly' but he reminds me that we *have* worked together once before – in Grant Park, Chicago, the day after Barack Obama won the US presidential election of 2008. That night, he admits, he kept falling asleep between our various live hits. He'd worked a two-day shift without stopping and had discovered a means of survival: a twenty-minute kip between twenty past and twenty to, so he was awake every hour on the hour for our headlines.

'No wonder you didn't recognize me,' he says. 'I was a zombie.'

Luke and I head into the demonstration to start filming. I am buoyed with possibility now we actually have the means to make a piece. In the thickest of crowds, in the middle of what was once the main thoroughfare towards the harbour, we see a raised platform. 'That's where you want to be,' Luke explains. I scramble up scaffolding until I have an unparalleled view of the protests now at my feet; Luke joins me on the dais. And as we brush our jeans down and clamber to our feet, I can feel a murmur of anticipation rustling through the gathered mass. 'Where are you from?' a young guy asks. I tell him we've come from London for the BBC.

And as word spreads through the crowds, the beat changes and I hear a strange new rhythm emerge, and some twenty thousand voices join in the chant.

'San qyu bi bi xie, san qyu bi bi xie, san qyu bi bi xie.'

I am trying to understand it, racking my brains to put my pidgin Chinese to good use, sort it into something intelligible to my rusty ear. Each time I catch a character or a sound, I quickly lose it. I turn to Luke, mystified, and he's laughing at me. 'Don't you hear it?' he asks. And I feel even more stupid. 'They're chanting, *"Thank you, BBC"*. They're thanking us for covering the protests.' The moment he spells it out, I hear it perfectly. And as my brain acclimatizes to the heavily accented English, I blush, forced to realize that I have just come here looking for good shots, atmosphere and actuality for my piece, but they have come here because the future of their country depends upon it.

For one glorious moment, frozen in time, I am standing there on a plinth, surrounded by thousands of voices shouting their support for the oft-beleaguered organization that employs me. Then I snap back to reality. I cannot film whilst they are chanting. It will look craven. Or organized. Or paid for. I must shut them up so I can film them properly doing what they were doing. I hear myself saying, 'Shhhh-shhhhhhh,' to twenty thousand people, my finger over my lips, like some horn-rimmed librarian. I look pathetic and Luke is once again laughing at me. It doesn't work until he puts down his camera and refuses to film. He is the one with the power; I am just the dummy on the plinth trying to do a piece to camera. Finally, they are still and we understand why: they have seen police advancing. And, suddenly, in the fifteen seconds of silence between the quietening of the crowd and the advance of the authorities, I realize I must do my piece to camera and I must do it in one take.

'They call this an awakening,' I yell, as Luke is rolling, and the crowd is fixated around us. 'It's a protest brought out by students, school kids even, without great organization – but one of their own free will.' I am hollering now, that it's about a promise guaranteeing their freedom and their democracy – 'A promise made to them in law, by Beijing, has been broken.'

It's definitely not the finest piece to camera I have ever done. Reading it here, I realize how little music or even sense it makes. I am shouting above the noise so my voice sounds hoarse; my hair has been scraped off my face to stop it going frizzy in the humidity. My eyes are a bit wild. I look, in fact, like a 3D version of an Edvard Munch painting, even though I'm having the time of my life. It is not perfect, but it is good enough – and, anyway, it is the only chance I will have before we are kicked off the platform and moved on.

Minutes after I finish, the tropical downpour starts again. We seek cover under the bridge. I watch as a thousand umbrellas open up below me, colourful semicircles filling the night sky. Tonight, their purpose is mundane – a response merely to the wind and the rain. But they have given the whole movement its name. They were deployed first as a defence against the pepper spray fired into the eyes of protestors by the authorities trying to disperse the crowds.

The umbrellas remain a literal and figurative part of this scene: not just a sign of shelter, but of defiance.

Surrounding the protests are skyscrapers and the fanciest designer shops. The Chanel and Gucci insignia high above the crowds are a reminder that this is one of the most affluent places on earth. Certainly, there is a sense amongst the older generation, the middle-class home-owners, that the students are damaging the social fabric. 'They don't realize how lucky they are to live here,' one businesswoman tells me. 'They have jobs and money and law and order.' Democracy, she suggests, can wait.

On the escalator, which is packed to the gills, I hear a voice speaking English. The Chinese face is familiar. He is painstakingly explaining something – possibly his location – on the phone. He may even be giving an interview as he walks. From the deepest recesses of my memory, I put a name to a face I must have interviewed a handful of times two decades ago. He is law professor Joseph Cheng, sometimes called Hong Kong's 'father of democracy'. I follow him until he finishes his call; then, Luke at my side, we pounce. We ask him for his thoughts to give our piece the context of history. I have my first interview.

We spend the next three hours chasing more voices: those of the student protestors; those of their parents beckoning them home; anyone in authority who can tell us how China will respond; even a survivor of the Tiananmen protests in 1989 – Han Dong Fang – who was detained, tortured and imprisoned for the part he played in that fatal uprising. It is nearly 1 a.m. by the time the crowds disperse and we hobble to a hotel – not to sleep, but to edit. We are shattered, starving and soaking. Tempers are fraying. I start to script, Luke begins to ingest his pictures, Warwick is pulling the piece together. We shout and we fight ('artistic differences') and it is partly therapeutic and partly because we just need a hot meal. In the heat of the moment, shocking things are said between colleagues. But they will be forgiven once the piece has made air.

This time, there is no moment of relief. As Luke finishes off the edit, I must get myself across town to the live point: a balcony somewhere looking down over the city as the next day begins. I will go live for the *Ten O'Clock News* at 5 a.m. Hong Kong time, then live for *Newsnight* with guests half an hour later. As I arrive at the appointed location, we find the building shut. The bolts on the front are drawn. No one answers our calls. It is a miserable, panicky moment where I realize I will never make it to air because a janitor has gone home. I am nervous and grumpy at the same time. Under my breath I am muttering – as I always do – that I will NEVER agree to do this again.

Then from somewhere in the shadows we hear a voice barking at us in Cantonese. It's a cantankerous-sounding language at the best of times, never more so when yelled by someone freshly woken. There is a clanking of keys and we are directed inside and up on to the roof, where we find the local crew setting up. Dawn is breaking; the camera lights are already insanely hot. And I can feel freshly applied foundation settling into little rivulets around my collarbone. There is, of course, no autocue – it's a makeshift affair – so I have committed my script to memory and I just have to hope it stays.

Below me, the streets are now quiet, the students finally in bed before a fresh day of school and protest. And I must paint a picture of the scene just hours earlier – of the noise and the bodies and the desperation and the hope. I do not mention the pro-BBC chanting, as it will all sound too weird and, in the fug of sleeplessness, I'm starting to believe I imagined the whole thing. One of the feistiest voices of the whole democracy movement, Emily Lau, will join me on the roof. And she will tell me something which will shock me to my core: that she thinks China learns only by its violence. She will remind me of Tiananmen Square and the thousands that lost their lives there, and her belief that only after tragedy can real change happen. And I will think of the bespectacled boys, and the girls in the gingham skirts, with their nerdy maths books and wonder if, as a mother, I would let my own children fight for democracy on these streets – where the stakes are so high but the punishment so brutal.

By the time we finish the sun is fully up. The air is already heavy with heat and moisture. The first clanging of construction noise – Hong Kong's constant soundtrack – is cranking up on the cranes around us. And I will head back to the hotel, passing a 7-Eleven corner shop on the way. I will buy microwaved dim sum and bad sweet wine. And at 7 a.m., finally, I will go to bed.

Jon Stewart:
The End of His *Daily Show*

He is sitting at the bar, with his back to me, ordering a coffee, when I get to the North London studio. And I have a moment just to contemplate the scene before I rush in.

Normally, I don't get nervous. This time I am. And it takes me a second to understand why. As I stare at the back of his head, I realize I am willing this Jon Stewart to be the one I fell in love with on *The Daily Show*. The one I have just flown back from an Alp in order to meet. The comedian who has managed to teach me so much about my own journalistic profession and has done it with an almost reckless ease for his own brilliance.

I do not want to find out he's a complete muppet in real life. That his thoughts are all tightly scripted, his jokes pre-prepped. I am desperate, in other words, not to be disappointed.

I order a coffee as his arrives and he insists on paying for it with 'this English money', which he throws around with abandon – like Belarusian roubles – as if he has no intention of returning to the UK, ever. We are here to discuss the film *Rosewater*, his directorial debut. It has been sent to me by the PR company ahead of the release date. And, in keeping with current practice in the industry, as a foil to piracy, they have burned my name across every single frame of the film so I can't share it.

All the subtitles now appear to end with the phrase 'EMILY MAITLIS', which I admit to him makes for slightly unnerving viewing.

'Yes,' he deadpans without missing a beat. 'Not just your copy – everyone's. We made sure every single version of that film has "EMILY" right across the screen.'

And my shoulders drop with relief. It is vintage Jon Stewart. His tone. His voice. Suddenly, I know it's all going to be fine.

Rosewater is the true story of an Iranian BBC journalist, Maziar Bahari, who was thrown in prison for 118 days for filming incriminating footage of the security services during the Iranian election of 2009. It was Iran's 'Green Movement', sometimes known as the 'Persian Spring', which brought social media – Twitter – to the fore as a powerful tool for telling the world about repressive states and fixed ballots.

So far, so simple. But there's another reason *Rosewater* feels so personal. Bahari had participated in a *Daily Show* sketch – a goofy spoof interview in which he was asked if he's a terrorist. Once he was incarcerated, this footage was shown to Bahari and fellow journalists in prison as 'proof' they had been spying for the Americans. So I am wondering, as I sit down with Jon Stewart on a massive stripy sofa in a completely empty room, whether the film is partially born of guilt.

'Not necessarily guilt,' he tells me. 'I think we became

involved based on an unlikely connection . . . Our main concern was that we still had [more] pieces to run and, if we ran them, would that put [the imprisoned journalists] in further jeopardy? Their families made clear they wanted more publicity, not less; they wanted to speak of it.'

I'm intrigued by this sense of personal responsibility. After all, I say to him, *The Daily Show* has always maintained that it's comedy. It's entertainment. It shouldn't be tarred with the news brush. Suddenly, *Rosewater* seems a million miles from that. One review called it 'unabashedly earnest', a phrase I have difficulty reconciling with Stewart.

'Well, it's not so much tar with the news brush,' he corrects me. 'I think that's somewhat misunderstood. When we say we're comedians, I don't mean that we don't stand behind the veracity of the research. We do. What I mean is, the language of news and the language of satire are two very different things. So they have to be judged on different metrics. In other words, the tools of satire may be a bit of a bludgeon, if you look at them journalistically. But we seek to come to some kind of real insight into something through juxtaposition, hyperbole, in the same way a cartoonist might say, "I'm a cartoonist." It's not a way of deflecting responsibility for their viewpoint, but a way of saying, "The tools of my trade are of a different essence from yours."'

The Daily Show, at its most brilliant, has captured moments of America's soul over the past quarter of a century. Jon Stewart nailed the anger about the economic crisis when he brought CNBC's moneymouth Jim Cramer to his knees. And, seven years earlier, a restrained but curiously moving address to his audience after 9/11 began: 'There is no other way really to start this show than to ask you at home the question that we've asked the audience here tonight and that we've asked everybody that we know here in New York since September eleventh, and that is, "Are you OK?"'

Viewers see him as a natural Democrat, but he can be just as merciless to those on the left. I remind Stewart of a *Daily Show* moment I watched from a Washington hotel room on the eve of the midterm elections of 2010 with Barack Obama as his guest. He asked the president if that totemic campaign slogan 'Yes, we can' could still be a realistic position for the Democrats. The president's bathetic response was: 'Yes we can, but . . .' A soundbite that perfectly encapsulated his struggle with delivering what Sarah Palin once called 'that hopey changey thing'.

So has Stewart been disappointed in Obama?

'I think you can make those black-and-white judgements in almost anything like this. I know the tendency is to want to make judgements on things – George Bush was this, Obama is this – but it's a far more nuanced picture than that. It's why we attach the word "gate" to everything. Because it's a scandal and it involves a politician, we put "gate" on it.'

It's a diplomatic answer – which perhaps conceals more than it yields. But Stewart's own political awareness was formed by the original one: Watergate – a seismic moment for a eleven-year-old that coincided with his parents' separation. Events, he now jokes, that have been conflated by his young mind.

'My father left at the same time [as Nixon],' he says. 'They both resigned and walked to a helicopter and did that wave.'

There was less to laugh about at the time. His father's 'resignation' took the form of estrangement. Donald Leibowitz left the family home. And never saw his son perform. Those looking for an understanding of why Stewart changed his surname may find it here.

There is an agonizing moment between us, alone on the stripy sofa, where I am trying to understand if there was reconciliation between father and son before his dad died. It is the only time in an hour and a half's conversation there are pauses. And the sense that we each, individually, want to be swallowed up.

'You hate talking about this?' I say.

'Yes.' Pause. 'Well, I don't know what to say.' Pause. 'Do you mean did I forgive him? And did he understand what that meant? Is that what you mean? Because I'm not sure what reconciliation is. Do you mean did we have a *Steel Magnolias* moment where we hugged and cried?'

It is the comedian's natural defence. And I am made aware I'm treading on territory he simply can't bear. He watches me trying to decide whether to hold his gaze and press him or drop it and feign invisibility. I feel like a huge, big, fat therapy cliché as I try to understand whether his adult success was motivated by an unhappy childhood.

'My childhood was anything but tortured. My parents split up; I didn't live in the middle of the civil war in Sarajevo.'

But there is, constantly, with Stewart, the sense of a man who has to be participating rather than just observing. Growing up, he would always rather bartend at a club than go to it.

'I worked in a punk club because I really liked the music – but just going there felt aimless so I thought, Well, shit, I'll just get a job here, then I can see the music and have a reason for being here.'

In February 2015 he announced his retirement from *The Daily Show*, his spiritual home for the previous sixteen years: 'I'm going to have dinner on a school night with my family – who I have heard from multiple sources are lovely people . . .', although he later admits to me they actually couldn't take more than about twenty minutes of him at one sitting. I ask if he fears that aimlessness he talks of, when he's no longer the anchor of a nightly show?

'It's a luxury – I have been fortunate enough in this business to make enough money . . . to be able to say [puts on voice of Skipper from *The Penguins of Madagascar*], "I've worked for too hard for too long, and I'm going to take some time with the kids." I love creating; I love writing. But you may be right; without that structure, my brain can eat itself.'

In fact, one of the things that made him love *The Daily Show* so much, he explains, is the sense of a rigid format that allows for 'inspiration to seep through the mechanics of it'.

For a man who manifestly hates doing film junkets he's been more than generous with his time. We have discussed how to fight ISIS; his answer is part pragmatic, part satirical. 'I'm not a military strategist, but I think the best way to fight them is, like, to fight them.'

I ask him if it feels like Islamism is winning against the West, and he says, 'I do think that, ultimately, that ideology does not offer a sustainable vision, so it can create a tremendous amount of damage and pain and fear but, ultimately, it's not a winning formula – as they say, the arc of history is long but it bends towards justice.' It is the same quote – from Martin Luther King – that Barack Obama will reach for as he ends his presidency two years later.

And then, before I know it, I'm asking him for something that feels like professional advice. I have just returned from covering the Paris massacres at the offices of *Charlie Hebdo*. It has ended with a siege around a kosher supermarket, and I am thinking very seriously about the role of the news reporter, live at the scene of the tragedy, when I describe to him my colleague's fear that he has been feeding terrorists lines by describing how many people may be inside the supermarket hiding for their lives.

He is engaging and fluid and thoughtful and unashamed

to have a view (often a novelty in my world). I am momentarily lulled — like a clingy groupie — into believing we are having a genuine conversation. Then someone from the production company tactfully reappears at the door and I am reminded he is simultaneously jet-lagged and about to fly home.

'One last question before you go?' I ask. And he shoots back, 'Sagittarius.' But my question is not about star signs, it's about star quality and the insouciance with which he shrugs off the impact he makes. At least from the quotes I've read. 'Can you,' I suggest, 'really tell me you don't care if there's an audience or not?'

He chooses his words carefully. 'It's not that we don't care if there's an audience or not, we don't think about them.'

In anyone else's mouth, it would sound arrogant. From him, it sounds liberating. He is someone who has pioneered an entirely new way of formatting news and comedy and satire and politics — and I'm excited about what he will do next. Right now, though, the answer is obvious: get some sleep. And spend those darn Belarusian roubles.

But I do hope he comes back.

The Migrant March from Budapest Central Station

It is September 2015; I am on the phone to my deputy editor, Neil Breakwell, using a llama farm as an excuse. I am trying to explain to him that I cannot easily go to wherever he is trying to send me because Saturday is my birthday and I have just booked a llama safari walk in Peterborough with my kids and nieces, who will be devastated if I now cancel. I mention this because the call is imprinted in my memory as the most perfect example of a journo brain-freeze. I am about to be sent on one of the most important stories I will ever cover, a story that will provide a backdrop to the most extraordinary changes our continent has seen, both geographically and politically, a story that will, in subtle and profound ways, change my own life – and yet, in that split second, I cannot think about anything except the llamas, the nieces and the unrefundable deposit.

All credit to Neil, who takes my odd response in his easy stride. He is a dog-lover and this appears to stretch to llamas too. We work out a way in which he can send me and ensure I will still be back in time for Saturday-afternoon llamas. Once this deal is struck, I can actually start thinking about the send. The story is this. A million refugees and migrants are marching through Europe in search of a better life. They have arrived in Hungary and are now camped out at the central Keleti railway station in the capital, trying to reach Germany, which has become Europe's promised land under Angela Merkel. The Hungarian authorities under Viktor Orbán do not want them there. They are trying to make life in Hungary as unattractive as possible so more don't follow. I must get inside that railway station, now a scene of hope and danger, chaos, potential and heartbreak.

It is not until I board my flight to Budapest three hours later and am staring out of the window that I am overcome with a wave of shame. I have come to recognize it as part of the job, a protective layer that lets you carry on thinking about family plans for a Saturday afternoon when the whole world around you is falling apart.

Jake Morris and Luke Winsbury, our producer and cameraman, are already there when I land. I find them in a café eating Hungarian chicken stew; they have been up filming since dawn and this is breakfast. My luggage is bulkier than usual. In the half-hour between the phone call and my departure, I have raced to my kids' rooms and thrown all their too-small football strips into a big pile. I have packed them for the youngsters we will find in Budapest, and at the airport I have purchased tiny gifts – sewing kits, aspirin, plasters – to give to those we find camping on the floor. I am not entirely sure of BBC rules on this one. I prefer not to ask. It is partly a knee-jerk response to something I have seen my own parents do when visiting Russia before glasnost, their own suitcases packed full of 'luxury' items – Tampax, books and women's tights – for the families they will be staying with there. It seems too obvious NOT to do it once I have thought of it. And I am wondering if and how I can hand them out without them looking like tacky TV bribes.

Over the stew, we plan what we need to film. It's obvious our first stop must be deep inside the station itself. There, we find makeshift homes, blankets, rugs, dinners being cooked on small burners, feet being washed under the emergency taps that have just been hurriedly fixed along a pole outside. Kids are playing skipping games, mothers are braiding hair, and in the middle of it all we find Zeta, a four-day-old baby, born here to a woman who left Syria nine months pregnant and gave birth on the concourse beneath us.

Youth is everywhere; many of the boys are travelling alone. One tells me his father was killed fighting the Taliban in Afghanistan and he has been sent here to pave a way for his mum and his siblings. He swoons when I pull an old Man United T-shirt from the bag and hand it to him. As he scrabbles it over his back, I realize, from his excitement and his frame, just how young he is.

Those amassed at the station are waiting for transport to take them out of here to the Austrian border. But there are no trains running. The government has put a stop to the journeys, realizing that any hint of a successful passage across Europe will merely bring more to the station.

The migrants have thrown everything at the chance to get inside the EU border; free movement is their holy grail and they are heady with the sense of life-changing opportunity it creates. But the clamp-down by the Hungarian authorities was not in the script. And now a sense of boredom, frustration and bottled-up resentment pervades the concourse.

In those few short hours we feel the atmosphere build and change. So it almost comes as no surprise when we hear that hundreds have now begun a country-length march on foot towards Austria. Clearly it is only the fittest, the most able-bodied, the least encumbered of the travellers, although many have families with them.

We leave the station and start to follow them. There is something biblical in this exodus. They are walking on the hard shoulder the length of the M1, which is literally what it's called: Hungary's main motorway, which will take them from Budapest to the Austrian border 170 kilometres away. We see families pushing strollers laden with household belongings and cases, toddlers on their fathers' shoulders – the universal gesture of a parental treat now rendered a necessity, for it is the only way these tiny legs will make it. As journalists, we are torn. Jake is keen to stay with the travellers, walk with them, get pictures and stories and conversations on the way. The downside is we have promised to do the whole programme live from Keleti station tonight. We cannot risk a journey which could take us miles away, with no chance of return through the congested traffic, if it means missing our live point and the broadcast itself. Reluctantly, we let them leave our sight. We will return to the city centre and try and make sense of the reaction of Hungarian people to what they are seeing. A mile from Keleti station we find a noisy bar. Football fans are chanting. Hungary will play Romania that night in a crucial Euro play-off. But the noise coming from the bar is more than just friendly rivalry. As we get close, we see they are all in black shirts. They are throwing flares that snap and shock on the pavement beside us. These are the Hungarian Ultras – nationalists. Their passionate, loyal support for their team converges with another passion – less definable, more disquieting. They chant of an 'old Hungary', of 'the way things used to be'. They are not political, they tell us, but they like to keep their Hungary clean. The strong whiff of xenophobia is hard to ignore. I am the only woman here, surrounded by these black-shirted men and their beers. And we experience the thrill of trying to go towards a crowd that every BBC handbook would tell us to back away from. Luke is trying to dodge the flares to keep filming; I am trying to find someone sober enough to talk on camera; Jake is juggling his health-and-safety responsibilities as a producer with his yearning to make the film richer. These voices will contrast so starkly with the ones from inside the railway station, we know we must have both.

On the fringes of the crowd I find Martin, who speaks some English. What does he make of the refugees at the station? I ask.

'It's horrible. They are demonstrating. They shouldn't be here. They should go.' He thinks it's bad for Hungary. 'Have you seen the smell, and the dirt? The rubbish? I don't mind to help kids, but it's not just kids . . . there's something else as well . . .' His voice trails away and he refuses to expand. But he is hinting at bad things. He means, 'They've come to do bad things'.

At the time, I remember thinking his was the unusual voice – the 'Ultra' voice. That he was out of step with the way the rest of Europe was thinking. Now, of course, I see how mistaken I was. His shirt was black and his words were blunt, but he was one of millions across the country and the continent who would watch this exodus across Europe with fear and resentment.

We almost have our piece, but before we finish filming our fixer offers to take us high above the city, where we can look down and back on Budapest and the meandering Danube. It is twenty minutes out of town and the Friday-night traffic is already choking us back. However, when we see the view I realize why we've come. It is not just the domed, gleaming rooftops as they catch the evening sun, or the ribbon that weaves majestically through the classical architecture. No, it is something more. This is a Budapest of stately nobility. A city that could once call itself the beating heart of Europe's greatest empire, now faded and caught up in its own financial struggles. It is a thing of pride to be able to remind visitors of seventeenth-century Ottoman Hungary, not the twenty-first-century mess of migrating humanity we have found.

The eyes of the world are once more upon it. But not in the way of old. A local man there explains to me, 'It's not that we don't like immigrants; we just don't want their problems here. It reminds us of what we've lost.'

I stand with the grandeur of the great city at my back as the sun goes down and film a piece to camera. Then we must run – to an edit – before getting in place for the live show itself. Luke transforms from cameraman to editor; he ingests the digital pictures whilst I write a script and Jake decides the look of the whole piece. It is all done in the cameraman's room – an editing tradition.

I sit cross-legged on the bed, Luke at the desk. We wire up the TV to watch our own edit taking shape upon the monitor. I normally write quickly and fluently, but this time it is hard and I cannot work out what is haunting me. I need somehow to get my individual stories – of baby Zeta, the Afghan boy, Martin the Ultra – into something that feels vast. I am trying to tell a story tonight without having any clue how it will end. Will the marchers reach Austria? Will that Syrian baby born in a Hungarian railway station be recognized as a citizen of Europe? And what will the Ultras make of it all if so?

I do not have to worry about what the Ultras think for long. By the time we've filed the piece to London and dashed back to the live point outside the station entrance, they have marched en masse from the sports bars and arrived there looking for trouble. The game has ended in a goalless draw and they are restless, visibly the worse for wear and ready to cause a scene with the migrants. They have brought bangers and fireworks and I'm trying to work out how I can broadcast over the noise. Neil has arrived from London to direct the evening programme and, as I am preparing to record the headlines, a line of riot police has formed behind me. I catch them out of the corner of my eye and cannot decide whether I feel protected or intimidated. The live camera crew we are using there have no English; we have no communications with the gallery in London; it is two minutes to air. And then it starts raining. It is the perfect storm of awfulness. I am trying to ask London whether they want us to include the riot police and take the scenes live if they kick off, or whether we must leg it to another, safer, spot, which is surely what the BBC handbook would recommend. Because I cannot talk to London, I will never know the answer. As it is, the decision is made for us by the simplest of things: an on-air cue to start talking.

I say out loud for the first time what I have learnt in the hours I've been here: that Europe's centre has shifted. We are no longer the hub, nor Spain, nor France; it is this great mass of what used to be the East – that is where the heart of Europe now lies. I talk live to a representative of the Hungarian opposition party, who tells me Europe as a whole needs a solution to this crisis; I talk to BBC correspondent Matthew Price, who has stayed with the travelling exodus of pedestrians and has extraordinary stories to tell of those he's met – pilgrims' tales. I talk to a spokesman for the Hungarian PM, who explains that their job is to protect Hungary, and Christian culture, and the values of this country and its people. I talk to the Slovakian deputy prime minister, who explains the deep background to Eastern Europe's response: these countries came to the EU looking for a better club than the Soviet regime – a club that would help them thrive. They didn't come into the EU to look after migrants. That was never the deal.

And then, lastly, we have a cultural discussion on the future of Europe with Anne Applebaum, the Pulitzer Prize winner who's written extensively on communism, together with the historian Simon Schama. It is he who tells me, 'Angela Merkel has become the new Jerusalem.' It feels profound in his mouth – a Jew who has detailed his own family tragedies in the Holocaust.

And I hear Anne say, 'Europe needs to create institutions on the borders of Europe to solve this crisis; Europe must see itself as a single entity, and Britain must play its role.'

At the time, I remember thinking it was obvious – boring, even – that she was pointing it out.

What I failed to see was how Britain, ultimately, would act. Not in its humanitarian response, but politically, in the referendum on Brexit that was to come.

If the choice was between becoming a closer part of Europe to take on these problems or exiting the EU to leave the whole thing behind, we chose the latter. The migrant crisis that many bleeding-heart liberals assumed would bring Europeans together had the opposite effect. It reminded us how complicated Europe's problems could get. It was something the UK population ultimately felt it had never signed up to.

An hour later, we are off air. It has been the most extraordinary programme. Not slick, not without its communication issues or its satellite-link delays, but rich in terms of the ground we have covered, the voices we have featured and the stuff I feel I have learnt.

My friend Kavita has watched and noticed around my wrist a gold bracelet. She remembered its story. The bracelet was made for me by my father from a gold bangle of his mother's, which she took with her when she and her family fled Nazi Germany in 1936. It is an observation so perfect it places me not only physically but personally at the heart of the story I have been trying to tell.

We pack up, like troubadours – travelling players finishing a performance on a makeshift stage, in near-silence. The riot police have left. But the barriers are up all over the city so no traffic can get through. We walk the long stretch across town trying to find a taxi, seeing nothing. We walk, and we walk, looking for a bar, anywhere we can stop and soften the edges of a long day and a fraught night. But it is 1 a.m. in Hungary and nothing is open. The walking itself is therapeutic, until, after an hour, Neil gently points out we are in danger of being confused with the refugee exodus of pilgrims we have spent the day filming. By the time we reach our hotel on the edge of town, we are too tired to think or drink.

It is a brutally short night's sleep. The flight next morning – my birthday – leaves at 5.45 a.m. I will land in London mid-morning, and by 2 p.m., against all the odds, we have made it to the Peterborough llama farm – an odd, happy bash of cousins and dogs and balloons and birthday cake and wellies.

The dislocation in my head between the confusion I have left behind and the celebrations I have entered is slightly too much. The kids and those llamas got hugged in a rather profound way that afternoon. I don't think I ever told them why.

David Attenborough:
One Hour in a Hot-Air Balloon

Some interviews wind you up. Some test your mettle. Some reduce you to a gibbering wreck.

But some calm your soul. The hour or so I spent with the ninety-year-old David Attenborough was one of the most beatific of my life. An oddly religious term, I know, for a man who doesn't have much truck with religion, but it was the serenity of that time that will stay with me most. He had just brought out *Planet Earth II*, a natural-history series that would go on to win BAFTAs, and the first episode was airing in the very week that America would elect Donald Trump as president.

Looking back, it is not surprising that, against that background of agitation and divide, of white noise and dark undercurrents, I would find the company of a man who offered wisdom and quiet thoughtfulness so nourishing. We meet at the BBC's Wogan House. I am chatting to his producers about the piece I am writing for the *Radio Times*. And I do not hear him come in.

Perhaps I should have guessed that a man who has spent a lifetime hiding stealthily in undergrowth should be able to enter a room without anyone seeing. But the first time I am aware that David Attenborough is behind me is when he observes: 'It's the small eyes – too close together – and the length of the nose. The rat is never going to make it.'

He has found me in the middle of a conversation about what makes some animals loveable to humans and some repellent. It is, of course, his home turf. Not just the understanding of the animals themselves, but of how we, the humans, respond to them.

He leads me off to a more private room to continue our chat, making his own coffee on the way. I confess to him I am still having dreams about a particularly vivid scene from his recent series *Planet Earth II*, where a newly hatched marine iguana has to escape a Medusa-like string of snakes as he runs to the sea to find food. It is my first reminder – spoiler alert – that not every animal in the series makes it out of there alive. And from Mr Attenborough it elicits a gentle rebuke to my way of thinking.

'We are very, very strange,' he tells me, 'that we think every child has got to survive. There are very few creatures in the world like that.' It will be a theme he develops later: passionate about population control and realistic in the part we should play in it.

He looks sixty, perhaps, not ninety. A head full of silver hair, a playful face that crinkles easily into laughter and his signature left wink. Maybe it's the youthfulness of a man who can say he has spent a lifetime doing what he adores. Or maybe – my eyes wander to the stash of KitKats on the table before him – he is fuelling his old age with the right stuff. Either way, it appears to be working. He's taken to the skies in a hot-air balloon for this series and seems shocked when I admit I have never done so.

'One of the nice things about it is that suddenly you will hear much nicer things. You hear church bells, you hear clocks strike, you hear distant conversations . . . there's nothing between you and a hundred and fifty feet of silence.'

There is poetry even in this thrown-away prose. If I shut my eyes, I can imagine his voice narrating the lift-off. I'm curious to know if he experiences what astronauts call the blue-spot effect: looking back on the planet with a whole different understanding of our place in it.

Not from there, he corrects, but he understands the phenomenon well from his travels. 'You've got no business thinking Africa has got nothing to do with you. I mean, you could just see the whole thing and you realize that you're finite, that you're cheek by jowl with one another, all in the same boat.'

I wonder if this intrepid explorer ever thinks about another planet. Does all the talk of water on Jupiter or life on Mars rouse his curiosity even further?

His answer is refreshingly direct. 'No . . . I know it's not the right thing to say in many ways but, really, I think it's irrelevant. We're light years away – it would probably take a hundred and fifty years to get anywhere. I'm not going to spend the next hundred and fifty years hoping I'm going to land somewhere and living in a space suit.'

They are the words of a man who clearly hasn't nearly finished with this planet yet.

Planet Earth II revisits a series first made ten years earlier, but the camerawork is more breathtaking, the landscapes more extreme. They are films he makes with obvious joy but also a sense of ecological concern; the series ends with him reminding the viewer, 'We can destroy or we can cherish – the choice is ours.'

He muses on this verbal ticking-off. 'I would love not to say it at all. I would love to say, "Just look at that, this is your heritage, this is where you belong, isn't it wonderful?" instead of saying, "You do realize that because of CFCs we are all doomed?" No, it's horrid to say it, but it's also an obligation.'

Does he worry, then, that the beauty is somehow too seductive? That it makes everything seem fine? Why, I ask, in this day and age, doesn't he show the reality of fish eating plastic bags?

'Er, I do,' he jumps in. 'I've just finished a film on them. An albatross chick waiting five weeks for its parents to come back with food, and when the baby opens up its mouth and the mother regurgitates the contents every single thing that comes out is plastic. Everything. Everything.'

This time round, the series includes an episode on cities and the wildlife that inhabits them. Should it worry us that we are building on places we don't belong?

'No, well, it shouldn't, because we are going to be on their turf and there's nothing you or I or anybody else can do about it. Population growth is terrifying. It's no good saying you shouldn't be there. What are all these people going to *do*? It wasn't their fault they were born.'

I remind him China has just ended its one-child policy and want to know what he advocates. He is against 'interfering with the basic human right which is having children' but says population growth is the most fundamental of the world's problems.

'Why is there urban violence? Why are there these problems with immigration? Why are we running short of food and polluting? Every single one of those comes down to . . . because there are more people.'

We now, I suggest, have a man in charge of America who believes climate change is a Chinese hoax. I am reminding him of a quote by Donald Trump. Attenborough's head is in his hands but the response is curiously phlegmatic. Or perhaps pragmatic.

'Well, we lived through that with earlier presidents – they've been equally guilty. Lyndon B. Johnson didn't take an enlightened view on the environment.'

That was quite a long time ago, I point out.

'It was, yes, and the world wasn't as badly overpopulated as it is now. No, I would avoid living through it . . . but do we have any control or influence over the American elections? Of course we don't. Or' – sotto voce – 'we could shoot him . . . ? It's not a bad idea . . .' He catches my eye and giggles.

It is clearly a joke. Nevertheless, the line will elicit the wrath of Trump fans when it comes out. Some will even make death threats against Attenborough. Of all the unintended consequences of my work, this one would be the hardest to explain to an adoring nation.

Talk of Trump takes him on to populism. 'There's confusion, isn't there,' he tells me, 'between populism and parliamentary democracy? I mean, that's why we're in the mess we are with Brexit, is it not?' He cites ex-Chancellor of the Exchequer Ken Clarke, who poses the thought that if people had to ask the state to fund a national gallery or a funfair, they'd say a funfair. 'Do we really want to live by this kind of referendum? What we mean by parliamentary democracy is surely that we find someone we respect who we think is probably wiser than we are, who is prepared to take the responsibility of pondering difficult things on our behalf.'

That depends, I suggest, on us believing our politicians *are* wiser.

He agrees. 'That's why people getting up and saying, "We've had enough of experts," is so catastrophic.' He's quoting Michael Gove from the Brexit campaign, but he moves seamlessly from politics to anthropology: 'I can see the arguments. I mean, I've said for years I don't think any human society is prepared to make decisions which they may not like if they're made by people who don't speak the same language.' It's funny to hear Brexit portrayed as a sort of survival call from an endangered species. I should have guessed.

Attenborough is not scared to call it xenophobia. But he recognizes it as truly primordial fear.

'It's very easy, as we all know
minorities until they become
yourself a minority. It's easy to
tation of middle-class liberalisr
people – I love the way they
tumes." You know' – giggle –
you find that they're actually te......
that they've actually taken over the town council and
what you thought was your home was not. I'm not supporting it; I'm saying it's what it is.'

He is passionate about using scientific evidence to
explain climate change, and says he refuses to be drawn
by people who ask him to 'prove it' using things he's
seen first hand. 'I know if I say I've seen a glacier in
South Georgia – I was there ten years ago – and it's
shrunk, they will say, "Well, I know a place in Green-
land where in fact the glacier is bigger . . ." You don't
want to be lured into the question of specifics because
you will lose. You have to go to science.'

I have heard somewhere an argument that if the Indus-
trial Revolution – economic development – had started
in Africa rather than Europe, then sun and wave technology would now be at the forefront, not the old fossil
fuels. Does he agree? His answer knocks me sideways.

'Yes, yes, absolutely. But a little voice inside says to
me, "Why are you going on about this?" Because it could
actually happen. And then will humanity have the sense
to deal with unlimited cheap power? What are they
going to do? Are they going to say, "WHOOPEEEE,

NOW LEVEL MOUNTAINS! WE CAN MINATE FORESTS!" I mean, it's Pro- eus stuff. Once you get infinite power, there are sequences. How are you going to use it?'

I am open-mouthed at the way he's taken a tangible commodity (electric power) and made it the stuff of Greek hubris so I actually have to think about it properly for the first time.

He sees my confusion and continues to explain, mimicking the voice of a greedy estate agent: 'Yes, why don't we melt the Antarctic, you know there must be stuff under there, *under* the glacier where you could build houses.'

'So,' I attempt, 'running out of power may *not* be such a bad thing?'

'No,' he says. It falls quietly between us. Silence.

I suddenly realize why David Attenborough is the giant he is. It is not just his geographic curiosity, not just his anthropological understanding, not just his gift for narration that simultaneously calms the soul and inspires the mind. It is that behind it all there is such a deep thinker. A man who, in his own words, doesn't aspire to 'the philosophy of Buddhist nirvana' but who recognizes the finite nature of the individual and the remarkably small part we play in something much, much larger.

It is hard, though, to reconcile this adventurer with a man who spent eight years behind a desk, as it were, in BBC management, as Controller of BBC Two. I'm surprised it didn't kill him. But he insists for a programme-maker it was 'the most fantastic job you can imagine. When I joined there was this absurd mystique that some-how there's magic about making programmes and only the BBC knew how . . . as if we gave it to the nation.' He laughs at the pomposity.

Well, I say, perhaps that isn't completely over. Look at *Bake Off*. That was 'gifted to the nation'. Was the BBC right not to renew the deal?

'Oh, absolutely right! To say, if you want another million – go ahead. We've got plenty more ideas where that came from.'

What about that other figure we 'gifted to the nation'. Was the BBC wrong to fire *Top Gear* presenter Jeremy Clarkson? I ponder.

'Well, yes, I regret letting Clarkson go because it's very good to have a voice that's anti-establishment or so profoundly anti-establishment.'

Even though he doesn't mind running over mice?

He shrugs. And I'm reminded of how we started: the rat with the too-close-together eyes and the pointy nose that no one really likes . . . I have to explain I'm not talk-ing about Clarkson.

There is a knock on the door, and his salvation comes in the form of someone offering to shoo me away. So I throw out one last thought. What, in his ninety-first year, are the things that bring him joy?

'People,' he says simply. And his eye flashes down to the one stick of KitKat that remains uneaten on the desk in front of him. 'Oh, and chocolate. It goes without question.'

And I leave feeling, somehow, as though I have been up in that hot-air balloon. Uplifted, and calmer. Life feels a bit richer, a bit bigger, a bit more exotic for having had one extraordinary hour to myself with David Attenborough.

An Airport Hotel with the Dalai Lama

Today I am off to meet a living god. Not just a celebrity superlative but a literal living god. I am trying to get spiritual but it is taxing because I am meeting my god in the Sofitel of London's Heathrow Terminal 5, TW6 2GD. Admittedly we are meeting in the Prestige Suite and I am wondering if the Living God always insists on the Sofitel Prestige Suite wherever he goes, or whether his entourage, feeling slightly guilty about the functionality of the location, have promised him prestige to cheer him up. Anyway, it is a very early-morning encounter, and the Living God, whom by now I should reveal is the Dalai Lama, is turning eighty, so, frankly, I am delighted to be meeting him wherever he dictates, suite or no suite.

It will be an extended interview on BBC Two as well as *Newsnight*, and the challenge is this: to take a much-loved national treasure and still make the interview challenging enough to hold the attention. This is a man (god) who fled his country, Tibet, in the uprising of 1959, fearing for his life, and with the help of the CIA's Special Activities Division crossed into India, where he lives in exile. We have spent a good deal of time working through the questions ahead of the encounter. I want to ask him if he believes Tibet will ever be an independent country, if he thinks China is a force for good or bad, and why he thinks the survival of his own lineage is in peril – after reading somewhere he believes he will be the last-ever Dalai Lama. I like to think that we have compiled a set of questions that are both personal and expansive, political yet spiritual, warm yet robust. Nothing can possibly prepare me for what happens next.

I arrive to find the crew already set up and slip into place to let them work out the shots. The Dalai Lama is next door, doing whatever lamas do by way of final preparation. Then the connecting door (Prestige-Suite glamour) opens and in comes this rush of warmth and the twitter of almost-human birdsong. I had been expecting colour – the ubiquitous saffron robe – but I had not been expecting quite such instantaneous laughter. It is the giggle I remember most, specs bouncing on his nose as it scrunches. He is powdered as he sits down, and the folds of his robes are arranged to fall televisually. The formal perfection is completely at odds with his own demeanour: an eighty-year-old man seeking fun.

I begin by reflecting on his longevity – it is a birthday broadcast, after all – in the most tactful way I can think of. Does he feel the same leader that he was? 'Are you a different man?' I ask. I am expecting a response with the weight of Confucius: heavy pauses; quiet reflection.

Instead, he starts pointing to his scalp, laughing and rubbing the top of his head. 'When I left, you see, Tibet

there was a lot of hair here. Now m
you see, I think I may say sometimes p
money – money is time – so, similarly, I th
say time is experience. Experience also, you see,
so time passes. And particularly difficult time d
period. Period to gain more experience. So I can de
itely now say today this person is more experience than
at the time of 1959 or early 1960.'

Less Confucius, then, more Yoda. Strangled syntax. Almost incomprehensible. I am nodding as if it's the wisest thing I've ever heard. But, on reflection, he is just telling me he is older and balder. Well, yes.

I ask him about his early memories. He was recognized as the Dalai Lama aged two. Does he retain any stories of those very early years? The question could lead anywhere. Childhood influences, early fears, family members. But no. He embarks on a complicated story about being disturbed by a camel whilst having a poo.

'One strange thing is no toilet, proper toilet. Just open toilet. So I went I think the hard work so I sort of sit like that.' He motions a squat. 'Huge camel. Black camel approaching towards me. I still remember the size and colour of the camel. Then I immediately run away, my bowel business was stop.' The anecdote ends in peals of laughter. I feel as though I've just walked into a *Carry On* film. I am wondering if this is what the BBC Two controller had in mind when he commissioned a full half-hour spiritual special.

His other childhood anecdote is about snatching a

nk, when he (the Dalai
thwacked by the cousin
e. But he got to keep it.
d devotion in the story,
ust laughing.
 childhood stuff whilst
ll-on existential. 'You've
Lama. Explain to us that,
re of your past lives, past

uch less. Of course,
eople say time is
ink I want to
like time,
ifficult
n-

'Now, we are twenty-first century. So you see this actually lama institution, frankly speaking, is develop during feudal system. So society's changed. Have to change. Some of these institutions some sort of . . . influence existing society sort of system. Now that out of dated. Therefore as early as 1969 I publicly officially I announced the very institution of the Dalai Lama should continue or not up to Tibetan people. If majority of Tibetan people at the time of my death feel now this essential old institution not much relevant then automatically cease . . . then my sort of basic sort of belief world belongs to seven billion human beings and each nation belongs to the people, with the respect, may I say so, that Great Britain belongs to the people, not the royal family.' He laughs again.

There's a lot to unpack here and, once I figure out what he's actually saying, it is interesting – curiously democratic. And socialist. And republican. Although it's worth noting he's not actually offering all this until after his own death. Which seems to delay the whole issue quite neatly.

I ask him if he thinks the same of our royal family but he tactfully sidesteps that. Indeed, he tactfully sidesteps just about everything that would entail an actual opinion about anything fundamental. When I ask him if he believes Tibet will ever be independent in his lifetime he goes off on a riff about quantum physics, common interests, the European Union and ends by saying he's not really seeking independence. I am starting to think he is using his broken English in the way England football managers often do when they're trying to say nothing at all. It is sort of weaponized into a pattern that seems intent on making no sense.

I persist, thinking perhaps it's just me. 'Do you think China is doing more good than harm for Tibet?'

'That may be too early to say.' He laughs. 'But possibility. Preservation of Tibetan culture, Tibetan tradition and environment is benefit. Now more Chinese leaders particularly now present leaders seems to be more realistic, look more wider perspective. Unlike other previous leader, they just see that way.' He makes a small circle with his hands to suggest a narrow vision. 'I will say a totalitarian country is sometimes unpredictable so difficult to say definite but there is some signs of hope.'

Nope, I'm thinking. Not a sausage. He's managed a five-minute answer – with gestures – in which he has neither condemned the Chinese regime nor praised it. And yet, unlike with a British politician, I cannot press him to define his answer without looking like I'm making fun of his language problems. I am stuck. I take to nodding again.

There follows a question about whether he feels Tibet was being used by the West to take on China. He replies referencing Korea and Vietnam and the CIA and Nixon in China, but it's more like a historical exegesis than an opinion.

Then I leave politics and try faith, which, presumably, is his thing more than anything else. Does Buddhism have a practical response to conflict?

He tells me about the news he has seen, about victims, and he asks questions. 'How to build a peaceful sanctuary. How in this century to depend on compassion. Sense of concern for their life, sense of concern for their happiness. And that respect for their right. Once that can develop, irrespective whether believer or nonbeliever, through education, through awareness.'

Suddenly, he sort of reanimates into a memory of the Iraq War, recalling his 'good friend Mr Bush – as a human being I love him very good on human level. His policy matter is concerned is sometimes is difficult. So after Iraq crisis happen and after my meeting with President Bush that I told him, "I love you, I respect you, but where some of your policies concerned, I have some great sort of reservation . . ." I told him! I am laughing like that.'

I am wondering why he didn't have the conversation with his good friend Mr Bush before the Iraq War if he felt so strongly. And as I am thinking this, a curious sensation overcomes me. A sort of sadness. I am loving our chat, and his ebullience and humour and warmth, but I start to feel – dare I say? – conned. As if really this Living God is like any other kind of parody politician. Obfuscating. Indirect. And prone to a mid-sentence change of subject. Is it our fault, I wonder, for setting him up to be something he cannot possibly be? Would I get a different response from any other spiritual leader? We rarely get the chance to find out. Should I really hold the Dalai Lama responsible for having no discernible views just because he seems more media friendly?

He will not talk about whether we should change our approach to euthanasia – allow dying with dignity. He will not talk about science and faith and whether they can cohabit. He will not elaborate about his response to Shugden Buddhism, whose followers say they feel outlawed by his kind of teaching. There are lots of words and more bluster and the giggle.

Finally, I reach for the question that would seem out of place in virtually every other interview but which feels as if it might be my best way to understand him.

'What are the things you love?' I ask. 'What makes you laugh? Your favourite joke.'

He tells me he hates formality. 'I say it boring, it too much formality. Unnecessary . . . I think laughing, smile is something unique about a human being. God give us that sort of special thing. So we have to utilize that. Our unique thing. But still be like tiger.' He pulls a comedy stern face. 'It's not use!'

We draw the interview to a close. I remind him that he once blessed Bradford City football club and they consider any improvements in performance a direct result. They gave him a T-shirt, apparently. I'm guessing it's more nightwear than day for the Dalai Lama. He won't admit to being a Bradford City fan but says he's delighted his blessing worked. He laughs one more time and punches me on the arm.

'Ow!' I shriek. 'I thought you lot didn't believe in violence.' And he's off again. That giggle. And another pretend punch.

I leave the Sofitel Prestige Suite in the shadow of Heathrow's first morning planes. Immediately I am outside, and start panicking about the edit. Did he give me enough? Did I get answers? Can I honestly make sense of anything he actually stated on camera? I'm not sure I understood anything he's just said. And then, as if imbued with a sense of his own deific inner calm, I feel my shoulders drop. I try the smile that only humans can do, and I remind myself of something few others can say. I have just met the Dalai Lama in an airport hotel. A man (god) who by any metric will almost certainly be the last of his kind.

Arrested in Cuba

Flicking through the Cuba photos on my phone, I'm reminded that Havana is one of the most photogenic places on earth. A broken doorway, a mural hailing 'Revolución!', a string of washing reaching through palm trees, a fisherman on the Malecón at dusk, the city sweepers at pink dawn. This is the land where neglected colonial buildings of empire seem romantic, where dilapidated cars seem vintage, where political slogans seem rousing. There is so much you want to take home.

But then I find the space on my phone where the photos suddenly run out. A place that we were never allowed to film. A lost few hours that showed me more about the country than a hundred guided tours of the Old City.

The day when we were forcibly detained, arrested and stripped of passports and phones.

I had been to Havana before – a sort of austere Christmas family holiday – hurrying to see this anachronism of an island before it was lost for ever. And my impressions that time were fairly bland. It had music and rum and smiley people and the constant air of sex. It had empty shelves and terrible food and long queues and no cashpoints.

It was, in other words, everything I had been promised. And everything I had been warned of.

A land I was thrilled to see. And to which I never really wanted to return.

But this time, I arrive with a task. Barely two weeks after the election of Donald Trump, Fidel Castro has died. My head is still reeling from covering one world-changing event. My family has hardly seen me for months. But this is a story I cannot miss. The end of a man who rewrote the twentieth century, who survived more than six hundred assassination attempts, who confused our whole notion of cold communism by making it flourish in the hot tropics, who elicited a flirtatiously starry-eyed indulgence from those quick to condemn dictatorships and censorship the world over. I want to see Cuba now to get a sense of the direction it will go in next. Beneath the state-decreed grief, are people really mourning? Are they scared? Are they jubilant but wary of showing it? What is rippling beneath the surface?

Some places are easy to work in as a camera crew – America is one. Most places offer their middling frustrations. Cuba is downright impossible. Even waiting to get the tripod off the plane takes more than two hours of sitting at the various luggage carousels wondering if it's been lost, confiscated or forgotten. It is the first reminder that Cuba doesn't work with hot tempers and high blood pressure: we will be forced to slow everything down. We are warned not to film without the proper paperwork and so we spend a painstaking nine hours in the foreign press centre waiting for authorization.

By the next morning we are on our way to Bejucal, a town an hour or so away from Havana but a world apart from the tourist trail. On the way, our old blue 1950s Cadillac ruptures its petrol tank. Our driver throws off his shirt and dives under the bonnet. His legs trail out from under the car as if he has just been run over by it. He bangs the tank with a hammer until it bleeds petrol on to the road, then hurries us back on board, telling us there is no time to lose: we need to reach our destination before the tank drips dry.

As the engine splutters into life, a man walking a pig on a rope passes by.

Just a normal sort of day in Cuba.

Bejucal is a small provincial town of the kind you might find the world over. A health clinic, a few empty stores. A well-maintained plaza. And a bunch of bored local kids. Pierced, shaved and tattooed, they appear to be channelling their inner Neymar. They have agreed to meet us, be interviewed for *Newsnight* on the public square.

'Don't sit on the railings,' they warn us. 'They'll come after you.'

How could these anarchic-looking punks be worried about parish rules? I wonder. Because it's Cuba, the voice inside me corrects.

They are excited to meet us. Particularly with a camera.

Intrigued by this combination of rebelliousness and caution, we start to ask them about their lives. They speak no English. I reach for Spanish. What do they want for Cuba's future? Would they call themselves socialist? Castro's long shadow has fallen over their whole lives and those of their parents – they have known no other leader besides his brother Raúl. Will they choose to bury Castro's idealism along with his ashes?

They are questions they have clearly been thinking about for years. But no one has asked them publicly. The answers, when they come, are brave and unyielding.

'We want to get out,' they tell us. 'To travel, to see the world. We understand everything that Castro did for us. And he did many things. But now it's time for change. Living under the embargo is like being in a gigantic cage.' I remember that phrase so clearly in Spanish: *una jaula*; the boy I'm talking to locks his hands together, miming the action of constriction. 'They push scraps to eat through the bars. You can see the trees and the branches beyond, but you can't reach them. Understand?'

We do. Encouraged by their openness, taken aback by their honesty, we want to learn more about this town they're from. We have heard about Cuba's legendary health system – often hailed as a shining example of everything the system has got right – so we head away from the square to the clinic on the corner. There are a group of doctors inside and we have nothing to lose by asking if they will share their experiences with us – on camera. They are happy to, providing, they say, we do not film their patients. We set up the camera away from the waiting area so no one is caught accidentally on film. I remember the interview for how reasonable it was. Nothing shocking – no propaganda. The doctor we speak to doesn't tell me they are on their knees. She doesn't tell me life is too good to be true. She speaks practically, of the education system and the way it's integrated, of the challenges and the opportunities. I could, to be perfectly frank, be in Reading general hospital.

It is only when Jamie Bowles, the cameraman, and I have finished the short interview and pulled the pale blue door of the clinic closed that I realize the atmosphere outside has changed. For one thing, our colleagues are nowhere to be seen. Jamie sits down and, as is customary for him in moments of reflection, lights up. At that instant, a plainclothes officer approaches us. She has cartoon comedy evil eyes and a slightly manic grin that makes her look as if she is enjoying herself, although it may just be a facial tic. The filming of a government building, which includes the clinic, she tells us, is not allowed. We show our press passes but they count for nothing.

'We have your colleagues,' she tells Jamie and me. 'They are at the university. Would you like to accompany us?' It seems a curious, unprompted lie. She is standing next to a police car, not a mobile library. Why would she tell us they are at the university, when clearly they've been taken to the county jail? I remain inscrutably polite as I tell her thank you, no, we will wait here until they return from 'the university'.

We stay put. Jamie is quite happy to be able to finish his fag. And is generally one of life's unfazed. 'What do you think we should do now?' he asks. 'How about a lemonade?' I suggest.

And so we head to the one store on the square that sells anything at all. Lemonade and water, razor blades and soap. We buy our drinks and sit, very publicly, in the middle of the square. If anything is going to happen to us, I would prefer there to be a scene.

Our phone batteries are running out and, even with chargers, there is nowhere we can ask for a charging point – electricity is in short supply and works for just a few short hours a day. I am torn between wanting to notify London and tell them what's happened and wanting to reserve the last bar of phone power for emergencies.

We stay in the square under the watchful gaze of the police for the best part of an hour.

Our driver, he of the leaking petrol tank, has been taken along with our colleagues, so we don't even have the means to escape if we wanted to. After an hour, something snaps with the officers. Impatience, perhaps. Or maybe a call from a superior. They come to us on the bench, stand us up bodily and demand this time we accompany them – without euphemism – to the police station. This is the emergency I've been saving my phone-a-friend call for. I dial Dan, our deputy editor, and tell him we are being arrested. An officer wearing a Ministry of the Interior uniform is trying to grab my phone from me. Between her and the dying battery I just have time to tell Dan Clarke where we are, but in the panic my mind has gone blank and I've forgotten the name. 'It begins with B and it's an hour from Havana,' I splutter. Dan is trying to reassure me and google at the same time. I hear him reaching for B words just as the battery dies. I shove the phone into my inside pocket before the officer sees what I've done. I'm praying Dan can pick up the pieces in London.

At home, my husband, half asleep, will receive a late-night phone call from my editor, Ian Katz. 'Ah, Ian,' Mark will say. 'If it's you the news can't be good.' 'No,' Ian admits. 'But not terrible. She's been arrested. They all have. We'll keep you posted.' 'Excellent,' replies Mark. 'Do you offer the same service in Iran? We're off there next month on a family holiday.'

Mercifully, no one, it seems, is taking our captivity too seriously.

They bundle us into a police car, threatening, but scrupulously courteous. It goes all of about two hundred metres before we arrive at the police station and jail. I had realized the town was small, but possibly not this small. They take our passports. They decide to separate me from the boys. I cannot understand why. Perhaps because they see me follow the interior ministry officer's Spanish and think I know more than I am saying. Perhaps it is pure vindictiveness. Or – who knows – an order from above. Every time the guard asks me a question and I answer she screams, 'MENTIRAS! MENTIRAS!'

('Lies! Lies!') at me. It is unsettling and has a profound effect. I search harder for the right answers, even though I don't know what those would be. 'Why were you asking political questions?' she wants to know. I do not know how to answer that. Does she mean of the teens in the square? Or of the doctors in the clinic? I must be careful not to say too much and implicate more people. After a couple of hours, we are all reunited in one room. It looks curiously like a sort of court of law, with a desk for a judge and several pews. My producer, Warwick, is back with us. He decides the best way to look in control is to sit at the judge's desk and start reading a book. He is aiming for nonchalance. Everyone has handed in their phones except for me – mine is hidden in the lining of my gilet. They know I have it still, and for reasons I can barely fathom myself I continue to pretend I don't, playing for time. Partly pride. Partly because I figure they will soon get bored and chuck us out. I am clinging absurdly to the reassurance of having a means of communication. The others in the room are shuffling, but it is my last stab at control of a situation that long ago left me powerless.

Then news comes that Dan, or Dan helped along by Google Maps, has saved the day. After extensive internet searches he's found our town and mobilized another BBC crew to come and get us out. When the fair Amazonian Washington Bureau producer Tara strides calmly into the station, the police think she is in fact a UK consul general. What is lost in translation in those moments is rather to our gain. By nightfall, we have been released, our pride dinted but our passports and phones intact.

Our encounter with the Cuban interior ministry ends there. But the story itself, sadly, does not.

The next day we learn that those we'd talked to in the square have been rounded up and marched off to the police station. Anyone we'd chatted with, anyone who'd been unlucky enough to show us round, was hauled in for questioning. One woman is asked about her employment; another about a loan for her sister's flat. Another has her papers checked – for six hours. And this is how it works: slowly, insidiously. The grinding down, the constant reminder you are being watched and followed. This woman is not accused of anything tangible but is asked to return the following week.

And this, we are told, is what comes next: her employer will be warned; she'll find it tougher to get a loan or a new job or a house. Her life will get steadily harder until she learns her lesson: that it's simply easier not to speak up.

We never use the shots of the scrupulously clean clinic, or the interview with the doctor, so calmly functional she could be from the Royal Berkshire. We never go live the next night with the guests we have set up. We feel somehow nervous about implicating anyone further in our work.

We are left with that sinking feeling journalists around the world know so well. That we have unwittingly created problems and then run away to the easy life back home.

For the next few weeks we stay in touch with those in Cuba. We want to know what we can do without making things worse. It's a big question. It takes careful thought. But perhaps it starts here: with a reminder to myself that dictatorships are not romantic. Even when they have a figurehead like the beautiful Che, or a photogenic fortress like Havana. That police states, even when the cocktails are plentiful and the sun shines constantly through the palm trees, are still police states.

A Gathering of Neighbours

Over the course of the last few years I've had several *big nights*. And I don't mean the traditional Margarita-fuelled hitching of skirts, table-top dancing whilst crooning to a mop as if it were a lover.

No, quite frankly, there weren't enough of those.

I mean elections. Those foundation-shifting, earth-shattering moments of political madness where the impossible happened. I was in Grant Park, Chicago, in 2008, on the night America chose its first black president, listening to Barack Obama's victory speech on the stage. I was live in Times Square for the BBC as America voted in Donald Trump eight quick years later. I was interviewing on air as Britain chose to leave the EU.

And I watched from the centre of the studio as Theresa May saw in the results of the election she would wish she'd never called. The image of the night was her face at the count – glum and aching – next to the Darth Vader-like character of Lord Buckethead, who was contesting her Maidenhead seat.

We spent a long time explaining that one to our foreign viewers.

Those were our big nights. Macho, and relentless.

Fuelled with adrenalin and Diet Coke. Offset by Mars bars.

But one of my personal favourites was much quieter and more gentle.

It took place in a snow-covered farmhouse in Iowa.

Any US-watcher will hear the word 'Iowa' and know it spells one thing: the very first caucus in the primary races in a presidential-election year. This was 2016. It was a year that would end in the election of Donald Trump. But we didn't know that then.

We had flown in from Texas, where we'd been on the tail of Ted Cruz, the senator there who will run against Trump, loathe Trump, attempt to sabotage his convention and end up with the unshakeable moniker 'Lyin' Ted'. We actually fly into Omaha, Nebraska, and spend two hours at car hire waiting for a snow-tyred SUV that also has a back seat phone-charging point so I can turn my bit of the Land Cruiser into a mobile office and plan my pieces for the next few days as we head across the state border from there.

In Iowa we stop at Darrell's Diner, in rural Hamlyn, where Ted Cruz has just spoken to a packed crowd. He's sworn to repeal healthcare, drop the nuclear deal with Iran, give pride back to gun-owners – all the things Trump will later do in office. It is outside Darrell's that I see a man smoothing a 'TED CRUZ' bumper sticker on to his car.

'Why Ted Cruz?' I ask, hoping for a sound bite I can use for my piece.

'Because . . .' He pauses to take me in. 'I gave Donald Trump a shot. I went to his event; I got the free T-shirt. But it fell apart after three washes.'

On such disappointments – or, who knows, the mis-reading of a washing instruction – are opinions formed. Votes cast. And in Iowa they take their responsibility incredibly seriously. This is the home of that strange thing: the caucus, a beast that sounds as if it's emerged straight from the pages of Lewis Carroll. 'Caucus' trans-lates literally as a 'gathering of neighbours'. It is where people will meet up, argue, debate and convince and then offer up to the rest of the country their preferred choice of party candidate.

It is voting in its most primordial form. It requires those who sign up to leave warm homes after dark, often in deep snow, and spend hours in a chilly church hall discussing the merits of their woman or man. There is no electronic database. Not the whiff of a chad, hanging or otherwise. This is firmly rooted in pencil and paper, torn up into little squares and passed around a room of half-familiar faces and strangers. It lies somewhere between a neighbourhood-watch meeting and an end-less card game. It is not for the faint-hearted.

And somewhere between leaving Nebraska after that over-long encounter at the airport car-hire place, meet-ing the T-shirt man at Darrell's in Iowa and driving through row after row of now snow-covered corn-fields to Des Moines, I decide, as if my life depends upon it, that I must attend one of these caucus meetings.

I must see it and film it but, above all, I must just be there.

So we spend the day – Vara Szajkowski, my producer, Peter Murtaugh, my cameraman, and I – ringing round and talking to people, trying to cadge an invite. There are big caucus gatherings – five hundred in a school sports hall – and there are tiny caucuses in someone's living room. I am thinking the smaller, the better.

In the end, with a couple of dozen phone calls, we land an invitation to a Democratic caucus.

It will take place at the home of Mary and Gary Weaver in Precinct 3, Boone County, Rippey. One thing I have never understood about America is how it can be so simultaneously armed to the hilt and wary of the outsider, yet so open and warm and welcoming to the complete stranger knocking on the door. Perhaps the two are not unrelated. The weapon in the desk drawer gives you the freedom to be fearless.

We have finished our live hit with London, sent our piece and because we are six hours behind it is only 6 p.m. We grab supper on the go and drive out of the capital, Des Moines, to rural Boone County, an hour away. As we pull up at a picture-perfect farmhouse snow is falling. Other cars arrive around us, a human flurry of boots and coats; some people carry plates of food for a potluck supper.

Mary is standing at the door, welcoming people in. She envelops one young man in a grandmotherly hug, pinches his cheek and says, 'Look, our first student tonight.' There is a raw romanticism to this whole evening and I sense their need to pass it on to future generations.

We are barely questioned as we unpack our camera equipment, explain we are with the BBC and try, as we block the hallway of the tiny space we enter, to look inconspicuous. Laid out on the table are traybake cakes: one vanilla, one flapjack. And white plastic cups of orange squash and a thermos of coffee: a curious mixture of the homely and the infantile. Subconsciously, I register with palpably British pique the absence of alcohol. But then this is a polling booth, not a party.

The living-room furniture has been rearranged into three separate areas to mark out the three Democratic candidates still in the race. Those backing Hillary Clinton will sit in the rows of chairs along the far side. Those for Bernie Sanders will be on the sofas around the front. The other candidate left in the race is Maryland's governor, Martin O'Malley. A rank outsider. They are clearly not expecting a big turnout for his supporters. He gets just one faded armchair, its stuffing escaping at the edges, with the word 'O'Malley' written on a sheet in felt pen across it.

It remains un-sat-upon all evening. It is the most pitiful thing I will see all campaign.

People find their spot, pull off boots, pour coffee, greet those they know, introduce themselves to those they don't. It is all immensely *civil*. A sort of textbook example of how democracy in action should work. I do, however, find marital tension. Roxanne and Steve Gunderson arrive together. But he has gone to the Clinton chairs and she is in the Bernie corner. She calls Hillary a hawk. Can't bear her support of the Iraq War or any other US military involvement since. She likes the peacenik side to Bernie. Her husband thinks she's bonkers.

When the introductions are over and the housekeeping announcements have been made, they will spend time hearing short ad hoc speeches from the floor – like a Quaker meeting, but one that will eventually send bodily representatives, in the form of delegates, to the convention. The maths is too complicated for me to follow as a first-timer but, broadly, the ratio is weighted in favour of the winner.

So far, it has been conversational. Suddenly, the political temperature rises.

There is exasperation from the speakers, shouting over one another. Iowa is famed for its Independent voters. They come open-minded but ready for debate. The Hillary corner is trying to convince the Sanders corner there's only one serious candidate for the Democrats. The Sanders supporters are infuriated that Hillary's camp cannot recognize *her* limitations and *his* popular appeal. From the Clinton chairs a white-haired man in his late sixties cries out, 'Are you not listening to what the Democrats are saying?' He is shut down by a young woman, long dark hair and glasses, Bernie fan personified, who is saying, 'But America is about being idealistic. We don't have to settle.' To which the white hair is back on his feet, saying, 'If he's the candidate, they will look for someone else, I'm telling you.'

My mind will return to this scene time and time again, wondering what I missed, what I might have spotted if I'd listened to the arguments more intently, without wondering about our camera shots for the piece.

And then for the moment of truth. A corporeal show of support – not the pressing of a button or the ticking of a box on a ballot card, but the actual, physical crossing of the floor when a candidate changes their mind. We wait and we watch to see if anyone will do it. There is no movement.

Then, slowly, deliberately, a gentleman at the back with a stick gets up. His name is Dale. Dale came unsure, took in the arguments and has now decided his vote will go to Hillary. He walks from the front to the back of the room to show his decision. We go to speak to him and find out how he arrived at it. He's had cancer, he now speaks through a voice box, and somehow the electronic monotone gives his words an extra sense of deliberation.

'I like both candidates,' whirs the machine. 'I liked a lot of what Bernie has to say, but I've been a Clinton supporter from way back [he's talking about voting for Bill in the 1990s] and I think that's why I decided to go to Hillary more than anything else.'

None of this is rocket science. In fact, it's not science at all. It's literally watching people's gut feelings play themselves out in the open, then watching what it does to the maths. They end up with fifty-two votes and break them down using a formula scribbled up on a whiteboard for everyone to see. Our farmhouse will send two Clinton delegates to the convention. One Sanders delegate. None for Martin O'Malley.

Later we will learn that history has been made that snowy night of 2016. The Clinton v. Sanders contest will be the closest ever of any Democratic caucus in Iowa. The paper-thin margin between them will throw Bernie Sanders into a new light for many here. He has opened up a race that seemed closed, almost dull, against a woman long considered to be unassailable – but who, ultimately, is not.

This is the night Sanders will show Democrats how to mobilize the working class, white vote – the one that will eventually go to Trump – and the youth vote, winning an astonishing eighty-four per cent of seventeen- to twenty-nine-year-olds, faring better with them than even Obama did in 2008.

And after the evening draws to a close, as neighbours leave their gathering, as we declutter the room of our camera baggage and help tidy away the chairs, we do not fully realize the enormity of the question that room was grappling with: who would best represent Democrats in that election year against a formidable Donald Trump?

But we know this: in an electronic age of data and polls, of analytics and tweets and, yes, of fake news, we have seen democracy in its most visceral form.

Where you leave your home in the dead of winter, to gather with your neighbours, argue with your opponents and show your vote by where you choose to sit in a snowy farmhouse living room in Iowa.

How I Was Accidentally Accused of Running a CIA Black Site for Torture

6.40 a.m., Friday, 3 February 2017

My eyes are not even open yet but I am already trying to look at a screen. My phone is a blur beneath sleep gunge and last night's eyeliner. Before I realize it I am looking at Twitter notifications. And my head cannot figure out what I am seeing. I have been accused of running a CIA black site for torture. It is a picture of me, from a *Newsnight* interview earlier in the week. But it has been posted by the Director of Human Rights Watch New York. Above the picture of me, a caption reads:

> Of all the people Trump could have picked as deputy CIA director, he chose woman who ran CIA black site for torture

I am staring and staring at it and still it doesn't make sense. But my initial emotion is nevertheless guilt. *What did I do?* I seem to be saying. OH NO, WHAT HAVE I FUCKED UP NOW?

Before I am fully conscious I am tweeting my innocence. But even that is slightly apologetic.

Erm. This is me. And I'm pretty sure I never ran a CIA black site for torture.. #Newsnight

↩ ⇄ ♥ •••

I run downstairs to get the kids off to school. I show it to Milo and we giggle. I wonder aloud if I could sue but he tells me he will defend the right of anyone who believes me capable of running a torture camp. I forget what provoked that but I probably asked him to empty the dishwasher or put his clothes in the laundry or do something really menacing like his homework. It is Friday, his school assembly, so I rush along to that and forget all about it.

By the time I emerge the thing has been retweeted seven hundred times. It's spawned a host of memes.

There is a picture of me with the Cookie Monster and the line:

confirmed image of you interrogating a detainee

↩ ⇄ ♥ •••

And:

those wild nights after a newsnight party and no one can remember how they got home or if they set up a CIA black site !

↩ ⇄ ♥ •••

One tweet imagines the new look of *Newsnight*:

minister, you haven't answered my question, now, put this
towel over your face

↰　　　⇄　　　♥　　　•••

Kenneth Roth, of Human Rights Watch, has, it transpires, confused me with Gina Haspel. Who did work
for the CIA and who did run a secret prison and of whom –
surprise surprise – there are few photos.

Throughout the day I am contacted by journalist friends
asking if I'd like to make my denial a bit more defini-
tive. One is Jim Waterson at BuzzFeed, who asks for a
quote confirming that I have definitely never run a CIA
torture site. I assume it is a joke: I know Jim and he's part
of the extended *Newsnight* family – partner of our deputy
editor – so I respond in kind. BuzzFeed had been reporting the latest Trump scandal: unproven allegations of a
salacious night in a Moscow hotel. His lawyer denied
culpability with the excuse that he'd never been to Prague.
So I write back (an in-joke between friends): 'You can use
the following: A spokeswoman for Ms Maitlis confirmed
she had never been to the Czech Republic.' It's a throwaway line, written with one finger as I am coming out of
TK Maxx on the way back from walking the dog, if I
remember. But Jim has actually been tasked with writing
the story up for BuzzFeed, so he publishes it – faux denial
and all.

By mid-afternoon, New York has woken up but I've
still heard nothing from Roth, the fellow at the centre of

this news storm. But I get texts from politicians and friends around the globe who are loving it.

Curiously – perhaps the most curious thing about this whole saga – is that I don't hear a peep from Roth until the following week. When I finally do, it is the most unapologetic, unfunny, uncharismatic apology I think I've ever received. And I laugh out loud because I was the one – of course I was – who woke up with the weight of guilt on my shoulders when I read it, not him. It is a reminder of how insane my world can be. To be accused of something so preposterous is one thing, but to carry it around with me all day wondering if somehow I'd accidentally done it is another.

Rachel Dolezal: The Black Human Rights Activist who Turned Out to be White

Of all the interviews I've ever done, it is perhaps not surprising that the most controversial was about race. Some would argue that it was not, truly, about race – or shouldn't have been, anyway: it was an interview with a white woman who believed she was black. That she had been born into the wrong race. It sounded ludicrous. And I couldn't get my head around it. Rachel Dolezal granted me the UK exclusive when she decided to explain to the world what happened after she was outed for 'lying' about the colour of her skin. We met at her home in March 2017, but the story begins some two years earlier.

It is June 2015; Donald Trump is about to announce his candidacy for president in Trump Tower, New York. The previous summer the shooting dead of an unarmed black teenager, Michael Brown, in Ferguson, Missouri, had ignited months of protest and a national debate over civil rights and law enforcement. And in the small town of Spokane, in rural Washington State, a civil-rights activist is talking to a local reporter in a coffee shop about race hate crime. The civil rights activist is Dolezal, who is an NAACP branch president.

And it is during this seemingly straightforward encounter that her whole life begins to unravel: publicly and humiliatingly. The interviewer asks Dolezal, face to face, if she herself is African-American. And it is a question Dolezal cannot answer. Stunned, she eventually responds that she doesn't understand what he's asking.

The clip goes viral. Not just in Washington State, or even in America, but globally. The response was visceral outrage, disbelief and incomprehension. She was accused by white and black people of being a sham and of trying to appropriate the experiences of a person of colour.

So when I am offered the chance to meet her I jump at it, because it is, quite frankly, one of the weirdest claims I've ever heard. I'm keen to hear her make sense of it.

I find Rachel at her home in Spokane two years after that clip made her world famous. Notorious. I have just finished reading her book. In it she describes an oppressive childhood at the hands of deeply religious, authoritarian parents who forbade her from wearing trousers (because of her sex) and constantly reminded her of her position in the family pecking order (last). She recounts that she was forced to eat her own cold vomit as a punishment for refusing her oatmeal at breakfast (she threw up into it and they saved it for her supper). And that she was left to find her own way home from a foraging trip in the mountains of Montana when she was young and afraid. It is, by her own description, a childhood that reeks of despair and negligence.

Then, she writes, things begin to change. Her parents adopt more children: four black babies, to be precise. Dolezal will claim it is to increase their household benefit payments. But the responsibility will fall on her, as the older sister, to nurture them. She immerses herself in black culture and history to better understand the questions they will have. She learns to cook – she has to feed and wash and dress them – and she becomes their de facto mother. She clearly relishes her new role. Suddenly, the whole bizarre premise starts to make sense. Not rational sense, but emotional sense. Here is a girl trying to escape her own skin – figuratively and then, perhaps, more literally. She writes of the need to 'rush headlong away' from the white world and towards the black one. The black stepbrothers and sisters had been the family that she loved. The family that had not cast her as the outsider. She simply went looking for more.

When I arrive at her house, she has just finished putting her toddler to bed. He is her second biological child (both have black fathers) and she has now also adopted one of her black siblings as her own child. She describes to me how her 'transition' came about: how she learnt to braid hair; how she felt she needed permission from black friends before doing her own. How she tanned her skin with sunbeds and creams; how she immersed herself into a world of black activism where it would come to seem unnecessary – crass – to question her ethnicity.

She explains to me that she never 'actually' lied; she just found convenient ways to answer the questions. So when asked about her race she just says, 'My mother is white' and leaves the rest unspoken. She wants to use the same argument transgender activists use but apply it to race: the sense of being trapped in the wrong body, of a fluidity that is far from binary. She calls herself 'trans-racial' and when I ask what that really means she tells me she can move between the two. And then she tells me that race, anyway, is a political construct: a totally invented hierarchy and a way to stigmatize or control those at the perceived bottom if you are one of those at the top. What she says makes a lot of sense conceptually, even if her own story seems to have come from a much darker, simpler place. I am sympathetic to her backstory even if I am tough on her logic. We finish the interview and she shows me her studio – she is trying to sell paintings she has done to make ends meet. She is on the breadline and was turned down by numerous publishers before she found one who was willing to publish her book. And she is desperate to turn it into a source of income to raise her kids.

I say goodbye, puzzling how to make sense of the interview we have just done. I had come to it expecting to find something freakish ('Look, this white woman claims she is black!'); instead I feel to even suggest this is about race is somehow to miss the point. Perhaps there are mental-health issues. Perhaps my intellectualizing of what she's claiming is way off the mark. She has fallen out with most members of her immediate family, she is broke and, if her own testimony in the book is to be believed, she had a relentlessly miserable time growing up. It is an all-too-familiar tale of childhood abuse. The struggle for me now is reconciling what I feel I know with the interview that everyone at home wants.

It is another week before it airs. I have left Spokane, Washington State, and I am safely home. To publicize the interview we tweet out a picture of Rachel and me standing together in her living room. Colour-wise, there is not much between us. The caption that goes with the photo asks, 'Can you choose your race?' The question is deliberately provocative. But, even so, I am unprepared for the level of vitriol that comes our way. My timeline is full of people accusing her of the worst: lying, profiteering, appropriation, insensitivity, cowardice.

Some people are genuinely keen to start a debate about race and what it means.

You only get to choose your race if you're white. Therefore no

↰ ⇄ ♥ •••

All race-normative discourse is fundamentally oppressive. Cisrace people need to hush and listen

↰ ⇄ ♥ •••

What a shame this eraser of black women's experience is given airtime, while so many brilliant black women are not

↰ ⇄ ♥ •••

Others just got personal.

> Pls stop enabling this failure of a woman and put her in a
> loony bin

> appropriating others peoples pain is not a good look

And then there were the smashed-up attempts at angry irony.

> I choose to be transfabulouslywealthy if we are going to
> play this game

The comments stop me in my tracks. They make me feel I have an extra duty of care towards the woman I've just interviewed. I worry for the first time that we have been exploitative in seeking her out. It is not that I want to protect her narrative – I don't, it's demonstrably false – and I can see how claiming 'blackness' could be deeply offensive. But I feel now I need to protect the person who's found herself in the eye of the hurricane. I have edited the piece with what I hope is balance. But I'm now doubling back on what we've left in and what we have lost. Did I recount enough of her childhood to put her claim in a clear context, even if I haven't spelled it out? Have I included the accusations that she has been racist in her attempts to pass herself off as black when she is not? What about her description of how she was raped: is that irrelevant to this discussion? Or relevant to the person she has become? I'm finding it hard to separate the academic argument from the woman I have met.

I remind myself that it was she who wanted to talk, she who had written of her experience and she who had been judged for the last two years, anyway, without anyone fully knowing her story. This was her chance to stop being one dramatic headline and become the whole person behind it.

Was it offensive to people of colour to see the prominence we gave that interview? Perhaps that's harder for me to answer. Certainly, I wanted to listen to those telling me she was taking up airtime that should have gone to black voices. In the office, I put forward my concerns. I explain that, having met her, it feels inappropriate to treat the encounter purely as an accountability interview. I want to portray her as I found her there, in her own home, as she herself struggled to make sense of what she'd done. The team are sympathetic but time is running out and we need to work out the debate we are trying to have off the back. In the end, we try and tap into both sides: in the studio a female critic who was appalled at her behaviour; down the line from Chicago a black activist who thought it absurd to aim so much bile at her. As I chat through the interview on the phone with him he tells me she's a misplaced target for people's outrage. He holds up the Kardashians, accuses them of appropriating black culture 'with their butt injections and their bling'. No one touches the Kardashians, he reminds me, because they're rich and successful.

It is a brilliant, brave, thought-provoking line. And it will take the discussion into a new direction, raising questions of class as well as race. But it never gets on air. Our Chicago guest will get stuck in heavy traffic. And I will be reminded, as I sit looking anxiously up at the clock in the studio, how often our editorial choices are hostage to such simple things as a dodgy mini-cab service.

And Rachel – what of Rachel, the white woman who believed she was black? As I write, she's been charged with welfare fraud. Benefits claims undeclared. I suppose that should make me less sympathetic – confirm her neatly in the narrative of imposter, be it with regard to financial dealings or her own identity. But, oddly, it doesn't. Perhaps her story had a more profound effect on me than I realized at the time. We love issues at *Newsnight*, we love the argument, dissection and debate of current affairs, and this – the whole question of 'choosing' your race – was as fascinating as it was contentious. But the interview with Rachel Dolezal was one where the issues had overtaken the person at the centre. I see more clearly now that race became a lazy shorthand for something much simpler: a deeply unhappy woman who longed to be a part of something she could not.

The Fire at Grenfell Tower

On 14 June 2017, I woke at 1 a.m. to the sound of sirens soaring past the house. Because we live on a main road in the middle of London, I barely gave it a second thought. But my husband was already awake, scrolling through his phone. 'There's been a fire,' he said. And at that point I remember the sense of relief that it wasn't terrorism. Fires, we know, don't really kill people. Not in London. Not in 2017.

By dawn, I was up, Hannah Mac and I running the dog on Primrose Hill. It was only when we reached the top, looked back, saw the heavy grey smoke from the direction we'd just come and searched the phone for the latest scraps of news that it started to sink in. It wasn't just a fire. It was a fire you could see across London. It was a fire that would leave more than seventy dead, many hundreds more homeless, sleepless and mentally scarred. It was a fire that would rewrite tragedy in twenty-first-century Britain.

Hannah's producer instincts kicked in immediately. She rang the desk and offered herself in whatever capacity they needed. She was directed straight to the scene. I wasn't working that day, and I didn't want to be; I didn't want to be the Hollywood version of a reporter with a microphone and cameraman intruding on grief and confusion when things were so raw. It is my job, unfortunately, to do that. And, of course, I do do it. But it's easier when you're a stranger, when you're operating in French, when you're asking American police to let you cross a line – even in Manchester at the Arena stadium bombing I was at one remove. This time, I felt no distance, just a weight in my solar plexus. This was my neighbourhood. The residents of the tower would include our school-bus drivers, sports coaches, dinner ladies and local artists. It was on my doorstep, as the early sirens had warned me. It was too close to treat as another story.

And so instead I ran home and called my friend and neighbour, Federica, a long-standing volunteer at the Rugby Portobello Trust. Without me saying a thing, she appeared on my doorstep and together we clicked into 'doing mode'. We started packing bin bags full of stuff from around the house: baby clothes and shoes, games for the kids, blankets and shampoos. Anything and everything we thought useful. It was, if I'm honest, somewhere between a gesture and a cathartic purge. A way of trying to feel useful even when we didn't really know what to do with ourselves.

We headed to St Peter's Church on Kensington Park Road, which I had known of old as a toddlers' playgroup. This became a focal point for people trying to do the same as us. We found a kind of well-meaning chaos. Bin bags and piled-up garments. A sign saying 'Miscellaneous' when, really, it all was. We arrived, unloaded and then stayed to make sense of the donations. Women's stuff in one place, kids' clothing in another. Amidst the deep sense of shock there were moments of unintended pure comedy. The chap who dropped off a bag of twenty unmatched socks fresh from his dryer. Or the moment I unpacked the diamanté-embossed Stella McCartney jeans. I have never folded so much skinny designer wear, never unpacked so many British Airways business-class wash bags. I understood it for what it was: that morning, the borough was heavy with a kind of raw, collective guilt, a recognition perhaps of the divide between those who appeared to want for nothing and those who had lost everything. We threw little away – and, as it turned out, the business-class wash bags were spot on: fresh toothbrushes, socks and sleep masks were probably the most useful starting pack we could have asked for.

I updated anyone bringing donations with posts via Twitter, telling them which collection points were stuffed full, which were taking deliveries. There was a call for headscarves and longer robes – the first indication the victims would include a large number of Muslim families – and my deputy editor at *Newsnight*, Jess Brammar, saw my tweets and suddenly realized I was on the scene. I explained to her that I needed to stay there as a volunteer first, but afterwards I would happily present the programme from location at 10.30 p.m. To her huge credit, she agreed, and let me be for much of the day.

Later on, we headed to the Rugby Portobello Trust HQ. It had opened its doors to survivors and residents still looking for family. They had set up a trestle table in the gym to mark the end of Ramadan. Many of the families were still fasting, in the middle of all this grief and upheaval.

One local pizza company had sent out a mass delivery timed to arrive at sundown when the fast ended. The charity was looking for drivers to take those newly homeless to hotels for the night. My sister Nicky (also a local) turned up and took one family down to the Premier Inn in Hammersmith. She returned confused. The family had asked her what they should do for meals – were they allowed room service? Should they eat communally at the centre? Was there spending money? She shook her head, not knowing, and asked me. And I shook mine, no clearer. We had been given responsibilities but felt deeply unqualified to offer direction.

Back at Walmer Road, and the Portobello Trust, more shell-shocked survivors turned up, looking for someone to tell them what to do, where to go just to sort out the next meal, or the next bed, where the babies could sleep or how to search the hospitals for those they hadn't found. I was with a doctor who had been on the scene at 4 a.m. and was still going strong at ten that night.

Council members popped down to the centre and at one point – in what felt like a parallel universe – Andrea Leadsom turned up to speak to reporters who were outside the front, waiting for news. The overriding sense was that no one in authority was really in charge. That day was powered by volunteers, amazing people who got their act together when no one else seemed to have a clue what to do. They made cash collections, sorted out every family with enough to help them get by for one night.

Just before 10 p.m. I left the Rugby Portobello – a powerhouse of activity and organization – and went down to our live point. There, Hannah Mac was waiting for me. She would produce live. It suddenly seemed an enormously long day. I caught her eye. She was thinking the same thing. We had cast our minds back to the early morning, the plume of black smoke, the unforgiving horrors the day had yielded. And the two of us back together – both of us still unchanged from the morning.

The fire was still burning on the twenty-second and twenty-third floors. I think – as I glanced over my shoulder at the orange glare behind me – that was the first moment I fully realized the scale of it: that the numbers of dead would be beyond imaginable.

My live on air was unpolished; I was still in that morning's running kit, with a shabby green-grey coat thrown over the top – I hadn't had time to change. There was so much I wanted to say and I was scared of rambling. But at that point, I said it all. About the gulf between the residents who shared that neighbourhood – the Westway Sports Centre was where both the Beckhams' and the Camerons' children played football. Tonight it was a makeshift refuge. I told them about the business-class travel wash bags and the Stella McCartney diamanté jeans in the collection bags, and I spoke to a vocal campaigner from the Grenfell residents' group, furious that the concerns of many had gone ignored for so long. She told us about the worries they had been voicing for years over the way the fire escapes were managed, the lack of sprinklers, the way building regulations had been flouted, about the materials used on the tower.

Normally, on air, we are cautious not to let one speaker voice allegations we can't prove. My job is usually to temper those voices. This time, I just couldn't: I let her shout and tell me how negligent the authorities had been. Behind us, the flames were still burning through that building. How could I possibly stand there, at that moment, and tell her to tame her anger and her accusations?

That night, I suddenly remembered, I'd been invited to a dinner inside Kensington Palace, less than a mile away. It was the annual gathering of the Founders Forum – tech entrepreneurs, the new masters of the universe. It still seems extraordinary that those two moments could coexist less than a mile apart. On any other evening it would have seemed a huge privilege, and a delight. I remember feeling quietly grateful I wasn't there that night.

After the programme, Hannah and I walked home through the streets of Notting Hill, which were still brimming with people. At first glance, it looked more akin to carnival night: the whole area pedestrianized; trestle tables set up and stretched across the road, laden with food for the first responders and all those who had lost their home. There was the most extraordinary scene of community. Outside one house we found hot food and pizza boxes set up on a makeshift stall. 'It's for the fire crews,' the owner told us. 'Please tell them there is food for them here at 190 Ladbroke Road.' Sure enough, further up we found the fire crews themselves and passed the message on. I asked one how high he thought the death toll would be. He told me he reckoned not much fewer than a hundred. At that moment, the official figure was still around twelve. That, we knew, would be wrong. But, thankfully, the firefighter's prophecy was too.

The next couple of days passed in a haze. My kids and I went back down to one of the centres, sorting shoes, taking old football shirts. Once again there was this overpowering sense of so much undirected goodwill. Everyone wanted to help; no one quite knew how.

The tragedy taught me things about this city, and my own borough, that I didn't know. It horrified and disturbed me and will do so for a long time to come. But it also exemplified what happens when your personal and professional worlds collide.

I would like to think that covering the story as a local reporter made me better. But maybe the opposite is true. Maybe I got too emotional. Too involved. I can hear a voice in my head warning that you can't be a volunteer in the morning and a reporter the same night.

I was not to know it then, but two days after Grenfell I would interview the prime minister with a pain and a ferocity I never knew I had.

Grenfell made me ask a larger question of my job that day: How much of you goes in – and how much should be left at the door?

Theresa May After Grenfell

The first I know of my interview with the prime minister of Great Britain is ten minutes before it happens.

I am sitting at my desk, watching my editor, Ian Katz, coming towards me and talking animatedly on the phone in a conversation I can see but not hear through the glass door.

Seconds later, he walks in. 'She's on her way here,' he says. It is the simplicity of those five words which makes me draw breath. And then a delicious realization that it's too late to panic. Or run.

Bizarrely, I just carry on doing what I'm doing: listening to an interview on the *PM* programme on Radio 4. A troubled voice is saying, 'There's a need for people to hear the prime minister say in words of one syllable, "Something *terrible* has happened. Something has gone *badly wrong*. It is *our fault*. We accept *responsibility*."'

And suddenly, easily, I know that will be my first question to Theresa May.

It is Friday, 16 June 2017. Two days after an inferno in a tower block in west London has left countless dead, burned in their beds, and hundreds more homeless. Moreover, the Grenfell tragedy has sparked an intense public debate – and rage – about inequality in our country, about austerity and about whether people's lives were put at risk by systemic failures to invest in their safety.

It is a period of oppressive heat – London hasn't seen rain for weeks – and there is a brittle atmosphere in the city reminiscent of the summer of riots of 2011: a sense that anger and grief and frustration and sweat are about to boil over into something bigger.

There are protests on the genteel Georgian streets of Kensington. In the shade of lime trees on Hornton Street, demonstrators have gathered. They surround the town hall and its officials – known to me in more mundane times as the gatekeepers to parking permits and children's library books. They flood the building to demand answers from the council. Later, they will take their demonstration across London to the BBC to accuse media organizations of being complicit in a cover-up of the numbers of dead.

Above all, there is fury that no one seems to be in charge on the ground, and they blame the PM for failing to meet residents, failing to meet the challenge of this tragedy square on.

It is within this context, then, that Theresa May appears at the BBC.

Our office is on the third floor; the interview will be on the ground floor. I am crouching in the lift, trying to do my make-up on my knees as we go down. The mascara is not going well and I am wearing a white jacket. The possibilities for disaster are endless. At the bottom, we are met by James Harding, my head of news.

'You do understand what's happened, don't you?' he asks. I am not sure where to start, so I just say no.

James explains that the PM had requested a quick exchange with the BBC at the location of the fire, Grenfell Tower, to get her statement across. Fiona Bruce has gone down there to present the *Six O'Clock News*. But the atmosphere is too febrile – people shout, '*Coward!*' at the PM as she leaves the community church there – and Downing Street has decided not to risk it. Instead, she will come to the BBC to do a pool clip (one all the media outlets can use simultaneously). And I will be the one to deliver it. James is keen that our viewers should understand *why* the interview is happening, like this, here, and it should be part of the interview. It's a complicated ask with minutes to go. I need to revisit the questions I have scrawled in pre-teenage handwriting in my notepad.

We have been allowed five minutes of interview time, which is generous by Downing Street standards. We have set up two chairs and two cameras in a meeting room. James and Ian now start to debate about what they want the interview to cover. Ian insists it must include questions about building regulations and safety – all the issues we have been unearthing on *Newsnight*. James tells him there won't be time for that now; he wants it to be about her immediate response, the public mood, the things she cannot just throw forward with talk of 'a public inquiry'. I'm wondering if I will get to ask about a change of political mood: the end of austerity; the ditching of the culture that hailed the cutting of red tape. There is far too much to cover, far too little time to plan, and I realize I do not want to stand there listening to men argue, as it's freaking me out. Instead, I go inside the interview room, sit down and shut the door. Good interviews happen once you cut out the noise and the rushing and the desperate search for stats and quotes. They are born in the silence, after you've taken one or two hermetically sealed minutes to work out what the interview is actually *about*. That minute on my own allowed me to find the composure to get my thoughts together and put them into words. Precious seconds before the PM and her entourage burst through the door.

We shake hands and she sits down opposite me. The TV is still on silently, and replaying scenes of Grenfell. She attempts a weak joke about having just come from there. Of course she has. And we know why. It's too painful to catch her eye and no one knows quite what to do.

The cameraman asks me for a clap to synch up the two cameras on to the same time to make the editing easier. I clap, and I begin. My two editors are crouching in a corner of the room, literally on the floor to ensure they don't get caught in the shadows of the camera shot. It feels vaguely ludicrous.

My first question is James's point: Why did you come here today instead of doing the interview at the location? She can't address the point – walks past it – and says, 'What I want to talk about today is what the government is making available to the victims.' I follow up by pressing her on the point the angry radio voice was making earlier: 'There is a need for the public to hear you say in words of one syllable, something terrible has happened, something has gone badly wrong, it is our fault, we . . . accept responsibility.' I ask her about whether she misread the public mood, whether she admits the response was not good enough, and each time there is this curious, clumsy sidestep away from the questions I ask. Later, it will be called robotic, unfeeling, inhuman. Even the *Daily Mail*, which had been Theresa May's biggest cheerleader up until the election of 2017, will splash it over the website with the headline MAYBOT MALFUNCTION.

It is – I won't pretend – a hard interview for me. I volunteered on the ground at Grenfell before I covered it as a news story, so my phone is already full of people asking real questions: Where will we sleep? How will we get food? Why is no one in charge? I have not had to dredge up a list of suitable issues; they are all there, in black and white, in texts I have received from residents. It is hard because I inevitably come to it with emotion, hard because my bosses are crouching in the corner of the room listening to each word, hard because Downing Street is trying to stop us overrunning, hard because it is a pool interview so I must ask questions that I imagine every reporter would ask in my shoes. And it is hard because – in truth – I have sympathy for Theresa May, who is in a wretched position amidst a tragedy of unimaginable proportions. The woman looks shattered, sleepless and distraught. I am in no doubt that she has felt this horror deeply but believed it more important to *do* than to *emote*. What else would you expect of a vicar's daughter from Eastbourne? It seems completely understandable.

But I learnt a very important thing that evening: I had to do the interview that the moment required. Would it have been the same interview a week earlier or even a day later? Almost certainly not. But you have less choice about these things than you realize. Less time to think or reflect than it may appear. These moments are not architectural structures, measured and executed to within a millimetre of the drawing on the draft. They are clashes of circumstance and situation, the product of sleepless nights and palpable nerves, where your make-up is done in the lift going down, where your bosses are arguing, where your own notes are scrawled in a handwriting you will never decipher and the entire preparation happens in a ten-minute window.

I'm writing this book in part to try and dispel the myth that everything that happens in television is planned. I would love to think that what we show on air is the product of hours of editorial analysis and foresight. We think about things *a lot*, but the actual broadcast is rarely the thing we had in mind. Much of my own work is the stuff of chance encounters. The ones we didn't see coming.

Sometimes it captures the public imagination in a way that will change the course of the story for ever. It's often terrifying. Rarely predictable. But that has come to be the essence of what I think of as my daily job.

Russell Brand: How Addiction Starts with a Penguin Biscuit

I am preparing to loathe Russell Brand. For a start, he has booked his own make-up artists and separate green room for our interview. He will come in via a different door and only appear when he is done. Secondly, he is running thirty minutes late and, as a prodigious and religious timekeeper, I cannot bear the waste of time or the power signals that it is meant to send out. For a third, I have seen what happens in his interviews. The interviewer gets tied up in knots and normally ends up holding his hand at inappropriate moments.

By the time he deigns to enter the room I am near growling. A low, throaty rumble of disgust is forming at the anticipated indignity. And my own producer is getting nervous. Sure enough, Brand's make-up is better than mine, his hair is longer and glossier, and he's not sweating from having sat under bright lights for half an hour. I am batey and determined not to give him an easy ride.

But then he comes in. And he has me at 'Hello'. That simple.

Of course, with Brand, 'Hello' is never simple. He walks in and somehow pretends to look star-struck. Like he wasn't expecting to meet me. It is genius. Flattering, warming and confidence-boosting. Then I remember that's what it's meant to be. He's wearing tight leather trousers and a white shirt whose buttons have been flung apart insouciantly to reveal a more than adequate amount of chest hair. We are here to talk about addiction, and he has written a self-help book called *Recovery*. Apparently – his three assistants clarify for me, powder brushes in hand – he needed the green room for pre-interview meditation, not make-up.

'Do you mind, Emily, if I take a picture of us for the purposes of social media?' he asks, with his comically faux-Dickensian courtesy.

Of course I do not mind. A photo! Of me! For Twitter! With Russell Brand!

See, I am grubbily keen already and he's only been in the room a minute.

Russell Brand's book is a sort of AA programme without the pomposity. It is funny and punchy. It is, more bizarrely, a step-by-step guide to how to stop being addicted to whatever you're addicted to. A guide to changing behaviour and rewiring the mind so you stop wanting to damage yourself. And it offers to help you clean out a lot of emotional closets.

I tell him I have been surprised by how practical it is. I always assume we will be blinded by the brilliance of Brand prose in his writing, but this feels different. He literally puts in bullet points. Charts. Spreadsheets. He looks pleased that I have noticed it has a purpose.

'Is the solution to addiction the same whatever the

addiction is?' I ask. And yes, he very much likes that one too. I am getting full marks for reading the book.

He himself came to this from drug and drink addiction. At the time of interview, he hadn't touched drugs for fifteen years. He recognizes that some addictions need extreme support if they are chemical dependencies, but most addictions run along the same lines. I tell him my own is late-night, post-*Newsnight* internet shopping, which leaves me feeling like I've drunk-dialled an ex-boyfriend when the parcels turn up the next morning. He nods – tells me addiction is a useful analytical tool. A good way of looking at attachment and dependency – an amplification everyone is searching for as a way of supplementing what he calls 'our experience of being'.

It's all a bit Hare Krishna, but then Brand is. I feel like I'm being lectured on an overpriced retreat weekend in the Cotswolds.

I remind Brand that his own addiction began with Penguin bars in front of the telly, shoving them into his mouth one after another.

'It was actually very gently done,' he corrects. 'I wouldn't shove them in. I would eat off the top bit then scrape out its little brown guts. Then nibble round.'

Clearly he is a Penguin pro. As I was at that age. The conversation then takes a turn for the more surreal. Why Penguins? I ask. If you wanted to get the chocolate sides off whole, then surely Club bars or even the now defunct Montegos are infinitely more satisfying. That chocolate comes off in hard slabs, not soggy corners like Penguins. I do not have Brand's backstory. His messy childhood hinterland. I cannot tell you the street names for smack. Well, only about two. But if it's 1970s after-school biscuits, then, look, I am hands-down unbeatable. I think he knows it. He looks crumpled and then explains that the Penguins weren't really his choice: his mum got them. I nod, fearing I've gone too far, and anxious to drive us back on to the subject in hand.

Brand explains his own early addiction as a worry about his mum's health. Of feeling unsafe. But it mutated over the years: 'The only consistency is this sense of longing, a sense of yearning you can be fulfilled somehow. You can connect through material.'

Then the time has come to ask about sex. The stories of Brand's sex life are rife. He once checked himself into a US clinic to curb his need for lap dancers and prostitutes. Surrounded by what he called a rotating harem of women, topped up by one-night stands and casual encounters – around five different ones a day at one point, or nearly twenty a week.

So would he call himself a sex addict? I ask. 'Possibly not at the time, but I think in retrospect it was pretty clear that I was using sex to medicate and to feel connected and to deal with that yearning and longing, so yeah, in fact I start to think that the object of the addiction becomes less and less relevant.'

So does he think – married now with a baby and a big fluffy dog – that sex addiction still threatens him?

He pauses. 'It's really challenging. I don't just think, Oh no I'm a rampant sex addict, how will I stay in a monogamous relationship? I think more, I hope this tendency towards destruction won't devour me. I've also come, Emily, to regard the yearning quite benevolently because I think it's a kind of longing for truth. A longing for connection. I will never be satisfied with placebos or ciphers because I've experienced the sort of promiscuous lifestyle. I've experienced indulgence in all kinds of other ways that I thought might resolve the way I feel, and I now know they won't.'

So then I come in with what I think is my killer question: our interview has fallen around the time when women are starting to come forward to open up about the abuse of Hollywood media mogul Harvey Weinstein. A bit of me thinks, Why am I treating Brand as the addict, the victim, in all this when he's perpetrating bad behaviour? So I launch at him:

'When you look back at that promiscuous lifestyle, do you think – does that appal you? Do you think, God, I was disgusting. Do you look at your daughter now and think, I hope she never meets Russell Brand when she grows up?'

I sound passionate and caring, disgusted and unafraid. Or at least I think I do. But he laughs in my face, making me feel like a head girl who's getting irritated about a hockey score.

'Emily, don't get so worked up about it. It's only a rhetorical device. Does it appal you? No, my dear, I don't look back at the past and get all worked up about it like Ebenezer Scrooge. I simply think those are some things I've done. I've amended for them and, as for the likelihood of some sort of Faustian kick up the arse from future Russell, if my daughter meets somebody who's caring and sensitive and knows how to communicate, then I think that will be a good thing.'

And like that – with a nod to Dickens and Goethe and a cartoonish cliché – I am demolished.

I'm not going to get tears of repentance; that much is clear.

A few years earlier Brand had appeared on *Newsnight* to say he never voted, as he was weary and indifferent. The clip was replayed millions of times. It became an anthem to his followers – a sort of justification for others not to vote either. I ask him if he stands by it or if he thinks of it as a result of his depression at the time. He gets agitated, defensive.

'Well, no, it's not mental illness, Emily, no, it was a reaction to politics at that time which I think, subsequently, it's borne out that a lot of people felt similarly that they were not being offered viable alternatives and, subsequent to me saying partisan politics is meaningless, we've seen a huge lurch to the right. We've seen Brexit; we've seen the rise of Jeremy Corbyn. I don't think that I was some kind of soothsayer, Nostradamus on a peninsula peering out into the bleak unknowable. I was simply taking the temperature and speaking on behalf of a lot of people.'

'But,' I say, 'a lot of people followed your lead and thought, Oh, Russell Brand's apathetic; I don't need to vote. The world is too crazy a place to be apathetic.'

'I'm not apathetic,' he says. 'I don't think people could ever mistake me for being apathetic. Do you really, meeting me, talking to me, think I'm apathetic?'

'I wonder why you didn't vote.'

'You know why? Because there weren't realistic options at that point, were there? I think the genie's out of the bottle on that one, Emily.'

'Don't you think it was irresponsible?'

'No, as a matter of fact, in my more optimistic moments I hope that it may in some small way have contributed to what we have subsequently seen. The Labour Party electing a leader that is engaged and engaging. That is authentic and that is truthful, and that is listening to people and that seems to be like a human being that connects, not some bizarre automaton, technocrat lunatic with a Richter screen staring at you out of the pages of a Quentin Blake book. So I think it's a great thing.'

And this is when things begin to get weird. I move on to ask him about parenthood – how he's finding it, is he a nappy-changer – and he gives me a new-dad-sweet-boring answer. Sorry, but he does. My mind has already drifted back to our previous conversation about political apathy. And I'm wondering if the encounter was robust enough when, suddenly, Brand calls me out for not registering the comedic value of his last answer.

And I realize, as he was speaking, I'd tuned out.

'You can't *ignore* that. Did you hear it or what? Sometimes I do wonder.'

'I did,' I say.

'That's what you do? You just edit the moment,' he insists.

He's right. I have. My head has already decided his sweet-new-dad-answer is boring and I've mentally edited it out. He tells me off. Right there, on camera.

'Don't edit things out, because if you listen properly you will get little jewels of spontaneity raining down from heaven. Like that last scene in *Charlie and the Chocolate Factory*—'

'*Elevator*,' we both correct simultaneously. For all our vast differences, we have clearly both been raised on a middle-class diet of Roald Dahl and Penguin bars.

There is a mutual pause.

Then, suddenly:

BRAND: Where do you live?

ME: Well, not very far from here.

BRAND: I'm not going to follow you. I'm not that sort of person. I'm just trying to imagine you in a domestic situation.

ME: I have an apron on a lot of the time.

It's true. I do. I signal my fleeting domesticity with a range of very cool aprons. Sometimes I even leave the house in them by mistake. But why do I feel the need to tell him that? Here and now? Could it be that I am flirting? Attempting to? That the apron is – gahhh, perish the thought – the sartorial aid I have reached for in a burst of *Sun* page-three coquettishness?

In my embarrassment, I try and draw the interview to a professional close. We talk briefly about self-harm. I am hoping he may show me his scars on camera (yes, I really am, that's what being in television long enough does to you; it makes you think of visual curiosity in the most inappropriate way). Then I say to him, 'Right, is there anything you feel you didn't get a chance to say that you wished to?' rather like a GP wrapping up their hurried ten-minute slot with an elderly patient who may not be back for a while.

Brand grins. 'No, actually, I like it when you do the energy spikes. They're my favourite bit, when you go: "Well, staring back at the past you're promiscuous you're in a pirate ship you're being sick over the side of it why are you doing this!"'

He is imitating me and laughing at me. And I apologize for sounding like a moralizing mother. I hate being somehow cast as Hockey Girl. Definitely time to go. Or maybe, I think, I didn't sound convincing enough. About the voting.

'Shall I do it again?' I ask. 'Shall I tell you off again? Let me do it one more time. And off I launch, *con gusto*:

ME: You came on *Newsnight*, what, five years ago, and you proudly declared that you hadn't voted. You encouraged apathy amongst young people. Why would you do that?

I finish my rant and he just looks at me. 'Are you

happy with the answer you got last time? 'Cause it's the same. You're just doing it for your own editing pick-up, aren't you?'

'No,' I say, 'I'm doing it again because you're saying it wasn't energetic enough.'

BRAND: It was full of energy. Loaded.

ME: Why don't you answer it again, then? It'll flow.

BRAND: No, you asked it really well, I thought, and I answered it pretty well. [Turns to the cameraman.] What do you think, Jeff?

'Jeff' (who is, in fact, called Keith) looks despairing. 'I think you've both broken television,' he says. 'It's all got too meta. You've broken the whole thing.'

And with that, Brand appears satisfied. He returns, emboldened, to our discussion of Penguin biscuits. 'Red, green, blue wrappers,' he muses. 'But they're all the same underneath. What a valuable lesson in anthropology.' Only Brand could extract an epigram on race from a multipack snack.

Piers Morgan Becomes a Feminist

I'm trying to remember when or how I first met Piers Morgan and all I can recall is a five-hour lunch at the Ivy – him and five of my great girlfriends – for which he generously picked up the tab. Piers was on a roll, telling us that 'thin women are atrocious' and we should all aim to be fatter. It was the kind of random bullet he'd shoot out just for effect. He has always known how to clear a room. And always relished the role of provocateur, sometimes deployed with more success than others. We became mates over fifteen years ago; my husband and his wife adore each other's company too. But, if I'm honest, whilst I would call Piers a friend and have confided in him – up to a point – I have never felt I came anywhere near to cracking his shell. There is a bombastic outer coating to Morgan that makes women everywhere – and possibly men too – roll their eyes to the heavens. When I was offered the chance to interview him for the *Radio Times*, I was curious to know if I could get him to open up. Curious to know how it felt to interview someone you knew well rather than a celebrity or politician you were meeting for the first time. I guess I was looking for a moment of human honesty, weakness or fallibility, because I have never really seen it. I wanted him to tell me something that had actually gone wrong for him and how it felt. The interview took place in January 2018 at my house, where he has been several times.

Piers Morgan helps himself to a cup of tea, sits down at the kitchen table and asks me how I am. For the next five minutes, I tell him. My week, my month, my anxieties. Then I suddenly realize what's happened. I'm doing all the talking. And that is wrong, because I'm meant to be asking the questions. And that is also very Piers Morgan. There's a reason he called his show *Life Stories* — because people talk to him.

'On the way here,' he says, 'just a twenty-minute walk, I had three taxi drivers calling to me out of their windows. At my café six or seven people came over to talk about Trump.'

Piers is very gifted at reminding you how successful he is. You might even say it's one of the things he's *really good at.* So when he starts down this road of 'all the taxi drivers want and adore me' my first instinct is to take the piss. Only this time, I can't. This time, I am, as it were, being paid to be here. Listening. And civil. It's excruciating.

He has six million plus Twitter followers and name recognition in at least two continents, but his USP has always been the man down the pub. So much so that at one point a decade ago he actually bought a pub. He became the pub owner down the pub. Talking to the other man down the pub, his brother, who ran it.

But this time the taxi drivers are talking to him about Trump because he has just been in Davos interviewing him. And that very act of the president giving his first international TV interview to Piers Morgan speaks volumes about the world we have entered. A world in which a contestant from a reality-TV show – *The Apprentice* – and the host of said reality TV show – now president – can cook up a friendship which will serve each of them nicely a decade or so down the road.

'It may not have been a traditional, conventional hard-news interview, but that wasn't my intention. My intention was forty-five minutes of prime time. They're different animals. And I've been really struck by the public reaction, universally saying, "I saw a different side to him." Not that they thought better of him, but different.'

He has pre-empted any criticism I might have of the interview itself by telling me how much 'normal people' enjoyed it. It is, I suspect, attack as a form of defence, because journalistic reaction hasn't been so generous. The veteran BBC broadcaster John Simpson weighed in on Twitter as it was being aired to rebuke him as a soft touch.

The art of the political interview, Piers, is to push your interviewee hard-not let them spout self-evident tosh

↰　　　♻　　　♥　　　•••

'I can't even remember a momentous interview that John Simpson has ever done with anyone,' Piers tells me. 'A perfectly good correspondent,' he continues, 'but he was of course most well known for "liberating Kabul", as *he* put it. Which was a bit of a surprise to the British armed forces who had *actually* liberated Kabul at the time.' It is a jab at an unfortunate and lasting legacy of a line in a Simpson radio interview, the broadcaster's excitement momentarily getting ahead of him as he declared on the *Today* programme, in November 2001, that the BBC had made it into the city ahead of the troops.

There is a bitchy streak to Morgan that makes him mention it now. Clearly the insult hurt, even if he thinks – as he often does – it was born out of envy. Triumphant in victory, graceless in defeat, Morgan was reduced to insults.

'Why always so personal? Did you have to call him an "old prune"?' I ask.

'"*Pompous* old prune",' he corrects me. There is nothing more satisfying to Morgan than the stiletto puncture of a hyped ego. Possibly because, as he would readily admit, he knows how it feels.

He drains his cup, reminding me of the last time he was here, for supper, tying my gentle dinner guests in knots. It was like watching a dawn SWAT team with a battering ram take down a Wendy house. Awkward, disproportionate but, ultimately, hilarious.

I recall how shattered he looked then, as he admitted the breakfast programme he presents was killing him and swearing his wife would divorce him if he stayed on it any longer. But he remained in the job after they allowed him to push his start time back an hour or more. He turns up at the studio at 5.30 a.m. nowadays, allowing him a mere half-hour before the show starts.

'I'm lucky . . . five minutes of slap and on I go . . . The female stars of the show all have to go and get ready. It takes them longer because . . . they get more attention and pressure on how they look.'

I am struck by how carefully he's tiptoed round that sentence. Where once he would have joked about 'looking fit' or 'not scaring the horses', now, post-Weinstein, or maybe post-sofa instruction from his clear-headed and tenacious co-presenter, Susanna Reid, he nods to a kind of external pressure women face.

He uses the moment to declare himself a feminist and will talk a lot about the movement over the course of the next hour. It is an admission I'm not expecting. Particularly after he found himself so publicly on the wrong side of feminism with his remarks about the Women's March on Washington the day after Donald Trump was inaugurated. Is he feeling chastised?

'No,' he demurs. 'The Women's March, particularly last year, was not about feminism or women's rights. It was about screaming abuse at Donald Trump. It was Madonna saying, "I've been dreaming of blowing up the White House." '

'She was only one person in millions,' I remind him. 'You chose to make it about her in your column. Instead of everything else.' But he's unrepentant.

'I will march for gender equality if I'm asked to. I'll do that and I'll march for women's rights. But I'm not going to join a march with a load of abusive girls banging on about Trump. To me, that's a self-defeating waste of time. It didn't achieve anything – what did it achieve?'

I cannot contemplate Piers Morgan ever marching for gender equality. My imagination has conjured up a strident voice talking over everyone else's communal chanting, emerging from beneath a pink pussy hat, and I want to giggle.

Instead I ask him what he, as a feminist, makes of an exposé of a men's dining society, the Presidents Club, which has turned out to be a front for a lot of grubby goings-on – groping, prostitution and unedifying behaviour by powerful men towards young women.

'Look, some people behaved very badly. But I've seen hen nights over the years. Is it going to be the same when the Chippendales tour Britain? I think women who go to Chippendale events and grope the men are no better and no worse than the men at that event but I don't see anyone calling for the Chippendales to be banned!'

I try and get a word in, but Piers is already frothing at the mouth, with his next column organically forming as he speaks. He suddenly turns on me.

'Have you ever been to a Chippendales event?' he asks belligerently, like a man forced to spend much of his life at one.

'I *have*,' I say emphatically. I am reluctant to be cast as the ingénue female in the presence of his macho worldliness even though I can't *quite* remember what I have seen. The trouble with being from Sheffield is that I occasionally confuse whole chapters of my life with *The Full Monty*.

These questions will haunt me long after Piers has left. So much so that on my next trip to Las Vegas I will seek out the Chippendales to ask them if they have ever felt exploited by women. (But you can read all that in the Chippendales chapter, page 260.)

'Right.' Piers nods. 'So you know what goes on at them. I mean, women paw these guys all night. I can see a big issue down the line with men just getting very resentful and feeling: why is it only about male behaviour?'

We are barely five minutes on from Piers I'm-a-feminist Morgan and already he is taking up the cause of the beleaguered male. A role he plays to perfection. His constituency is, after all, the hard-done-by bloke bemoaning a (needlessly!) changing world. In this vision – what you might loosely term the Brett Kavanaugh vision of world events – men are the victims of merciless women striving and conniving to make them fail. I am once again stumped by whether it's something this smart man in front of me actually believes, or whether it just suits the persona he presents to a raging audience. I take a deep breath and quietly point out that his view ignores the politics of power: the men usually have the money and the clout. At the Chippendales, the men probably earn more money than the women in their audience too.

'Yeah, I completely get that . . .' He pauses. 'But I would also say to people that the five or six most powerful people in the country right now are women.' He rattles off his well-honed list of women in power. 'It's not bad. I think we've moved very fast in a short period of time.'

It is a weird pivot. A non-answer to the question I've raised. A sort of all-male-golf-club toast to the Queen.

Piers has become, in recent months, master of the benign controversy. The only man on earth who can pick a Twitter fight with a sausage roll and a papoose. Occasionally it's like watching a Michelin man crash around a padded cell. I wonder how hard he has to work to constantly go against the grain of public opinion.

'No,' he corrects me. 'I often think I *am* the grain – most of the time – of public opinion. It's just not the same grain as social media. The two things are very different. Whenever we do polls on *Good Morning Britain* Susanna will tell you my gut instinct is almost always reflected in the polling of the viewers. Because for ten years my job as editor of the *Daily Mirror* was to get the gut feeling for the British public. When you've edited 3,500 newspapers you've got to get your finger on the pulse of the country. You can't afford to be wrong too often.'

He cites his position against the Iraq War as a prime example. The rest of the establishment, he points out, has now caught up. 'I don't ever argue an opinion I genuinely do not think is my opinion, but I can have my opinion change.'

I want to believe this. Believe there is an intrinsic honesty to whatever position he's taking. But more than anything, I'm struck with how much he wants to be making waves. That the only real insult to him would be silence. A failure by the public to register and react to whatever he's just said.

'I don't see how you can be a columnist and not want people to talk about you. Every opinion columnist wants to be read as widely as possible; otherwise, why would you do it?'

'Even when they talk about you in a way that would make most people want to leave the country?'

There wouldn't, I muse, be many people prepared to share a cartoon picture of themselves licking the presidential backside. He posted the caricature to condemn a BBC comedy show for featuring it at all. And ensured – as he did so – global pick-up.

It can only have been intentional.

When I ask him about the insults, the endless ribbing, the criticism, he talks about it being 'annoying', 'frustrating'. Nothing more. It's not that I want him to mistake me for a therapist and burst into tears, but for all the time I've known him I've never understood if it goes much deeper. If he actually finds it really hurtful as it would do with, say, a normal human being.

'It annoys; it doesn't hurt. Celia [Walden, his wife]

will tell you, I just laugh at most of it. I do. I laugh at most. Although some days you wake up and they say, "I hope you and your family all get beheaded by ISIS, have a good morning," and you're like, What . . . ???!!'

It isn't just the daily trolls, of course. In his life he's been accused of actual things. Crimes: fake photos, insider trading. Phone hacking. Lord Leveson described his testimony on that as 'utterly unpersuasive'.

'He was talking about a very specific part of it, and I would dispute it,' he retorts. 'Yeah, look, I've been accused of lots of things. But I've not been found guilty of any of them. Much as people would like me to be. I actually prefer to stick to the facts. I was not found guilty of insider dealing, I was never even arrested for phone hacking, and nor were any of the thousand or so journalists who ever worked for me. I've never hacked a phone or told anyone to hack a phone and yet, on Twitter, every single day I get twenty or thirty people saying, "You hacked a dead girl's phone." Everyone in the media knows that was *another* newspaper. It's probably one of the most awful things you'd be accused of doing and every day I have to bite my lip and think, OK, OK.'

What is the legacy of that, I wonder, on his soul? Is it corrosive?

'It's fine, because I wasn't found guilty. It's not corrosive, it's annoying, just annoying. I have a very thick skin so I can deal with it. Every public figure has stuff that's not true written about them which gathers momentum on social media.'

Has his own sense of what should be public and private changed over the years?

'It changed towards the end of my tenure as editor. Because when you get older – I mean, I was a twenty-eight-year-old editor, I didn't really understand the complexities of life at all. By the time I'd left the *Mirror*, I'd gone through a few things in my life [divorce] and seen a different side. When you're living them in the goldfish bowl you suddenly appreciate how much harder it is.'

And Piers, I imagine, can't be that easy to live with. I ask him how Celia would describe what she loves most about him and what she loathes about him, and he quickly says: 'My self-confidence. My ability to ride the storm and survive the jungle.' I genuinely don't know for a second if that's in the loves or loathes column. It transpires he's talking about what she most admires. And, tellingly, perhaps, he completely forgets to tell me what she doesn't like. I will text him to ask only later when I find it missing from my answers. And he will tell me she hates him licking his fingers when he reads the paper. I know I would get a far more revealing answer from Celia herself but I've promised not to check.

Piers's answers come – for the most part – fluently and generously. Except when I ask him which politician he currently admires the most. There is a pause. Then a longer pause. Then we laugh, and he says, 'It's not easy. Leave that as a pause, yeah.'

Loyalty, whether to beliefs or people, has always mattered to Morgan. He was one of very few high-profile friends to have visited his old mate Andy Coulson, David Cameron's former Director of Communications, in prison on charges of conspiracy to intercept voicemails.

Does he find loyalty lacking in public life?

'I think a lot of people, when the going gets tough, are quite capable of running a mile.'

'People have done that to you?' I ask. I am preparing my mental couch now. Encouraging him to lie back and shut his eyes.

'Yeah. Well, I've been through such tumultuous periods in my career. Leaving the *Mirror* was huge, leaving CNN. You always just slightly notice how people respond and you work out their mettle. It's a real reckoner.'

It's true. I've noticed how his annual Christmas party (at the pub) often acts as a strange barometer. Old mates and emptier rooms when he's fallen out of favour. Jam-packed and bursting at the celebrity seams when he's riding high on public opinion.

And it strikes me afterwards that his 'real reckoner' phrase is the moment I will understand him most. How seriously he takes his friendships; how tightly he holds his family. Indeed, I can think of no one who has introduced me to more of their own relations. Every social gathering has the slight air of a wedding-party knees-up – mums, dads, sisters and brothers usually pouring the drinks.

It is clear they ground him; they are indeed the 'eye-rollers in chief'. But maybe their devotion also liberates him, allows him to play at being the most reviled man on telly. An inbuilt gyroscope that lets him enter the storm and find calm at its eye.

Piers Morgan mocks a world he himself belongs to. Bursts the celebrity bubble he hovers inside. He lambasts hypocrisy but vehemently agrees when I suggest he – everyone – is actually a hypocrite. He sees himself as the renegade outsider but is actually a key pillar of mainstream media. When I ask if he hankers to be taken more seriously by newspaper peers – if he'd relish the opportunity to edit, say, the *FT* or *The Times*, which he's certainly brilliant enough to do – he turns it on its head.

'No, I have a far, far more fulfilling journalistic career right now which entirely surrounds me and offers my opinions to a massive platform. TV, Twitter, columns – it's almost like I'm running my own newspaper and I'm the only member of staff. I love that.'

He has rewritten the rules of journalism in the same way Trump has rewritten politics. You can love it or loathe it but most people would have to admit it's breathtakingly audacious.

Towards the end of his time at CNN, when he had entered the gun debate full throttle, he became the subject of a public petition asking him to leave the US. And another one – here – asking him not to come back. He relished it all.

'You will never,' I suggest gently, 'be called a national treasure?'

He bursts out laughing. 'I think you're being a little

hasty there. You'd be surprised. People would be very surprised if they walked around the streets with me. I think more people see me as a panto villain. But with that comes the possibility of a morphing into an international treasure, which I'm not giving up on yet.'

He's joking. At least, I think he is, and it seems the right place to wrap it up. We end, pop the mugs in the sink and say goodbye.

It will take me another twenty-four hours to realize he might not have been joking.

And it will be another forty-eight hours before I reflect that maybe, just maybe, he's right.

Emma Thompson on
Harvey Weinstein

The movement against Hollywood mogul and alleged sex offender Harvey Weinstein began with an article in *The New York Times* when a few brave women began to break the silence. That was at the beginning of October 2017. Ashley Judd and Rose McGowan were amongst the very first.

Three days after the story broke I texted the actress Emma Thompson, whom I'd interviewed before. We had discovered that time a shared love of vodka Martinis, so I have her number. Would she like to comment about Hollywood, Weinstein, or the culture of men and power? She calls me back. Says she's thinking about it. But has a lot going on.

Two hours later I send her another text.

> So, what you reckon? Heading into work wearing a ghastly blue granny dress you only get to see if you say yes. We will come and find you with a crew?

I am somewhere between trying to make light of what I know would be a big interview and apologizing for asking in the first place. It is something I've been told

I do a lot. Even in my brief spell as *Newsnight*'s political editor, I remember being told by friendly politicians of all persuasions that I always sounded as though I regretted the request – which, naturally, I made anyway because that was my job. I guess the English, wincing side of me just hates asking anyone – but particularly 'celebrities' – for what I never completely stop seeing as 'favours'.

I watch the grey dots on my phone. The sign the respondent is reading, perhaps writing, perhaps deleting their response. The final response doesn't come for two more hours.

> No chance for me today darling. Sorry. Right up against it. Sorry sorry.

It is the rush of words of a busy actor fleeing around the place and I don't take it personally. But I know hers would be an excellent voice to have on this and so I persist. Reminding her of the three new rape allegations that have emerged that day, offering to make it as painless or as seamless or as technically uncomplicated as we can. It will only, I say 'take ten minutes on camera'.

She responds saying she will 'get to it when I can but not today'. My heart sinks but I know that any more and I will start to sound annoying. So I leave it. We have tried. I assume it's her way of saying a kindly no.

Which is why when my phone pings with a text the next morning, in the middle of a leg wax of all things,

I am beyond excited. She has read a piece in the *Guardian* and asks me why we don't do a *Newsnight Special* on the whole shebang. 'I'll commit to that.' I leap up and in my rush to action there is hot wax dripping in hugely uncomfortable places. I ring the *Newsnight* desk, asking what we can make possible.

In the end, we decide on the following day. She has a gig at a theatre in Westminster. She can give me half an hour before the final rehearsal. We will see her there ready to roll at four thirty. There is an awkward moment when I ask what the play is and she tells me it's a fund-raiser for Syrian refugees. 'I asked you to chair the debate,' she reminds me, 'but you said you were working.' It is both true and slightly shaming. Here I am attending the very event she asked me to be at, months ago. But I'm here for me, not them. I can feel myself reddening.

It is the same day I have also been given an interview with Keir Starmer, Labour's spokesperson on Brexit. Looking back as I write now, I realize I had always assumed we would lead the programme on Brexit and Starmer. And get to Emma Thompson for 'watchable relief'. In the end, what she says to me during that half-hour is so profound and so articulate and speaks to so much and to so many, not only do we lead on it, we run the interview in its entirety. Nearly twenty minutes. It is picked up around the world, by broadcast and print media, and garners five million hits on YouTube. My Twitter timeline will reveal a rash of new followers hailing 'Emma Thompson for PM'.

The interview will take place at the Emmanuel Centre in Westminster. I will leap from there to Millbank, our studio, for Keir Starmer, provided we are not running late. The crew are setting up by the time I arrive, perfecting the shot, the lighting and the connectivity. The newsroom has sent a satellite truck to take the interview the moment it has finished and feed it back to the *Six O'Clock News*. No pressure, then, I think. I really, really don't want to get this one wrong.

Emma Thompson is running five minutes late. When she comes she is immaculate. Dressed in a sharply tailored jacket; short new hair; good make-up. She looks – and this will sound odd – powerful. She looks like a woman who knows exactly what she wants to say, who isn't bowing to pressure or publicity but who has decided that she feels a responsibility to speak out. She wears her celebrity, her glamour, lightly. I ask if she's ready to roll and she throws back: 'I'm not spiritually ready – and I'm spritzing like a menopausal buffalo.'

It is her very English way of saying, 'It's as good as we're going to get so we might as well go.'

I have heard and read stories of her encounters with Harvey Weinstein. I'm not sure how many of them are true. So that's where we start.

'Is Harvey Weinstein somebody that you would call a friend?' I ask.

'No. The understatement of the century. I had only some business contact with him . . . His bullying behaviour patterns also existed in his business world and so my really main contact with him was shouting at him down the phone that I never wanted to work with him ever ever ever, and so when I came into rooms where he was, which often happened, you know, he would look, well, actually frightened. Because I think that's the sort of thing that happens. If you call out a bully on their behaviour, they tend to avoid you.'

'So you called him out for being a bully to women?'

'Yeah. No, not to women. This was in his business practice. I didn't know about these things [the sex-abuse allegations] but they don't surprise me at all. And they're endemic to the system anyway. And what I find sort of extraordinary is that, you know, this man is at the very top of a particular iceberg, you know. And he's – I don't think you can describe him as a sex addict. He's a predator. That's different. He's an actual predator. He's dangerous, and what he was doing and has done was actually criminal. But he's, as it were, at the top of the ladder of a system of harassment and belittling and bullying and interference . . . This has been part of our world, women's world, since time immemorial. So what we need to start talking about is the crisis in masculinity, the crisis of extreme masculinity which is this sort of behaviour and the fact that it is not only not OK but it also is represented by the most powerful man in the world at the moment.'

In my hurry to keep the Weinstein conversation flowing, I completely miss that this is an allusion to Donald Trump. I will replay the recording on my phone back at the office and berate myself with loud curses for not following up on this more nimbly. She has, in that one phrase 'crisis of masculinity' – words that will resonate for weeks to come over social media – made the whole interview about so much more than one perpetrator and his victims. She is trying to help me appreciate what we will all come to understand in 2017: that the Time's Up movement has the power to be a game-changer in terms of how power is wielded and by whom.

As I say, I missed it all at the time. Caught up in the moment of the live interview, I am looking for newslines, not philosophy. So I casually let the line sail blithely by, and plug on.

'So when you describe him as being the tip of the iceberg,' I continue, 'do you think there are others *like that* in your industry in Hollywood?'

The next tranche of stories has not broken at this point. The next individuals have still to come forward with tales of Kevin Spacey, Mario Testino, and more.

'Of course,' Emma tells me. 'Many.'

'To that degree?' I ask.

'Maybe not to that degree. Do they have to all be as bad as him to make it count? You know, does it only count if you really have done it to loads and loads and loads of women? Or does it count if you do it to one woman once? I think the latter.'

It is the single moment of the whole interview that will most chime with our audiences. The moment it stops being about Weinstein alone and starts being about something every woman listening can relate to.

I have heard that she once rebuked Weinstein on the set of a film for trying to put her co-star on a diet. I am keen to hear the original story. But she tells me it wasn't actually him. It was another producer. Her co-star had been told by producers to lose weight and Thompson had said, in no uncertain terms, she would walk from the film if she heard anything like that again.

At the time I remember thinking this anecdote was an irrelevance. A distraction, because it wasn't Weinstein. Now, as I write, I realize it actually makes her point better than anything else. This behaviour and all sorts of abuses big and small were going on the whole time. It didn't have to be Weinstein. It didn't have to be rape. It was, as she explains so brilliantly, 'just the little run of small cruelties, humiliations that women all experience. There are sixty-six million people in this country and maybe thirty-five million of them are women. Now, you speak to any of those women . . . and they will all have a story to tell you about some kind of harassment. Whether it's being felt up on the Tube . . . whether it's being nine years old at a children's party and some magician sticking his tongue down my throat, whether it's being in a lift with an older powerful man who I was getting on with quite well when I was twenty-four and who suddenly lunged at me. Everybody's got stories like that – everyone.'

I am trying to get us back on track, not realizing the power of her universalizing.

'So when you knew Harvey Weinstein as a bully, is

that something you would have passed on to other people? Did you tell people that that was what you encountered or did you feel it wasn't your place?'

'We discussed it,' she tells me. 'I discussed it at length with my producer Lindsay Doran. We discussed the fact we were really glad to get our property [films, projects] away from him. And I often expressed the feeling that I had of . . . I mean, whenever I was in a room with him he gave off the most appalling aura of someone that you didn't want to be anywhere near on any level. I could never have worked with him as a producer; I could never have done it. But I mean, you know, he was incredibly powerful, massively powerful and that kind of power holds great sway.'

She recognizes how she herself has escaped much of it.

'I've had education. I'm white, you know, which makes it easier for me to speak up, for instance, than any woman of colour. I've worked sort of independently until I was thirty so I was always extremely feminist, extremely aware of the oppressions.'

'So how,' I ask, 'would you explain the silence? We know now that people knew about this for decades, his sexual behaviour. The directors, the agents, the fixers who seem to push these women actresses into the lion's mouth. How do you explain that?'

'Isn't it the same story as Jimmy Savile? It's the same story, Emily. If someone's powerful, you can say, as the nurses used to do in those hospitals, be careful . . .'

'Pretend you're asleep,' we both say at the same moment.

It is a spine-chilling quote from the Jimmy Savile revelations that has clearly left its mark on us both. The phrase nurses used to try to help patients he was preying on, because they didn't have the power or the clout to actually stop him.

She returns to Weinstein. 'Some of the agents may have said, "Look he's a little bit, he's a bit ... Don't worry. Again he might pester you a bit but, you know, go in." Because one of the big problems about the way in which our systems work at the moment is that there are so many blind eyes. And we can't keep making the women to whom this happens responsible. They're the ones who've got to speak. Why? We've got to look and say, this is HAPPENING.'

What is she trying to say, I wonder, when she talks about 'the millions of blind eyes contributing to every one of these crimes'? It's the first thing she's said that I don't understand. At least, I understand the words but don't really understand what she's implying. Is she suggesting she's missed a trick? We've all missed a trick? We've accepted it for so long?

She tries to explain. 'It's all the little things, the little things that mean you don't feel quite safe going into the room, or getting on the tube. But you don't want to say because nothing really specific has happened. In a sense it's easier to say, "Oh my God, he absolutely jumped me." But a lot of the time women will sense that, you know, they would have just got, "Oh well, Harvey will be Harvey."'

They made jokes about him at the Oscars, I remind her. Jokes, innuendos, hints. Was that a missed opportunity?

'I think', she reflects, 'there were probably about a million missed opportunities to call this man out on his disgusting behaviour.'

'You will have heard, as I have heard,' I say, 'of certain women who choose to play the game in Hollywood. They know it's a huge and competitive industry and they reckon a sexual favour may be worth a part in a block-buster movie. It does go on, doesn't it?'

'Of course,' she concedes. 'I'm sure it does.' But she tells me it comes as a result of women holding so little of the power at the top of the tree. They reach for a differ-ent, alternative kind of power which feels like a choice but which isn't really.

'So this is part of our difficulty. This is part of the rebalancing. This is a gender dysfunction. It's a public health issue. This is not about one man's crimes against women, this is about our system's imbalances, our sys-tem's gender crisis. We have to act on this. We have to turn this on its head. Because what it means is naturally vulnerable people are going to continue to be preyed upon whether Harvey Weinstein goes to jail or not.'

I'm wondering whether there's a liberal hypocrisy at the bottom of this. Whom we condone. Whom we con-demn. How we explain bad behaviour within the world of Oscar-winning aesthetes.

'One word,' I say. 'Polanski?'

I am reminding her that despite allegations of sex

with a minor – a thirteen-year-old girl – and despite being wanted in the US on charges of statutory rape – horrific, paedophilic behaviour – French film director Roman Polanski is still hailed and defended by many in the film world as an artistic genius. Is it a licence, I ask, for horrific behaviour?

She admits this is something she's thought about and got wrong in the past. She once signed a petition against the extradition of Polanksi, allowing the artist his freedom.

'I signed it without really thinking about it. And then I was called on it by some young feminists at my son's university and they said, "This man's a rapist. He raped this woman" . . . I decided that I'd had been wrong, that I had been absolutely, as you'd say, bamboozled by my respect for his art. Absolutely.'

She had her name removed from the petition. She says she's grateful to the younger women for pointing it out. I ask if the abuse is disproportionate to her industry. And she accepts it is.

'Because of the objectification of women in our industry. Because it's about pictures of women, representations of women on film all the time. The pressure is absolutely enormous and it's very easy, particularly on set, for a woman to be abused – especially if they're doing a sex scene or having to take their clothes off. They're put into really difficult positions and there isn't enough protection.'

When Thompson speaks I feel that she is suggesting we are on the cusp of change. That she thinks Weinstein will be a watershed moment for her industry, for women and perhaps for what she calls the 'public health issue' of systemic abuse. But I am more doubtful. I can think of a handful of phoenix-like creatures who've risen again from the ashes of disgrace. The actor Mel Gibson not only survived the fallout after his homophobic and anti-Semitic outbursts but also the restraining order from former wife Oksana Grigorieva after suggesting if she got 'raped by a pack of niggers' she would be to blame, as well as a guilty plea to a charge of domestic abuse. He has won countless roles and awards from the industry since.

It's quite immoral, Hollywood, isn't it? I suggest. If somebody can make money, Hollywood doesn't care.

Thompson admits it's all true, but implores me to 'think ... especially because of Trump, there's a real groundswell happening now. Especially with the young women who are saying, "No, we're not going to have this. We're not going to go back to business as usual because it's good business."'

She wants the men as well as the women of Hollywood to say no to second chances.

I wonder how much of it comes back to America's forty-fifth president. She's mentioned him twice now, I realize. Why, I ask, when we have a commander in chief who is a self-confessed groper do we not respond to him in the same way? Does democracy somehow overwrite criminality?

This will be the question I return to in my own head

time and time again. Do we have to listen to voters? Because somehow they 'know best'? And anyone who calls out the electorate is somehow an anti-populist elitist?

Thompson chooses her own words more carefully. 'It's difficult, isn't it, with Trump, because so many women voted for him . . . The same way many women in South Africa said, "Well, I wouldn't mind being raped by Jacob Zuma." So what we have to remember is that there is often part of a system that's already in place, that's already oppressing them, already depriving them of a voice, actually.'

'So is this,' I pursue, 'the moment you say, hand on heart: Hollywood will now change?'

'No, no, I can't. But I do see and hear a lot of voices and I do want to add mine to theirs and say that Hollywood can and must change.'

She unleashes vintage Emma Thompson. 'You know, I spent my twenties trying to get old men's tongues out of my mouth.' The words are accompanied by her miming something huge and grotesque that looks akin to dental extraction. 'They just thought, She's up for it. So I would imagine that happens really very regularly. And so perhaps this is a moment where we can say to men and women, Open your eyes, and open your mouths, and say something.'

She suddenly bursts out laughing after this lyrical tirade, hearing an exhortation gone slightly wrong. An inkling of fellatial innuendo. Off camera, she whispers:

'Oh no, I suddenly heard "Open your eyes, and open your mouths." I thought, Oh fucking hell, what have I said?'

It is that winning, very English streak of a woman who, even in the full sweep of majesty, turns to bathos. A need to prick what she perceives as her own pomposity. I am keen not to lose the moment or – to tell it bluntly – the soundbite. I want her back on track, in full swing. But it seems the moment is lost. We laugh. And I draw twenty-three minutes of interview to a close. I'm not at that stage sure how well it's gone or even if we've managed to cover the things I wanted to cover. I'm still not sure how to use her reference to Donald Trump who, within months, and with a new sex scandal, will earn himself the unofficial title Sex Pest in Chief.

I check down my list at all the things that still lie there unasked. Was Weinstein exposed only when he stopped being economically useful to the industry? What happens if the women just say no to him? Do they never work again? Does she know of friends, actresses, denied parts because they refused sexual favours? But our time is up. She must run back to rehearsal and I to poor Keir Starmer to discuss Labour and Brexit for the eighteenzillionth time.

Hovering at my chair will be the producer from the newsroom. She will grab the camera memory cards, race outside and feed them into the satellite truck waiting at the door. By the time I have thanked Emma and waved her goodbye and turned on my phone, I will see her words already quoted back to me: on Radio 4, on the

BBC News channel and in the form of message upon message from friends and strangers alike who cannot get enough of what she is trying to say today. That night on *Newsnight* we will be debating which bits to run, how to sort out the strongest moments. Until my day editor, Adam Cumiskey, suddenly sees the wood for the trees.

'Why are we even trying to decide?' he says. 'We'll just run it all.'

And we do.

Steve Bannon Emerges from the Shadows for His First International Broadcast Interview

I don't think I've ever worked harder to secure an interview than I did with Steve Bannon, the political strategist and architect – many believe – of Donald Trump's electoral victory in 2016.

Before I interviewed him he had been a creature from the undergrowth, concealed in the shadows and unknown. He rarely, if ever, appeared on television. He talked widely to journalists, but almost always off the record. He was known to be fiendishly bright, hilariously blunt and, quite possibly, extremely dangerous.

Everything I'd heard and read about him suggested an arch-manipulator. A man whose greatest thrill was to see a kind of chaos – his chaos – take hold around the world. He wanted to shake things from top to bottom, upend the world. He called his mission 'The Movement' and wrapped it in a populist guise of giving the people back their true voice. But a little bit of me has never stopped thinking of him as a kind of Prospero: staff in hand, out to raise tempests for his own sheer bloody entertainment.

After months of prodding and poking the beast on email – to no avail – I was finally introduced to him in person by a friend, Niall Stanage, of Washington's The Hill news site.

One night, after *Newsnight* had gone out live from Capitol Hill, DC, we were summoned to Bannon's house: the notorious Breitbart Embassy. The setting was like something out of revolutionary Cuba (if Che had been extremely right wing). Everything that was said in that first meeting was off the record – and has stayed that way. But I committed all I saw that night to memory and can still call it up photographically. The half-bottle of red wine on the table, label peeling with a kind of decayed grandeur. The photograph of his daughter – a second lieutenant in the Screaming Eagles Division deployed to Iraq – seated on the throne of Saddam Hussein shortly after he'd been deposed. And the surprisingly ornate chintzy loo – seemingly at odds with the guerrilla austerity of the rest of the building. We had arrived at his basement door at 6.30 p.m. and been escorted upstairs to meet him. I had expected a fifteen-minute hello and handshake. But we stayed until nearly midnight, never running out of things to say, questions to ask. I left disorientated and thrilled, attempting to embark on an hour's walk home fuelled by adrenalin. I had kept it together for five hours but suddenly the wine had gone to my head and I was desperate to write everything down before I forgot it. I thought he had agreed – in principle – to a BBC interview. But the further away from that night we got, the less and less sure I became of what I'd heard.

Since that first meeting I had tried to keep the channels

of communication open, but a fog of radio silence had descended. I started to think I'd made the whole thing up. I cannot recall how many texts and emails I sent drifting off into the black hole of cyberspace, barely a whisper of reply. I cannot remember how often I had petitioned this man, often through his deputies, to consider an on-camera interview with *Newsnight*. I have interviewed plenty of US politicians: Anthony Scaramucci, memorably, on the White House lawn, in his rather bijou ten-and-a-half-day stint as Trump's Director of Communications (see page 303); and, of course, Trump himself, long before he became president. But Bannon feels different. A man who actively shuns the limelight. Who prefers 'off record' to 'on'. Who welcomes comparisons with Satan and Darth Vader. But whose political nous and gut feeling for what voters care about helped seal the deal that brought a political earthquake to America in the exuberant shape of Donald John Trump.

This time, I text my request almost by accident – late at night, post-party, worse for wear – after Niall emails me to point out that Bannon will be visiting Prague in three days' time. I fall asleep whilst waiting for an answer. It comes at 4 a.m. the next morning. It's not a yes. But it's not a no. It's enough for me to make a full pitch and – as is my slightly OC habit – to put hotels and flights on hold just in case it happens. Thus begins a lurching four days of uncertainty. I spend the entire gloriously sunny Royal Wedding weekend holed up inside rereading *Fire and Fury*, Michael Wolff's political kiss and tell that seems to have Bannon in its soul. And I have endless conversations with Dan Clarke and my superb team of editors at *Newsnight* which always begin, 'This may not happen but . . .' until they agree to set a double camera crew aside for me 'in case it does'.

The morning of our flight, an urgent email tells me the interview has been put back. I am torn between bringing everyone home from the airport to save a day and ploughing on in case it should change again. What I'm saying, essentially, is this. Until the moment I am sitting opposite him, I will not believe it's happening.

I am perched in the ballroom of Prague's Žofín Palace. Up on stage is the affable Lanny Davis, who served as Special Counsel to President Clinton. And beside him is the former power behind the throne of Donald Trump, Steve Bannon. They're debating each other in a session called 'What the heck is going on in America?'

Lanny opens with a sweet, weak joke. He's sitting and talking. The important thing, he goes on, is that they can agree to disagree. Steve and he come from radically different points of view, but they are here today having a conversation where they meet each other halfway. He speaks of the need for civility in modern discourse. The importance of America as a place of welcome, of openness. He is quiet, modest and, dare I say, ineffectual. When he finishes, the audience claps politely and he passes the microphone to his fellow speaker.

Bannon shuffles to his feet. A figure who constantly

strives to appear newly woken, unkempt, as if prematurely disturbed from hibernation. He takes the mic and he stands, now towering over his fellow speaker and their moderator. He makes no joke. Makes no concession towards a friendlier kind of politics. He doesn't do 'half-way'. He pauses. Looks out to the audience and says:

'It's ten a.m. on September fifteenth 2008.'

And as he utters those words, my mouth hits my stomach. He is talking about the Lehman crisis, the financial crash, the moments of history which will, he says, ultimately deliver Trump to power. It's a day I remember well – the day all the banker dads turned up at the school gate as they no longer had anywhere else to be.

But the reason my heart has lurched is because half an hour from now I will be alone with him, in his first-ever international broadcast interview. And in that one line he has just torn up the rules.

This is no longer a genteel think-tank debate; it's a stump speech with an angry agitator. A man who has campaigned with the Front National in Paris. Who supports the anti-migrant Italian party La Liga. Who told Trump – after the *Access Hollywood* scandal broke, in which contender Trump admitted to grabbing women 'by the pussy' – that he still had 'a hundred per cent chance of winning', and who introduced the travel ban from seven majority-Muslim countries into America.

This is a man who doesn't bother to hide his contempt for the liberal media elites, of which the BBC sits fairly near the top of the pile.

And I must get my head around what that looks like in combat.

We have set up in the basement of the palace, a low-ceilinged, echoey room with no daylight and no noise. It seems the right place to begin a conversation with the man who thinks darkness is good.

He arrives fresh from the debate and asks what I thought of it.

'I think you got an easy ride,' I tell him, a remark I instantly regret. Why am I trying to sound macho? Why would I put him on his guard so needlessly? He laughs. Seems flattered.

He is friendlier in person than his on-stage persona allows. His is a large presence. Black jacket upon black shirt upon black T-shirt; grey, slicked-back hair. The air of a university professor recently suspended for fomenting a campus uprising.

Moments before we record, my phone alarm goes off – to remind me to set the record button. It is an omission I have made so many times in the past, I dare not get it wrong this time. But the sound blaring from my phone is not the neutral ping of a buzzer but the opening chords of *Hamilton*, the musical that tells the story of a mixed-race immigrant who becomes an American founding father. It is sung by a diverse cast so appalled by the Trump administration that they delivered boos and a lecture to the vice president, Mike Pence, when he went to see the show. I smack it off, sweating and mortified that it will have confirmed his prejudice of liberal-bubble old me.

I ask Bannon how he thinks the first eighteen months of the Trump administration have gone and it unleashes a torrent of policy successes and statistics.

He talks too fast, dropping names the UK audience will barely recognize. He is fluent, oddly nervous, un-interruptible. It is nearly two and a half minutes before he draws breath.

By his second answer we are in the depths of the Robert Mueller investigation into Russian collusion. He believes the Deputy Attorney General Rod Rosenstein should be fired, Mueller should stay, Trump shouldn't testify in person but should answer questions in written form.

Does he speak to the president? I ask. I want to know, essentially, if he still has an 'in' with the man he helped to power after their legendary parting of ways.

'I take everything to attorneys because I'm in the middle of the Mueller investigation. The very first thing when Mueller brings you in there, one of the very first things he wants to know is your conversations with the president.'

It's said that even mid-level White House staffers nowa-days have to get themselves 'attorneyed up'. But when Bannon says it, I can't help thinking it's a convenient explanation to cover up the fact they don't communicate any more. It's nine months since he was fired. Bannon will try and tell me, later, that he left on his own terms.

When he speaks, it's like listening to someone who still thinks they're off the record. There is no order to his sentence structure. He's constantly interrupting himself from one thought to start another; his flow is littered with 'by the way', as if the newest, freshest sentence has to take precedence over the end of whatever he was about to say.

I ask him if he sees himself as the architect of the 2016 election. The deal-closer. And he cannot reject it quickly enough.

'No, that's totally not fair. You gotta remember, Trump is unique in American political history. He's his own closer.'

I've been told that senior members of Trump's administration talk to their president by way of the television. I'm wondering if this is Bannon doing the same. Reminding his leader of his very public loyalty.

He cannot help reminding me, though, that when he stepped in Team Trump were sixteen points down. He helped them refocus and, yes, told Trump that voters wouldn't care if he'd been caught on tape admitting he could 'grab [women] by the pussy'. He got Trump back 'on message', repeated to him that voters wouldn't care about individual behaviour, that the team were 'fighting for their country'.

But this Bannon – I'm guessing more as strategist than feminist – tells me he's now convinced 'the Time's Up movement is very powerful. It's trying to upend five thousand years or ten thousand years of the patriarchy . . . It's

Handmaid's Tale as a political movement ... It took a
kind of divine intervention but in the great irony, you
know, President Trump for some reason triggers this
Time's Up movement.'

He looks like he's trying not to laugh.

It is too cute. Too benign. And I have to remind myself –
and him – that in many of our viewers' minds he is the
man who's driven a nationalistic, divisive, dangerous and
arguably racist agenda right into the mainstream. He's
allowed – as one person put it to me – 'the Ku Klux
Klan to take their hoods off'.

Cue explosion. It is satisfyingly large. The touchy-
feely Me Too Bannon has gone, to be replaced with a
man dripping with contempt for the mindset of the
organization I represent.

'See, this is the opposition party. This is why the
media has no credibility; this is why the great BBC and
the *Financial Times* [he lists more] are basically the communications department for the global elites.'

He tells me economic nationalism doesn't care about
race or gender or ethnicity or religion or sexual prefer-
ence. It cares about your citizenship. Mass immigration,
he wants to explain, is a scam by globalists to suppress
the wages of the black and Hispanic working class by
giving unlimited competition on labour. Not only are
Trump's immigration policies not racist, they are actively
helping blacks and Hispanics. He will later claim that
Martin Luther King would be proud of Trump's economic record. It feels like he relishes provocation.

He segues into his thesis on trade. 'The United States is a tributary state to China. We're Jamestown to their Great Britain . . .' He thinks the great geniuses of Wall Street, 'the globalist elite and their mouthpieces . . . make it seem like its the second law of thermodynamics that these jobs happened to be shifted to China. That's total BS! Those jobs can come back if you enforce reasonable trade. They're a mercantilist power, they don't play by any of the rules and yet the elites in this country cheer them on.'

It is a passionate, eloquent riff on trade imbalance, the most cogent and lucid argument for it I think I've ever heard. It could come just as easily from the Occupy movement, from a Bernie Sanders or a Jeremy Corbyn.

My head is working out where to go. But my mouth is already ahead of me.

'You make such a forceful argument,' I hear myself say. 'If it is all about trade, why do you go around the world befriending fascists?'

I'm thinking of his support for Marion Maréchal, the latest Le Pen in France, or Viktor Orbán, whose resounding re-election in Hungary saw him defend 'Christian Europe' and call for an end to 'the multicoloured country'. A phrase even Bannon struggles to defend.

People only use words like 'fascist' or 'racist', he tells me, when they can't debate the facts. 'I wear it with pride when they call me a racist. I go, "You know why you're doing that? 'Cause you don't want to talk about economic nationalism."'

His anger is synthetic. My sense whenever I challenge him is that he's energized by attack, delights in the testosterone it fuels. The whole encounter will force me to ask myself uncomfortable questions about the interview process itself. Whether it's right to air opinions our audience can use to understand his world, or whether we are oxygenating and empowering these views.

When our interview is broadcast there are many comments and questions about why we have 'platformed' this 'racist/neofascist/satanist'. But because it's the BBC there are also comments asking why I was so mean and others asking why I wasn't tougher.

An interview can always be better. I don't think that feeling ever quite goes away. And this one was no exception. But this time, at least I can reassure myself it was an international first. It was an on-screen encounter he'd never done before outside his own Washington circle.

Since that time, he's become almost omnipresent – a fixture on the European circuit promoting his Grand Tour brand of populism. To some extent, it's made me re-evaluate how I perceive him. Bannon had always seemed to me to have the extra-sensory perception of a wild animal predicting an imminent tsunami. Except his antennae brought him towards the scene of crisis, not away from it. Perhaps I thought I saw the finely tuned machine behind the bravado that Trump wore like a Superman suit. Bannon was, after all, pivotal to the greatest shakedown in American history.

Now, I'm not so sure. I had always assumed he raised his magician's staff and made the waves crash himself.

But now I wonder if he's less kingmaker, more glory-hunter: posing with the players, arms around their shoulders, hanging out in the changing room when the goals are scored. He arrives on the scene at the moment of maximum disruption – a political photobomb in the corner of every shot.

Sheryl Sandberg: Good Grief

Four months after Donald Trump won the presidential election, I went to interview Sheryl Sandberg, the Chief Operating Officer of Facebook. The tech giant had found itself right at the centre of a storm about fake news. Had the company unwittingly allowed the spread of false accounts, Russian bots, the proliferation of made-up stories and lies – having hailed itself as a platform without an editorial hand on the tiller? Had it relinquished responsibility? Had it – the accusation went – helped Trump to victory?

There were so many questions for Facebook, the interview couldn't have fallen more perfectly. Except for one thing. We weren't really allowed to talk about any of it. The hard-earned interview had been granted to *Newsnight* in a much more personal capacity. To deliver a tale of grief and offer a passage through. It was the story Sandberg herself wanted to tell about the time in her life where her world had fallen apart.

Two years earlier the highest-profile female in Silicon Valley, Sheryl Sandberg, lost her husband, Dave. They had been holidaying with friends in Mexico, chatting around the hotel pool. Then he headed off to the gym, she for a walk. It was the last time she saw him alive.

Dave suffered a cardiac arrest on the running machine. It was Sheryl who discovered his body on the gym floor some hours later when he'd failed to return.

She wrote about her grief, and about how others dealt with her state of grief, in an extraordinary post on Facebook – visceral and raw – that coincided with the end of the official mourning period in Judaism. The response was overwhelming and, from that post and conversations she had over the period, a book was born, *Option B*, in which she describes how to deal with and even grow from grief.

A month before the book was published we were granted an interview – the UK broadcast exclusive – with Sandberg, at Facebook headquarters in Palo Alto. It was one of the most difficult professional encounters I can remember.

That Thursday morning, 23 March 2017, we headed to meet her. We'd stayed overnight in San Francisco. The team were excited but also fractious. We were tired, we'd travelled relentlessly in the week before, crisscrossing from Seattle to Washington DC to Pennsylvania and back to the West Coast. It was that time in a work trip where you've run out of clean pants and empathy. Your body clock is confused, you miss your kids and you still have to deliver what feels like – always feels like – the interview of a lifetime. Our planning team had fought hard to secure this interview and we felt charged with responsibility to deliver them a knock-out TV moment.

We arrived at a newly remodelled Facebook headquarters in Menlo Park, which my producer, Vara, described as a West Coast Ikea car park. It is a functional, utilitarian kind of place, designed as a hub for worker bees. Not a glamorous HQ. We were ushered inside with name badges and the Californian welcome: the Silicon Valley tech façade, corporate but upbeat, lots of people thanking each other ('You're so *welcome!*'). And free lollipops.

We had an hour to set up for the interview. And it felt odd lugging huge cases of heavy lights and tripods into a place where everything is done on technology the size of a phone. We represented the cumbersome glare of old media in a digital age, but the quality had to be good, and we took our time adjusting every angle, every light, before Ms Sandberg was due.

At eleven o'clock she walked in. Petite, birdlike, gracious, she thanked us for coming so far. She was nervous, she told me. Even though she'd written the book, this was her first broadcast interview about her husband's death. We had promised it would not be aired before publication, a month on.

She wore a navy denim-effect skirt, a crisp white blouse that no one could fix a mic on to and a cardigan. Somewhere between preppy smart and Silicon casual. Chic, but almost swamped by her clothes. She kept looking across at her assistant for reassurance. It was so odd to see this superwoman rendered quite so vulnerable by, well, us.

We begin to roll. By the end of her first answer, she is already crying. She describes finding her husband's body on the floor of the gym, already dead. Describes how she has to make the call home to her mother and tell her children, describes how she punishes herself for not looking for him earlier, believing – originally – that it would have been within her grasp to save him.

The book is her attempt to help others understand 'pre-traumatic growth': in other words, the way you can cushion yourself against the worst despair in grief by knowing the steps through it. It is part psychology, part personal story. And she is at her strongest when she's describing the isolation she felt in grief: the 'non-question-asking friends', the people who say, 'How are you?' and leave her grappling with an answer they don't really want. She describes in essence the crashing of a life and the rebuilding of it. Honest about her new quest for love, her sense of being a single parent, her regrets about the way she wrote her previous book *Lean In*, without acknowledging quite how many women have to do it all on their own. Her voice is still raw and constantly breaks up. There's a moment in the interview when I think I might cry too. She's describing an experience that could so easily be mine, in another circumstance. Another hotel gym on another family holiday.

It would have been easy for the whole interview to concentrate on the story of grief and survival, so passionate is her advocacy, so articulate is her pain. But I am also aware that I am sitting in Facebook HQ, Silicon

Valley, with its most famous daughter. A woman at the heart of the social-media empire at a moment in history. We've witnessed an election mired in accusations of fake news. We've seen Google under fire for the ad revenue they've made from dodgy jihadi video postings. We've had accusations of screen addiction and questions about whether the web is now doing more harm than good. It is Miracle-Gro fertile territory for a journalist and I can only think how odd it will sound if we don't attempt to cover any of it. At my shoulder I feel my editor, willing me on to ask the difficult questions. At my other shoulder, I feel my mother – a therapist – willing me to be sensitive to this woman's grief. They are irreconcilable and for a second I have an almost out-of-body experience, watching to see what I will do next.

In the end, ironically, it is Sheryl who paves the way for me to go off script.

She describes the way social media has helped her with her recovery. A gentle Facebook plug, perhaps. It seems natural then for me to also ask about trolling: the flip side to grief played out on social media. I remind her of grieving mothers who find that, far from being a consolation, social media can amplify their agony: nasty messages, uncompromising in their cruelty, left with the intent to wound. I wonder if she herself has experienced it in the past two years?

At that moment something happens. A tonal shift: she dispenses with grieving Sandberg; she embraces corporate Sandberg. It doesn't feel deliberate; perhaps she's not even aware of it. But the tears stop and the patter emerges. She tells me that, with more than two billion Facebook users, 'Things happen and those are things we don't want to happen and we take very seriously and try to take the appropriate action,' and she explains that Facebook, for her, is where her husband Dave's memories are stored. She has sidestepped anything about her own experiences of trolling; she hasn't even addressed the concerns head on. So I persist: she has such a positive sense of what social media can do, but there's a change now. 'We used to think of [the internet] as providing unambiguous improvement to the world. And now it feels like the mood is shifting – whether it's polarizing us politically, or eating into our privacy or our relationships. Do you sense that backlash against the digital revolution?'

Her patter continues: any technology that's ever been invented can be used for good and also for ill purposes. She diverts here to recount what is clearly a well-trod anecdote about the car replacing the horse and cart. 'It's our job to make sure that people can share and connect on Facebook and that we take the right steps to mitigate the harm when the technology is used in the wrong ways.' She goes on to explain that Facebook is different, as it is harder to be anonymous, that 'people behave better when their names and their faces are attached to it'.

All this is irrefutably true. But I am still left feeling that this is a press release – wheeled out and rehearsed with barely a change of gear.

I ask her about fake news – the part it may have played in the recent presidential election that brought Donald Trump to power; I ask if she thinks it's with us for ever. I ask about screen time and whether the rumour is true that Silicon chiefs ban their young from having too much as they recognize how harmful it can be. And I end up talking about what it is to be a female voice in the male-dominated world of tech. She answers all of my questions with fluency, if not with inspiration, and I end with a thank you.

The moment the camera stops rolling the tone changes again. She is furious and looks to her assistant. Then to me. Then to the cameraman and to my producer.

I am frozen to the spot as I hear that this was not what we had agreed – we had come to talk about the book (her assistant had actually permitted us in writing one question on fake news as part of this agreement).

I am utterly confused. I have just seen her, fluent and unfazed, respond to everything before her without the need to stop or redirect my questions. But suddenly, seeing her face, I'm feeling evil.

It would be riveting to watch the exchange if I weren't centre stage. But right now I am wishing for a great hole in the floor to swallow me up. I tell her that the interview is and has been predominantly about her book and how to learn from grief, but it would be *weird* to be sitting opposite her and *not* ask the things that everyone is so eager to hear her talk about right now. I have slightly lost a sense of who I am, wondering whether I have indeed been out of line, or whether I'm now being mind-controlled by a Silicon Valley conglomerate good at playing games.

I can do a Facebook interview any time, she says. This was meant to be special. And the assistant tries to tell me I will be pilloried for asking about Facebook in the middle of an interview about grief. (As it turns out, I will ultimately be pilloried for not asking her *enough* about Facebook – but that is for another day.) And the trouble is, I literally can't tell if she's right. The human in me wants to reassure her and promise we will ditch the rest. The journalist in me is getting angry at being told what is or is not fair – particularly when she's already answered my questions.

In the end, I am very frank. 'Look,' I tell her, 'I can't promise we won't use the answers you've already given us, but I promise you that all the interesting stuff you said *was* about grief.' I pause; then, realizing I have little to lose, continue: 'The other stuff came out sounding corporate and boring, actually.'

She listens. Her worry is that I 'hardly asked about grief at all'. And that's when I realize she's had a completely normal reaction to anyone who's just done an interview, or sat an exam, or made a speech – the post-adrenalin crash where you can't actually remember a thing you just said.

Luckily, I have listened hard in her interview, an interview in which a good twenty minutes were spent on grief, and I am able to quote back virtually everything she has said – the very metaphors she's deployed to say it. I reassure her we have talked about so many of the things she's written about in the book and, gradually, I can see the trust coming back on to her face. She wants to believe it will all be fine; I want to reassure her it will all be fine (it will); but for these extraordinary few moments the two of us are locked in a fragile, figurative wrestle, trying to work out who will blink first. I am trying to be comforting but not compromising. I say my editor will be in touch and we will work out what goes in and what ends up on the cutting-room floor. We sign off with a selfie together, and a big hug – she tells me I'm great at my job. It is confusing but a relief. I am reminded that she is – as she honestly admits – a woman in grief still struggling to re-enter a normal world. I am an over-tired, jet-lagged journalist constantly asking myself if I'm making things better or worse by the job I do.

At the airport that night, as I fly home, I suddenly burst into tears. I can't tell if it's because some of her grief has washed off on me or whether it's the pressure of feeling I've done it all wrong. Or whether – easiest thing to fix – I just badly need a drink. I write to her assistant. I write to my editor. Then I pass out on the plane (one neat vodka on ice, one 'may cause drowsiness' hay fever tablet, my perfect cocktail these days).

When the interview airs it will include some but not all of the Facebook questions. Jess Brammar, my deputy editor, will tell me – as I told Sheryl – the interesting bit was all the grief stuff anyway; the rest sounded mechanical. It does not cause a headline splash, but it is one of the most watched videos of the day on BBC News. And I will hear from Sheryl Sandberg herself, as she wakes up on California time and tells me she's seen it and she's happy.

And what do I feel?

How honest do I feel like being?

I will feel relieved that she doesn't hate me, happy she is happy. But I will simultaneously feel annoyed that, in these unprecedented times, this post-factual age where we are only just starting to recognize the unintended consequences of the social media behemoth, I didn't feel braver about asking the Chief Operating Officer of Facebook that little bit more about how Facebook Chiefly Operates.

Gordon Ramsay on Cocaine

'Seeds,' Gordon Ramsay is telling me. 'Seeds should be inside a fucking cage. Fed to your parrot. Or your canaries. Seeds should go inside a cage and stay inside a cage.'

It is vintage Ramsay. I have unleashed a small tirade by asking the multi-Michelin-starred chef what food fads most annoy him.

'And foam,' he adds for good measure. 'Foam should go in your hair. Not on a plate. In the 1990s, I had a cappuccino with white beans but I moved on. Foams have to be *abolished*.'

We are sitting in the Union Street Café, one of his thirty-three restaurants worldwide, drinking coffee.

He takes his short and black with – almost incongruously for a man with such a finely tuned palate – an injection of artificial sweetener on the side. But it is another ice-white chemical substance we are here to discuss today: cocaine and his loathing of it. And this is where shouty chef departs and in his place I meet a man who passionately wants to spill the beans on what he calls 'the hospitality industry's dirty little secret'.

He's been making a documentary to expose its prevalence and its power – not least over those he has loved. He lost a head chef, David Dempsey, in 2003 in a

cocaine-related death. His younger brother Ronnie is a
long-term heroin addict who's now been missing for six
months. But the momentum for this film came, he tells
me, at Christmas last year. 'A customer took a side plate
from the table, went into the bathroom, snorted a
couple of lines of coke and handed the plate back to the
waiter and said, "We've just done some lines of coke for
lunch; can you change the side plates . . ." This started
the whole dilemma of how far this is going on and the
pressure restaurants are up against from customers.'

The diners got a ticking off from the manager. Gordon Ramsay says if he'd been there he would have asked
them to leave immediately. He was shocked about the
openness. And from that he decided to test the loos of
all his own restaurants, including the Union Street Café,
where we've met. He found traces of cocaine in every
single place he owned (bar one).

Ramsay tells me about the celebrity book launch where
a foil wrap of cocaine was pressed into his palm during
a handshake. 'The chef came up to me, shook my hand
and said, "It's on me." No one saw that wrap. I put it into
my pocket, went to the bathroom and flushed it down
the toilet. It was about two and a half grams.' The chef
came back ten minutes later and asked Ramsay if he had
any left, and high-fived him when he said no. 'Being tar-
nished with that image, you know, not only upset me but
started to worry me. That's how they think you roll with
money and success. He couldn't be further from the truth.'

But it was the moment he was asked by diners to garnish

his own cuisine with cocaine that things really hit home. Where once a dusting of icing sugar would suffice, now it was class A drugs, the ultimate status symbol of a bizarrely indulgent host.

'I got auctioned off for a big charity dinner three years ago. Someone paid seventy-five thousand pounds [for me] to go round to their house for a good cause . . . You cook for twelve to fourteen people and literally have to stand there – do all the meet and greets and photographs. And when dessert arrived the couple came to me and said, "Look, everyone on the table is happy you're here but can you make a soufflé like never before and combine icing sugar with coke and dust it?" I laughed it off but there was no way I was going to go anywhere near that. I dusted the sugar on top of the soufflé and caramelized it purposely in a way that – with the blow torch – they had no idea whether it was on or off. I set the soufflé down. Didn't even say goodbye. I just left out the back door.'

Ramsay admits he was put off drugs very early through his brother. He recalls the day of their father's funeral which they went to via the drug-dealer.

'The condition that Ronnie said he'd attend the funeral was that I went [to his dealer] and sorted out his debt, paid it off and got him a fix. But I had to sit there and watch this brown, murky water being fired up with a Zippo lighter in a spoon, a rusty spoon, through a needle. So yes, pretty shitty.'

So is a relationship with Ronnie possible now?

'No, I can't. No. And everyone's panicking in the household discreetly because no one's heard from him for six months. Last time we heard he was in Portugal, busking.'

Ramsay tells me of a situation one December. 'He turned up outside the [three-Michelin-starred] restaurant at Royal Hospital Road begging customers for money and we actually had to get the police to move him on. It was that bad.'

He speaks with sadness but also the frustration of someone who's tried everything and seen it fail. Ronnie, he says, has been 'clean' on six occasions but always ended up back on the drug. Now, the chef tells me, his own family has to come first. The father of four teenagers was not shy about throwing the horrors of drugs before their eyes. Gordon being Gordon, it came in the form of a recipe.

'I sat them down and showed them the process of not just chopping or cutting up the coke – but also the cement powder, sulphuric acid, the battery acid – and then doused it in gasoline. And that scared the life out of them. Now it may be a bit cruel for a fifteen-year-old to see but – no disrespect – if you can start talking about contraception and sexual education at twelve, then I think at fifteen they need to understand.'

He says he and his wife, Tana, who's Montessori-trained, have been very disciplined with them. No music festivals – for now, 'until they're in a smart enough group that they're not going to be influenced and persuaded'.

Does he think he's a good dad?

'You've got to ask them. I'm a fair dad and I'm an honest dad. Things change. It's not a yearly thing, or six months, it's every three months we tap in and open up, and that's the secret of being a great dad.'

The horror of his own childhood is something he's written of extensively: an abusive, alcoholic father who beat up their mother. 'In many ways that's been a huge advantage for me, on how *not* to be a dad. I don't think there's many circles in life that you look at – bosses, mentors – and you think, Christ, what a dick. What you've done and how you treated me is going to set me up to do the opposite and it can only benefit.'

In fact, nothing about the extended Ramsay family is uncomplicated. When we meet, his father-in-law, Chris Hutcheson, has just come out of prison, where he was serving time for hacking Ramsay's emails – the culmination of a ten-year-long bitter feud.

Neither Ramsay nor his wife visited him in prison but, he tells me, there's been a big breakthrough.

'Tana had lunch with him here. And I think, if anything, it's helped secure the relationship going forward. He apologized. I met him for breakfast. Took him to the Breakfast Club in Battersea at half past seven.'

I'm trying to work out how their marriage, which has had its well-documented ups and downs, including a seven-year affair, survived the imprisonment of Tana's father. Ramsay admits it wasn't plain sailing. 'Until the truth came out it was very testing for Tana and me because I think there were moments in Tana's mind where she thought: Was that Gordon or was that my dad?' Ramsay managed to access the hacked emails through the server to prove what had been going on but, up until that point, he says, 'it was a hard pill for her to swallow. Knowing her father was out to destroy us as a family.'

I am about to go on and ask further questions on this when his publicist, Jo, steps in and gently but firmly reminds me this is off topic – we are meant to be talking cocaine and cooking, not family bust-ups. Then something remarkable happens. I can't actually remember a time when it has happened before. Gordon Ramsay cuts across her and says to me, 'NO, go on.' I get the sense of a man so confident he has nothing to hide, no particular side or edge, that I momentarily forget what I was going to ask.

'About the kids?' he prompts me.

'Oh, yes,' I say. 'Thanks. So will they still have a relationship with their grandfather?'

A wry smile. 'Yeah, I mean, they've got to. But if my daughters approach me in the next ten years and say, "Hey, Dad, my boyfriend's a chef and I want to invest in him setting up a restaurant," it's going to be a very polite NO. With a big capital N and a big capital O.'

Business and family, he's learnt, don't mix.

So how does the businessman with thirty-three restaurants view Brexit? Will a curb on EU migrant labour be OK for the industry?

'That level of influx of multinationals in this country sadly has sort of confirmed how lazy as a nation we are – when individuals from across the seas are prepared to come and work twice as hard for less money. And so, if anything, it's a big kick up the ass for the industry, and it's going to get back to that modern-day apprenticeship. So not only do I welcome that kind of change but I think it's going to put a lot more emphasis on home-grown talent, which I think we need to do.'

Our time is running out, and I'm keen not to let him go until my mind is at rest. All those cuttings I've been reading about rows with celebrity chefs: the Marco Pierre Whites and Jamie Olivers of this world. I don't want to sound gullible so I say, 'They're all confected aren't they, these rows? Sort of fun publicity.'

And I see a shadow fall across his face. 'It *was* fun,' he says, but then describes how he felt Oliver had crossed the line. 'Jamie turned round and said [in a newspaper], "I've got five kids; he's got four kids." To judge someone else's family on the amount of kids you have, that's . . . that's . . .'

He tails off, speechless. It sounds such a preposterous silverback boast I have the urge to laugh: it seems so nakedly alpha male. Until I realize why it's hit so hard.

It came after what he describes as 'a shit year'. He and Tana lost a baby at five months through miscarriage, his daughter had a collapsed lung and he ruptured his Achilles tendon. The throwaway, misaimed machismo from Oliver couldn't have come at a worse time. The hurt is palpable and he launches his own blistering attack on Oliver's hypocrisy.

'The problem with Jamie is that it's all commercial Jamie. It's all very well to spout off now about sugar tax and supermarkets. None of that was spoken about when he was label-slapping with Sainsbury's for ten years. So you can't be that much of a hypocrite . . . And no disrespect, but we're chefs, not politicians. When you breathe that stuff down the public's throat and say, "I'm leaving if we have Brexit," then, I'm sorry, the door stands open. Stand for what you say. Sadly . . . the only time he opens his mouth is when he's got something to promote.'

He tells me he will never talk to him again until he has the decency to apologize to Tana. 'Boys will always fight and butt heads but Tana was mortified, I mean, really mortified.'

'And Marco?'

'When Marco turns around and says he made me cry when I was nineteen, you know, he made me cry in such an amazing way. He helped shape the guy I am today because he pushed me to the absolute limit. Whether you're an athlete, a lawyer, a journalist, when you have a mentor that's that good, yeah, crying, I had no issues with because I knew what I was becoming. What he was giving me.'

If Marco Pierre White launched Gordon Ramsay, then the figure looking back at me right now is a man who's – broadly – exactly where he wants to be. He remains intensely workaholic – throwing extreme physical endurance in there for good measure – and a man who's unafraid to admit that family life, even for the most loving and devoted, can be messy and awkward and complicated.

For the last hour, sweary, shouty Gordon has barely been seen, and I've had the thoughtful, intimate reflections of a man who's witnessed death, drugs and disaster first hand and has a lot to tell.

But that, of course, is all before I dare to ask him about food fads, and yes, whisper it quietly . . . seeds.

Tony Blair: When the Interview Comes to You

'Hello, My name is Tony Blair and I will be speaking around this level.'

I am sitting opposite Labour's most electorally successful prime minister ever.

And I do not know why I am here.

The camera crew are doing the sound checks: making sure the microphones are at the right level, checking everyone's phones are off. It is March 2018, the week of the Brexit anniversary, a year since Theresa May triggered Article 50, which will begin the process of Britain leaving the EU. And a year until the deed itself is finally done. I am about to conduct an interview with Tony Blair, but I cannot shake the feeling it's not about this.

Let me explain a little what I mean. We do, of course, bid regularly for former prime ministers, of all persuasions and nationalities: Sam McAlister and Jack Evans have been fastidiously calling the Blair office and seeing if he might be encouraged on to *Newsnight*. Often it's a no, occasionally it's a yes: none of that is unusual. But the reason I am here right now is not *just* as a result of endless and thoughtful team bidding, it is because his office has reached out to us.

It was a mere two hours earlier that my phone pinged

with a message from my editor of the day, Stewart Maclean:

> Blair's office are offering us a sit-down before 2 p.m.
> We have to go to them.

The note from Blair's PA has explained it in full.

'Mr Blair is making a speech this evening on Brexit, extracts below. I wondered if at long last you would be interested in doing a pre-recorded interview with him on the speech. Appreciate there may be a question on anti-Semitism, of course.'

It is not unusual for a politician to take questions on another issue – the interview equivalent perhaps of the 'and finally' news story. But it is quite unusual to be given such a direct hint. Are we quietly being encouraged to ask about anti-Semitism? Or is he just acknowledging that a story leading the bulletins will be hard for us to ignore?

The reason it has been front-page news is because the party is currently in a kind of crisis of its own making. The Jewish Board of Deputies and others have written to Jeremy Corbyn, Labour leader, to complain that he has tolerated anti-Semitic behaviour, including Holocaust denial, within his own party and particularly within his own circle for too long. They write to tell him that mainstream Jewish communities will be rallying on Parliament Square that afternoon to protest at his inability to recognize the conspiracy theories and dog-whistle phraseology for what it is: a form of racism. Previous attempts by commentators to raise this concern with the Labour leader have been met with accusations that they are trying to 'smear' Corbyn, to replace him with their own brand of Labour (or Tory) leader. Or accusations that 'powerful Jews within the mainstream media are trying to poison the discourse with their own agenda' (neatly summing up, maybe, the whole problem of anti-Semitism in the phrase itself), or perhaps that people are guilty of conflating a disapproval of Israeli foreign policy with a dislike of Jews. The idea that the problem is entirely confected has served to support the Labour leader in the past. But this time it feels different. The voices of protest are gathering momentum, the problem is not going away, and now Jeremy Corbyn appears to be ready to listen. Is that why Tony Blair has called me in?

When I get the text from Stewart I am still in my running gear, one child sick at home, another going off to sit an exam. The urgency of the interview means we can't, as we normally would, sit down and plan the whole thing out. And the fact that we still don't know the exact time or even if it is definitely on means it's hard to know what to do first. I phone into the office and we plot out a skeletal line of questioning. What do we want to know? What will he 'show leg' on? Tony Blair is a pro. I have interviewed him four or five times before – often enough to know that, if he has something to say, he will say it. He rarely makes mistakes in an interview; he has a disarming way of making you feel like you're the first person ever to ask him that question. It's momentarily empowering. He pauses, repeats your name, and then says, I assume, roughly what he has always wanted to say.

Adam Cumiskey, Stewart and I are all on the phone call. Do we start with the anti-Semitism? Or the stuff on Brexit, which they have briefed in advance? Do we want to know about other things? Russia – following the poisoning of Sergei Skripal, an ex-spy, in Salisbury? Or perhaps about claims recently reported in the *Observer* that the Brexit vote was helped along financially by unorthodox accounting within Vote Leave? We get about ten questions together. The order is fluid. And I feel a kind of lightness of being; it doesn't really matter what I ask, as long as I provide pushback on what he tells us. We are there because he wants to say something big: I am intrigued.

We arrive at 1 p.m. and the interview is scheduled for one fifteen. Sick teenage son has come with me; I forbid him from mentioning Corbyn, Trump, the Iraq War or Brexit in front of Blair. He is to hide at the back and keep quiet. He looks terrified.

Just as we are ready to go, Tony Blair's assistant pops her head around the door.

'You're going to talk about Brexit, aren't you?' she checks. I assure her we will.

Tony Blair is an ardent Remainer. A man who in recent months has been happy to cross political divides, to find common ground with Tory politicians, Lib Dems and others in their shared belief that the EU is a force for good. The trouble, as we always note, is that it's hard to find a more polarizing figure in British politics. Still adored by many in the centre, seen as a calm voice of reason in the maelstrom of increasingly hysterical discourse on either side, there are plenty more who continue to find it impossible to forgive him the Iraq War, and implausible that he should continue to justify it as the right course of action, waiting for history to prove him right.

When he walks in, fifteen minutes later, he looks ageless. His hair is now grey but his face is tanned and he is wearing the kind of skinny black jeans that wouldn't look out of place on Sick Teenager. He's balancing a coffee cup on his hand like a sort of graceful Frisbee.

Seeing him, I am spirited back to the first time I ever spoke to him, as a freelance pup reporter at Sky News who had just landed in London after six years covering the Far East. It was a summer day exactly two decades earlier when Gazza (Paul Gascoigne) had been left out of the World Cup squad and the Spice Girls had just broken up. I was tasked with asking Britain's prime minister his thoughts on the issues dominating British public discourse. Was it right that Gazza had been dropped? Would we cope as a nation without the Spice Girls? He kept a totally straight face when I asked the question. Paused ('I'm treating this seriously and considering it') and then said (I paraphrase slightly from memory in this pre digital-clippings age): 'As Prime Minister of Great Britain I have to make decisions about a great number of things. I'm utterly delighted that is not one of them.'

I had run off with my clip, back to a delighted news editor, leaving a prime minister slightly startled that that had been the alpha and omega of my interest in current affairs. Here I was, twenty years on, doubtful he even remembered that encounter. And this time the whole interview is up for grabs, as I try to work out what I want to ask and what he wants to say.

His speech on Brexit will already have been made by the time this airs on *Newsnight* at 10.30 p.m. How do I find a way of making the interview still relevant? I begin with an open question: he is petitioning for Parliament to be given a free vote on the deal once the shape of Brexit is actually known. Won't it look to many like he's asking for the referendum to be rerun?

'There are many different versions of Brexit,' he explains. 'The role of Parliament is crucial here because MPs have got to insist first that we know the precise terms of the new relationship with Europe before we exit in March 2019 . . . It's right that MPs have their say, but then it's right also that the people have their say . . . It's important, I think, that we define what the will of the people is. I mean, the will of the people is undoubtedly to leave the European Union, and the government was given a mandate to negotiate the terms. But what's become apparent since June 2016 is that we know a lot more about the situation now than we did then. But also even within the government itself and within the Cabinet there are different versions of Brexit. One version of Brexit keeps us close to Europe. And closely aligned to

Europe. Another is a clean break from Europe. Once the government resolves the central dilemma of this negotiation and plumps for one of those two options, then that's the point at which you can really compare the future relationship we will have with Europe with the relationship we have now.'

So far, so fine. But I have heard it all before. This isn't why he brought me here.

I press on to ask him about Northern Ireland. One of his proudest achievements – a core part of his positive legacy – lies in the Good Friday deal which brought the parties of Northern Ireland together in a power-sharing deal, and then a second deal between the British and Irish governments. We are coming up to the twenty-year anniversary. Will he tell me something bold? Will he go further than he ever has before and prophesise bloodshed through Brexit? He will not. He is measured and thoughtful. He tells me there is no easy answer to Northern Ireland (we know that). Then he tells me he fears the government will fudge it. 'It's really important,' he says 'that MPs – they are the last bastion of ensuring that the people do know very clearly, before we leave, what it is we're leaving to.'

So it is not Northern Ireland that he wants to focus on today. That much is clear. He returns to his theme: the importance of Parliament. I am struck by the irony. Tony Blair, I remind him, never seemed to care two hoots for Parliament when he himself was in power.

'It won't be lost,' I point out, 'on people who think

you were the King of the Sofa Government. You didn't even care about Cabinet, let alone Parliament itself.'

'Not true,' he fires back. 'We certainly did care . . . but it's true we did have a huge majority. Even in my last term. So it didn't matter so much. But we were never dealing with an issue like this. This is unique. It's going to decide the future destiny and direction of the country for generations to come . . . No one is saying people were ignorant when they voted back in June 2016. But the fact is they couldn't know what the new relationship was because we hadn't started to negotiate it. Now we do know.'

He is passionate about the need for a second vote on the substance of the Brexit deal. But again, we know all this. It's not new. My head starts fidgeting. Why am I here? I try various Brexit-related questions. Does he think there's a case to be made for reconsidering the result of Brexit, given claims now being made in the *Observer* newspaper about the campaign spending of the Vote Leave organization? This is an open goal for anyone who wants to tear down the Brexit wall. And yet, once again, I hear a peculiarly measured response.

'I think if there were breaches in the rules then, of course, they should be taken very seriously, but I actually don't think – you know, people weren't tricked into voting leave. They voted leave for reasons I completely understand and one part of the argument that people like myself have got to take on board is that you've got to deal with the reasons why people were so disaffected that they thought Brexit – which is, by the way, not an answer to any of those problems – was the answer to those problems.'

So he has not, then, come to tell me the whole result needs reconsidering.

We have nearly exhausted the Brexit part of the chat, and I turn to the story on which I've been told he is expecting a question.

'Let me ask you briefly. Do you believe Jeremy Corbyn is anti-Semitic?'

Blair is ready for it. But he goes with caution. 'I don't believe he is personally anti-Semitic. No, I don't actually. But I do believe that he and the people around him particularly do not understand the seriousness of this problem. I think up to now at least they haven't really got it. And I think they would be very wise to listen carefully to what the Jewish community is saying today and to act upon it.'

Corbyn has, I remind him, already said he recognizes 'pockets of anti-Semitism within the Labour Party'.

'I appreciate that. But I think what the Jewish community will say is, "Look, we've had statements over the past two or three years but what we actually need is to see clear action." And I think if that's not done it's going to . . . I think we already have a very serious situation in the Jewish community, in the Labour Party, and that causes me, personally, a lot of pain . . . What I would urge the Labour leadership to do collectively is to recognize this is a real problem. This is not got up by people who want to oppose the Corbyn leadership.'

I press him further. Is it as serious a problem as some in his own party seem to think it is now? 'Do you think Jeremy Corbyn is in trouble on this one?'

'I think if he doesn't act it's going to carry on causing real dismay. In the sense of alienation in the Labour Party.'

'What is "acting"?' I ask.

'Well, I think, you know, the Jewish community and people like the Jewish Labour Movement have set out a series of things, but I think he . . .' He pauses. 'I'm not going into stuff. Telling him, like, he should do this or he should do that. But I think he needs to realize that it's gotten beyond the stage where words will solve this.'

The line is strong. But it's not – how can I put this without sounding hyper? – *that* strong. It's moderate and it's sensible and it is – frankly – unremarkable. Was I really called here then just to allow Blair to warn his successor to recognize the problem he's already vocally recognized?

I bring the interview gently to a close. We fill in the editing shots we need: a two shot, a wider shot – the usual bits and pieces. All the while I am racking my brain, which has gone into overdrive. What have I missed? What have I failed to ask? Did I forget a follow-up? Was this *really* what Tony Blair wanted? 'Maybe,' my producer says, 'you're thinking too much. He gave us some interesting lines. The interview will be lively and watchable.'

We pack the stuff away and head back to the BBC.

The *Newsnight* office has its own rather primitive watering hole. A single filing cabinet constantly laden with cakes and dubious sweetmeats brought back from around the world and arranged for communal sharing. I am never far from it. And it is here, chocolate in hand, that another colleague, the wry, quiet and fiendishly funny Sarah Teasdale, finds me lost in thought. 'How was the interview?' she asks. 'Did you feel dirty?'

The question makes me laugh. I think she means dirty because the interview came to us – which never feels quite kosher. 'No,' I tell her. 'I didn't feel dirty enough.'

What I mean and what she will understand is that I was expecting to walk back in here with the line that Tony Blair wants to sail around the BBC. The soundbite that he wants to be everywhere. But actually what I have is a fairly calm and thoughtful exchange. No fireworks. No slogans. What was it for?

I have recorded the audio for myself on the phone, so I can get it transcribed. I hide away at my desk and start to play it back, wondering where the strongest lines are.

I relive our Brexit conversation. I relive the stuff on the funding, Parliament, Vote Leave, Russia. Then I turn to the section on Labour's current anti-Semitism problem. As I listen I am struck by how many times Tony Blair has mentioned conversations with the Jewish community in his responses to me. He's talked about his friends. About his own personal pain. It is not unusual. But second time around it is noticeable. I have the strangest epiphany. Just there. Utterly unprovable, but somehow instinctively right. I suddenly realize that he has not, perhaps, been speaking for himself. Or should I say not *only* for himself. He is doing an interview that someone else has leant on him to do. It immediately explains so much. Why he has come to seek us out. And yet also why he has refrained from saying anything more strident. More arresting. Has he made an almost charitable intervention? I wonder. Has there been a donor, perhaps, or an old friend – a prominent figure in the Jewish community and the Labour Party, or even someone who is lending their support to him right now over his plans to help forge a new anti-Brexit movement in the country? I throw down my phone and rush out to find Stewart, today's programme editor. I explain my thoughts and he listens and nods. He thinks I may be right.

There is no one I can turn to for proof on this one. As I say, it is more of a gut instinct. And in terms of how we will play the interview tonight, it changes nothing.

Over the coming weeks, I will share this story with a few journalist friends. I will pick up the phone to Labour donors, well-known Jewish figures and muddle my way through a tentative question: did they lean on Tony Blair to make the intervention?

In just a few calls I've established it's true. My hunch is confirmed to me in an off-record conversation.

And now, perhaps, you want to know why it mattered? Why it was important for me to know? Quite simply, for my own sanity: I went to interview a man with the power to say so much, who chose to say so little.

I had beaten myself up for not asking better questions, cajoling better answers, being somehow *more interesting*, but perhaps it was always going to be this way.

This interview was done as a favour. It was the interview he was always going to give: no less, no more.

Zelda Perkins: Harvey Weinstein's Personal Assistant

Zelda Perkins was just twenty-two years old when she went to work for Harvey Weinstein. A young British woman, she became his personal assistant almost by mistake, stepping in to cover another assistant on sick leave. She remembers being warned about him from the off: 'Always sit in an armchair. Don't ever sit on the sofa, next to him. And always keep your puffa jacket on,' she was told by those keeping an eye out for her safety.

Zelda learnt to 'deal' with Harvey, his idiosyncrasies, his power games and his abuse. But it was when a junior colleague came to her distraught, claiming he'd tried to rape her, that she finally broke.

In the middle of the Venice Film Festival, she hauled him out of a dinner and relayed what she'd just been told by her sobbing co-worker. He denied it all.

Back home she sought help from Miramax, Weinstein's company, and wanted to go to the police to take the accusations of attempted rape forward. She was advised by the company to get her own lawyer. Not only, she says, were they not interested in pursuing a prosecution, they warned Zelda she would need her own legal advice. Zelda quit the company – and for reasons which will become clear as you read – she signed a controversial non-disclosure agreement that paid her £125,000. It seemed an utter fortune at the time. It was intended to buy her silence for life.

In fact, Weinstein's company kept her quiet for two decades: a combination of power, legal threat and money. But in 2017, as women around the world began to speak out about Weinstein's abusive sexual behaviour, Zelda decided enough was enough. She gave her first broadcast interview to me, for *Newsnight*, a world exclusive. She wanted to use it to change legislation – to petition Parliament to outlaw legal agreements being used to cover up criminal activity.

It was the work of my brilliant colleague Lucinda Day who convinced Zelda she wanted to speak to us. Zelda had seen my interview a couple of months earlier with Emma Thompson and decided that when she was ready to tell her story in full it would be to us. But there was a long way between being willing and the recording itself. It took many weeks before Zelda agreed to go on camera.

When I meet Zelda, at a central London hotel, it is just before Christmas 2017 and I have read her notes so fully I feel as if I already know her well. She has told me she is nervous. Nervous because she doesn't want to do a 'victim' interview: 'There are plenty of those out there already,' she explains, 'and actually, what happened to me personally was nothing in comparison.' She is nervous because there is a really, really important story she wants to tell and it's not about being sexually abused or even about the 'monster' that is Harvey Weinstein. It's about what happens when you try and tell the world something and the world stops you speaking. As soon as we meet I am struck that she has been carrying a weight. Is she worried others would blame her for knowing so much about Weinstein and saying so little? Her job here today is to tell me why she tried and why she couldn't. No wonder she's nervous.

Zelda, remember, was not a film star. She was an assistant. She is my age, mid-forties, and completely without vanity. She saw plenty of starlets, she tells me, on the other side of the camera when she worked in film. It never appealed. She is not doing this to have her face plastered around the world. Although that is where it will end up. She turns up in jeans, boots, a jacket. Slim, attractive but without making any particular effort. There is nothing coiffed or manicured. It is raw Zelda. She has a complicated story, and she needs to tell it well.

It is not just nerves that have forced her to keep pushing our interview back. The reason, she explains, is that she has been trying to see the actual copy of her own non-disclosure agreement, kept by her then lawyers Allen & Overy. Part of the difficulty with an NDA is that – by its very nature – no one is meant to know of its existence. She cannot take the NDA out of a safe, she cannot, when she seeks therapy, tell a therapist that it exists, she cannot share it with anyone else, she cannot even be alone with it. She has never actually seen the signed thing without lawyers present. Zelda shows me a covering letter. She points out a paragraph which stipulates that she must, to the best of her ability, 'seek to discourage any criminal or civil prosecution'. It is the moment my blood runs cold: the letter that she has signed is enabling the cover-up of criminal activity.

Why would she *ever* sign anything like this? I think it, but I do not say it. It worries me that I don't feel able to ask her such an obvious question but I am terrified of pushing her back into her shell.

And so we start at the very beginning, and I ask her, very simply, what it was like to work for Harvey Weinstein. And she explains that whilst on the one hand he was 'this sort of repulsive monster', on the other he was also 'an extremely exciting, brilliant, stimulating person to be around'.

She is trying to be fair to him but also trying to explain why so many people were so quiet for so long. Seduced – if that's not a terrible word to use – by his sheer talent.

'He was at the top of his game at that time,' she tells me. 'He held all the cards. Everybody came to him, and I'm not just talking about people in the entertainment industry, I'm talking about people in politics and in, you know, big business and industry. And so to be in the enclave of somebody that powerful was very exciting.'

I realize it is the first time since the scandal has broken that I have heard anyone say anything positive about Weinstein. It is so obvious, but it has been missing.

As if reading my mood, Zelda catches herself.

'He was also very unpleasant to be around. But he was a master manipulator and he – you know, his moods changed very quickly, and you never knew whether you were his confidante, or whether you were going to be screamed at. So it was a very highly adrenalized environment.'

I ask her when she first noticed he had a problem with women. How could she not have seen the film stars coming and going from his bedroom the whole time?

She corrects me. 'Everybody now says, "Why did everyone go to his hotel room?" Wasn't as simple as that. Everybody went to his *hotel*. This was where he did business; it wasn't in his bedroom, it was in his suite. You know, you had top agents, top movie stars, male and female, coming in hourly for meetings. This was his place of business, so it wasn't sort of this spurious weird thing that you had to go up to his room. However, he had a lot of meetings with actresses, and he clearly had girlfriends, you know, he had regular female visitors . . . sometimes aspiring actresses, well-known actresses, and they clearly had a fairly intimate personal relationship with him.'

So she assumed the relationships were consensual? Part of the 'film world'?

'Yes. I presumed they were consensual, but there were obviously some women who were reluctant to come. You know, when you'd ring up to try and make a meeting they'd always come up with excuses, and Harvey would get very angry and threatening and would threaten, you know, you personally, that you had to make sure that this meeting happened . . . With Harvey, there was no such word as "no" and I think that's really the crux of the matter.'

She reminds me then that she had had these initial warnings. She is thinking back to the colleague who told her to stay well wrapped up around Weinstein – a woman she thanks for 'saving her honour', which strikes me as an oddly discordant euphemism from such a smart mind.

'It was an incredibly important and good piece of advice,' she goes on, 'because it meant that I was ready, actually, when he did start behaving badly. And it also meant that I wasn't as frightened because I knew that it had happened to other people. So, you know, I was very robust in the way that I dealt with it.'

When I ask what Harvey did to Zelda herself I see a flicker of concern. She doesn't want to be the story – she's told me as much – and she *definitely* doesn't feel like a Harvey sex victim. Her tone is deliberately offhand, insouciant.

'He didn't have a very original repertoire, you know, but it was a system that worked. Massages, inappropriate suggestions, expecting people to work with him unclothed . . . Pretty much everything that you've read I've had to experience at some point or other.'

It was a warning she passed on.

'I said, "I'm afraid he's a pain, he will behave inappropriately; you just tell him where to go, you're tough with him, nothing will happen." But I was wrong.'

The bald statement is left hanging between us. As if she realizes then she must tell me the events that led up to the moment her life would change for ever. How it came to a head when she was with him at the Venice Film Festival. How a colleague came running to Zelda – after being left alone with him for the first time – to tell her he had tried to rape her.

'She was shaking, very distressed, clearly in shock. Didn't want anybody to know, was absolutely terrified of the consequences, what would happen.'

Zelda tried to calm her down, talked with her for half an hour. And then, perhaps, reached her own boiling point in the process.

'I went straight downstairs to where Harvey was having a business meeting on the terrace and told him he needed to come with me right away. For me to have broken into a meeting like that was very unusual. And he did not question me, he got up and came with me straight away, because he knew why I was as angry and serious as I was.'

I spell it out to check I have understood what she is telling me. 'So you accused him of attempted rape.'

She nods.

'And he denied it?' I am trying to understand what this conversation sounded like on the warm terrace of some extravagant Italian hotel in the middle of the Venice Film Festival.

'Yes. He said nothing at all had happened. And he

swore on the life of his wife and his children. Which was his best get-out-of-jail card, that he used quite a lot.'

As I am wondering if it ever crossed her mind that he might have been telling the truth, she offers up her own sense of visceral evidence – inadmissible in a court of law – which has come from seeing a young woman distraught. She explains she had come to know Weinstein's mannerisms and phrases well, that she could spot when he was lying from the four years of being at his side. And she reminds me that movie moguls do not jump to the every word of their personal assistant – in the middle of hosting dinner – unless they suspect they are in trouble.

It was not until they returned to the UK from Venice that Zelda spoke to her senior in the Miramax office and they suggested she got a lawyer. It felt like a kick in the gut. Zelda and her assistant both resigned from the company at that point, saying they felt they had been constructively dismissed because of Weinstein's behaviour. They informed Miramax that their solicitors would be in touch. At that point, Zelda explains, she assumed the whole thing had escalated into criminal proceedings and that he'd face trial and, ultimately, punishment. It was, in her mind, the only way things could go.

But that first meeting with her newly appointed lawyers was to change everything. They made it clear the two women had few options. Because they hadn't gone to the police in Venice there was no physical evidence. And it would in any case have been impossible to prosecute a crime of attempted rape in a different jurisdiction.

Suddenly Zelda was faced with the cold light of reality: the words of two twenty-something women against Harvey Weinstein, Miramax Film Corporation and Disney. The company built on the aspiration of making dreams come true was turning Zelda's life into a living nightmare.

Where once Zelda had assumed Disney would fire Weinstein and help them with proceedings, she was about to find out how the commercial world worked. This, she explains to me, was where the trauma of the abuse really began.

'I could deal with Harvey. He was an unpleasant, difficult man but I had ways of dealing with him. What I couldn't deal with . . . was the legal system. Essentially I'd gone to the parents to say, "Somebody's done something bad," and there was no recourse, it seemed. And that was really shocking, and very frightening, to discover that the law couldn't help me.'

Zelda says she realizes now the advice her legal team were giving her was ultimately meant to protect her from being dragged sideways through the courts and eventually destroyed by a beast so much bigger than her. But it seems too convenient that at this point they suggested the NDA – what, in a dirtier world, would be called hush money. Was that the moment Weinstein realized he could get away with more of his behaviour? From Zelda, a vehement 'no'.

She explains how she was told that the only way they would get Miramax to the table was by making a monetary request. She and her colleague shared a payout of £250,000, which seemed to her an utter fortune two decades ago. But at her own insistence she sowed extra demands into the contract: that he attend therapy to try and change his behaviour.

It never happened, of course. And she ended up broken and exhausted, anyway, by the whole legal process, eventually quitting not just her job but the whole industry. She moved to Central America to train horses. A euphemism for PTSD if ever I heard one.

I ask Zelda if she accepts the description Weinstein gave himself: 'a sex addict'.

She corrects me. 'He's a power addict. Everything he did, everything that drove him was about dominance. With men and women. He put an enormous amount of energy into humiliating men and an enormous amount of energy into getting women to submit . . . That was what drove him, you know, an overarching need for power.'

She stuck to her silence – written into the fabric of the non-disclosure agreement – for nineteen years, and I'm wondering, if she'd been listened to then, whether everything since could have been avoided? Would this resurgent Me Too movement feel quaintly superfluous?

She has clearly been thinking about it too. It's why

she's here, after all. But she reminds me it's not one woman and one man, it's a system. A system that could compel a young, vulnerable woman to cover up a serious crime. With the help of the best lawyers and a legal framework that condoned it.

'I dread to imagine,' she tells me, 'what other things are being covered up . . . You cannot have a legal document that protects a criminal, that protects somebody who is raping. This isn't someone selling you a dodgy car! . . . You can't change the Harvey Weinsteins of the world. There are always going to be people who follow the darker side of their character. But if the rules and the laws that we have to protect ourselves enable that, then there's no point in having them . . . We're a civilized culture. This has to be debated and the law needs to be changed. It needs to happen here.'

She stops. But it is what she has come here today to tell me. It is said with the passion and the kind of articulate precision that comes from having mimed saying the words over and over again in your head for twenty years. She delivers this masterpiece of feeling and thought without drawing breath, without self-correction, without hesitation, because it is everything she's been trying to say out loud for two decades. And when I ask if the retelling is distressing for her, she corrects me again to say no, the one thing it isn't is distressing. The last twenty years, she reminds me, where she hasn't been allowed to speak, have been distressing. The freedom she has found from breaking her agreement has finally given her peace of mind, released her from the trauma of silence. It has made her feel both validated and vindicated.

'The process I went through was legal [but] it was immoral. And now I feel that maybe I can be instrumental in some sort of change, and if I can make one good thing happen out of something horrific . . . then that makes this year a fabulous year for me personally.'

It now feels there is little more for either of us to say. Her piece is done. And I wonder if the responsibility now lies with us – the power of our media – to carry on pushing for this change in the law. Is that what my role should be?

We switch off the cameras. End the interview. We have been speaking for two hours and we are both red and baking hot. There is a silence where she is wondering if she has said too much and I am wondering if I have asked enough.

After it is aired on *Newsnight* it is picked up around the world. I see articles in Dutch, German, Hungarian, Italian and Spanish. It's in *Time* magazine and on CBS News, in Canada and Australia and India.

But none of this has piqued Zelda's interest as much as one question asked by an MP in the House of Commons that week. Our own lawmakers have started a debate about a change to the legal system on NDAs.

Because a former personal assistant, Zelda Perkins, had the courage to tell them to do so.

James Comey and His Part in the Election of President Trump

All US presidential campaigns are brutal. But the election of 2016 was in a league of its own.

Towards the final months, during the Democratic convention in Philadelphia in July, Michelle Obama made a rousing speech in which she appealed to the better nature of all involved. She referenced the difficulties of raising her daughters in the goldfish bowl of the White House. She segued – without bitterness – into the levels of vitriol she and her husband had experienced as a First Couple and how she urged her young children to ignore those who questioned their father's citizenship or faith or birth certificate.

'When someone is cruel or acts like a bully, you don't stoop to their level,' she told enraptured crowds. 'When they go low,' she said, 'we go high.'

She never mentioned Donald Trump by name.

It was a poignant cry by a popular First Lady: the speech would enter the history books and it would be hailed and repeated by all those looking not just for a cleaner, kinder rhetoric but for the politics of accountability and responsibility.

It would take me months to realize that she might be wrong. That, in fact, the opposite would become true.

Donald Trump's visceral, bombastic language was hugely successful in placing his opponents exactly where he wanted them. The nicknames he gave his enemies – Ted Cruz became 'Lyin' Ted', Marco Rubio became 'Little Marco', Hillary Clinton was 'Crooked Hillary' – were both comical and unforgettable; paring complex characters down to one simple weakness was reductionist, brutal and brilliant. And the question of how to find the right language to deal with that would remain a live one for the Democrats for years to come.

The 2016 campaign demonstrated to those who supported Trump – and, just as intriguingly, those who would go on to lose to him – that the lofty rhetoric of Roosevelt or JFK was over.

That election we learnt that whatever low we had imagined could go even lower.

The rules had been ripped up.

Alongside the nicknames, there were the chants. Three or four words of Trump catechism to fire up an entire room. 'Lock her up' became one of the most emblematic of the campaign, shouted by supporters, emblazoned on T-shirts and placarded through rallies.

They were calling for the imprisonment – without trial – of one Hillary Clinton, Democratic nominee for president, 2016.

The first time I heard it directed from the stage itself was at the Republican convention in Cleveland. Rudy Giuliani, former Republican Mayor of New York, encouraged a rowdy rendition from the audience. He threw it out to the crowd. It came back at him faster and louder and faster and louder: 'LOCK HER UP! LOCK HER UP!' *Us and them, us and them.* It was perfect warm-up material; it brought from the crowds a sense of grievance and injustice – that Clinton was trying to 'have one over them'. And that this time they wouldn't let her get away with it.

Hearing it chanted in the hall was a profoundly shocking experience. It was ritualized noise, punctuated with the percussion of stamping feet and banged chairs. It felt deeply, primitively primordial: an attempt to silence debate and exile political enemies without trial.

But it's worth remembering that at its core and behind the white noise was something many Trump supporters believed: that Hillary Clinton had acted illegally and dangerously by passing classified government content through her BlackBerry and her own personal email address.

It was the claim that pursued her for two years. The use of a private email address for secret material was a mistake, she said, made in good faith, but one she nevertheless came to regret enormously. Her course of action may or may not have ultimately decided her defeat. But it nevertheless opened her up to an investigation which would prove cataclysmic in the weeks leading up to the election.

The inquiry was conducted by the Director of the FBI, James Comey. A man whom history is still struggling how to judge. It fell to him to appraise whether she had done wrong and, crucially, whether she had intended to do so. In the summer of 2015, when rumours were already rife, Director Comey announced that he had opened a criminal investigation into Hillary Clinton. Over the course of the next two years, his actions – opening and closing the investigation, then reopening and reclosing it just hours before Election Day itself – would make him, unwittingly perhaps, one of the key players in the 2016 election.

Comey was no ingénu; he had held top legal positions in the land, served under Presidents Bush and Obama, and given legal counsel in some of the most controversial circumstances. He had known, in other words, that it was not possible to please all of the people all of the time. This election, however, he would discover how you could end up pleasing no one. Hillary Clinton would blame his actions for the part they played in her defeat. Donald Trump would blame him for clearing her of wrongdoing just as America went to the polls. He would be fired by Trump six months into that presidency, hearing the breaking news of his sacking via a TV screen in his own office.

James Comey was a man who evangelized the importance of staying 'above politics' in his FBI role. In 2016 he waded deeper than any of his predecessors. He avoided interviews with the press during his time in office and his subsequent testimony about his actions before Congress. But in March 2018 he published his memoirs. Everyone wanted that interview with Comey.

And after a certain amount of indecent begging we landed a UK exclusive for *Newsnight*. I flew out to New York to meet him.

Ahead of the interview, we knuckled down to one of the most serious briefing sessions I can ever remember. Briefings are tricky things. A roomful of people, each one with their own sense of what the interview should achieve and which direction it should go in. Sometimes, with a last-minute booking, briefings end up being the stuff of rushed and frantic thinking. This one was planned out, and I am so grateful it was.

I had received the book two days earlier (under a non-disclosure agreement) and the moment I had it in my hands every other bit of work seemed awkward and dull. That weekend I took the book to bed and devoured it. Not because it was the finest work I'd ever read, but simply because it answered – or at least broached – so many of the questions I'd been carrying around with me for two years. I began my annotations in gentle soft pencil. By the time I got to page 100 the pencil was a lime-green highlighter scrawled across pages. It became for me a quasi-legal document – the ordering of what had happened when, who had known what, how decisions had been reached and whether they had been regretted. It was, of course, only one man's version of events. But it was a man who had been right at the centre of everything. By the end of the week the lime highlighter had been joined by a pink one to go over the bits I *really* didn't want to forget. All in all, I read key bits of

the book three times. I felt I had to know my subject –
and indeed my Subject – inside out.

My sense in that briefing was that we needed to
explore the part Comey had played in the 2016 election.
It was what I felt our audience would most remember.
But the Dans – Clarke and Kelly, both brilliant in their
understanding of US politics – were adamant that we
focus on his time with Trump: what the president had
demanded of him in private; the conversations they
had shared; the awkward moment when an FBI director
would talk to his president about compromising material
and Russian prostitutes. My producer, Rhoda Buchanan,
wanted a wider context for his actions: hadn't he had
tricky encounters with George W. Bush? she pointed
out. And even Obama? Maybe Trump wasn't this excep-
tional caricature at all – maybe all FBI directors have
conflicted and complicated relationships with their com-
manders in chief. We locked ourselves into a little glass
box in the *Newsnight* office for maybe three hours and
round and round we went. I argued hard for 'the Hillary
stuff'; the Dans were reminding me we needed newslines –
would Comey tell us something new about Trump and
Britain? Trump and Mueller? Trump and Theresa May?
Rhoda was pushing stuff that gave us and him hinterland, and the interview longevity.

We didn't emerge until we suddenly started feeling
that the oxygen level in the room was depleted and everyone had a raging headache. It was time for fresh air and
the chance to let it all sink in.

The following day I head to New York. On the way over I read the book again, and highlight over my high-lighter until the thing is broadly illegible. Or would be to anyone but me. I revise and revamp and shorten my questions. I cut down the Hillary section; I enlarge the section on the Russian collusion investigation. I move Trump up and world affairs down. Never have I been so grateful for a seven-hour flight. Something to do with being locked in time and space, without Wi-Fi, gives me the headroom to realize what it is we should be asking.

We land at Newark at 7.45 p.m. and hit the ground running. I have made a set-up film that will run before my interview and I also need to shoot a couple of pieces to camera on the ground in New York.

We are met at the hotel by my cameraman, Peter Mur-taugh, who's flown in from Washington, and in the time it takes him to set up lights and camera, I have learnt my lines off by heart so I can deliver them in short solilo-quies. Pete and I have worked endlessly together: he knows I enjoy doing things straight off the plane when my adrenalin is high and my hair is still straight from the cabin pressure; we can rattle these off within fifteen minutes and they will be edited into the piece that night and sent back to London for when the desk wakes up the following morning.

And so by nine thirty we are done and back at the hotel, a whistle away from the Flatiron Building, home of the interview tomorrow. I intend to go for supper but sud-denly I realize sleep and solitude are what I'm most craving.

I curl up in my bed with the US networks shouting at me, switching between Fox and MSNBC to get the extreme version of news in which America excels. All the talk is of Comey: what he's said, how the president has responded, and where he's appearing next. Our interview will take place before many of the big American networks will have theirs. It is an extra layer of pressure to make this the best interview I've ever done.

I wake too early the next morning in a stuffy room and march around midtown in search of biting fresh air and a strong coffee. I'm in a slight panic. I cannot tell if it's real nerves or silly nerves. There is a subtle difference. This is the time I would normally go for a run, but my hair is already blow-dried. So I go for something that looks like a strangulated march through the streets of New York instead.

I text Niall Stanage, my Washington friend who introduced me to Steve Bannon. He is a proper Beltway insider who lives and breathes the politics of the Hill. I'm confused, I tell him, and ask if I am right to go with the Hillary stuff? Or are the Dans right that we must push for Trump?

In one text he sets my mind on a completely clear path. He says, trying not to offend me:

Put it this way, if the FBI director hadn't been fired by the president, the memos he wrote of their meetings would never have come to light.

And suddenly I understand. It is Comey's sacking by Trump that has started the whole process of the Russia investigation. Comey kept detailed notes of their meetings and finally went to Congress to tell them what he had witnessed. His accounts resulted in the appointment of Special Counsel Robert Mueller and a full investigation. It is like the last missing jigsaw piece has suddenly turned up, and I've been sitting on it the whole time. A brilliant clarity comes to the whole structure of the interview. And I know it's going to be fine.

The interview is scheduled for 11 a.m. and we get there early to set up and light the room. I have watched clips of James Comey to get a feel for how he speaks, but he is still largely an unknown entity. The book, called *A Higher Loyalty*, has been criticized for being sanctimonious. It is all a little too neat. It begins with a startling account of an attack by a serial rapist in his own home; it goes on to talk about school bullying and how he faced it down; he details his work as a lawyer dismantling the Mafia tribes of New York and how he got around them, and then goes on to describe how he stood up to the Bush administration when he was pressured to approve an unlawful anti-terror policy on torture. Everything he learnt in those early years comes back to be of service to him when his mettle is being tested. By the end, there is not a string left untied. The author writes as a believer in the power and importance of America's institutions, but it is hard not to see him looking for political and spiritual exoneration in its pages.

In his writing he comes across as a good man. But also as a man now desperate to come across as a good man. I cannot tell if I am just being British about this. We like our heroes accidental. We enjoy a bit of hidden, grumpy philanthropy, not the stuff that comes with a motto and a gift-card-style quotation. Is it just a sort of Anglo cynicism that won't let me relax? Or is it that, more fundamentally, I fear he will be humourless and the interview – for all its controversies – a bit dull?

My concern makes me harden my questions towards him. I cannot afford to be his confessional. I have to put to him charges that are being made against him by all sides: Hillary Clinton has accused him of helping her lose the 2016 election; Donald Trump, with characteristic colour, has called him a slimeball and a leaker. Everyone else has called him either self-righteous or lacking in judgement. What will I make of him?

At eleven o'clock on the dot, he enters the room. I have made a mental note not to remark on his height. I know that at six feet eight inches it is almost impossible to ignore, but it is clearly what everyone comments on straight away and I don't want to feel part of the pack. I am five feet seven – more in heels – and yet when we shake hands I feel dwarfed. I am anxious to get him sitting down before I lose my composure, but he makes a tour of everyone in the room, shaking the hands of cameramen and make-up artists alike with a kind of overt attempt to be inclusive.

As we are mic-ing up, I ask if the toll of the book tour has been getting to him. He tells me he slept an astonishing nine hours that night, so feels fine. Or would have done if the hosts of the show he's just come from hadn't tried to make him drink wine on set. I laugh. 'Hopefully they've made my job a bit easier,' I say. But I know that this book, and this interview, will mean too much for him ever to be unguarded, loose-tongued.

And then we're off. I have just thirty minutes to get through around thirty questions and allow room for follow-ups. There is so much I want to ask and so much I want to debate with him, but I have promised the team I won't get tangled in the weeds: we must keep the interview linear with a sense of direction.

'If I described your role in the 2016 election as pivotal, will you accept that?' I begin, the camera rolling.

'I would try to say I hope not, that it was certainly an important role and a prominent role. Whether it made a difference in our election, my honest answer is, I don't know and I hope not.'

'Arguably,' I pursue, 'after Putin perhaps, no one outside had more influence on what happened there?'

'Yeah, that's the thing I hope is not true. Certainly no one had a more difficult role than the FBI but I don't know the answer to the ultimate question.'

'You stressed how important it was for you at the FBI to remain above politics. Do you accept you didn't achieve that?' I am conscious that my questions are quite cutting, but my tone needs to be calm, unemotional. He pauses before he agrees.

'Sure. I believe that we were stuck in the middle of an amazing five-hundred-year flood of politics and political venom, really, in the United States, and I think we stayed away from making decisions for political reasons, but waves of partisan anger washed over us.'

At this point, the framing of the interview – why he's there – is broadly done. Now I start at the beginning, with the forensics.

'Let's go back to July 2015. You opened up the first criminal investigation into Hillary Clinton, her personal email account, as she was running for president. Do you accept that when you made that public, you crossed the line? Your role changed and you unwittingly then made your position political?'

He looks me in the eye and then delivers a punch.

'I don't. In fact, I politely reject that.'

'Because,' I continue, 'you didn't have to go public. You could have opened the investigation [without saying you had]. Others before you perhaps would not have gone public.'

He tells me at this point – as if steering a child away from a dangerous toy – that this one was not the controversial decision. That the case had been opened in response to a public referral and that it was a fairly uncontroversial thing to confirm an investigation everyone already knew about.

A younger me would have been chastened by this simple explanation. But the grown-up me has read the book three times and underlined it now in two different highlighters so it is relatively simple for me just to point to the contradiction in what he's saying.

'Uncontroversial, and yet the attorney general at the time, Loretta Lynch, asked you *not* to call it an "investigation". Why do you think she did that? Did she not believe that you should be going public?'

He tells me she did. It was her decision. But admits he was concerned by her choice of words: she directed him to call it a 'matter'.

'The Clinton campaign at that point was working very hard not to use the term "investigation" so it worried me. But I decided not to fight about it because I thought journalists would miss the distinction.'

There is something in what he's saying which suggests – to my ears – that he believes Lynch was playing along with the Clinton campaign's terminology. Is he hearing a compromised judiciary? Is that why he felt he needed to stand his ground perhaps harder than he might have?

We move on to – arguably – the biggest decision of his life. The move, just twelve days before the election, to reopen the investigation. It came after a tip-off that the laptop of the disgraced Congressman Anthony Weiner, ex-husband of Clinton's top aide, contained hundreds of thousands of those Hillary emails, which they thought they hadn't seen before. Comey explains that he never understood how the emails had got there, but once he knew about them he called for a warrant to search the computer. And at that moment he told the world once again that the criminal investigation into Hillary Clinton would have to be reopened. I remember hearing the news in London, an hour or so before we were going live on air and, critically, whilst Clinton herself was still airborne, on the campaign trail, and out of cyber touch. There were pictures of Hillary Clinton's jet coming in to land; all the world's media already knew what the presidential nominee and her team were just learning. It was the rawest kind of political snuff movie. And no one could take their eyes off the screen.

I am recalling that moment, those images, as I say to Comey: 'Why didn't you wait? Wasn't there a rational position that said, "Do you know, I need more time to look at this? This is a critical moment in US history. I just need more time to work out what this is about?"'

He sighs. I imagine how many of his own side, his family, his friends, have asked him the same question. How many times he's asked it himself since that day.

'Yeah, that's a really good question, and look, reasonable people might take that path. My view of it was: that would be dangerous and potentially catastrophic to the justice institutions in the United States. We had told Congress and the American people months earlier, "We're done here. You can rely on this. There's nothing there." And now that's not true in a materially huge way. And the result may change. So what do you do? Do you speak, or do you not speak? Well, to my mind, speaking would be really bad. Not speaking would be concealing, would be covering up something that was no longer true. And that would be disastrous.'

His explanation is not an excuse. And it makes total sense. Of course, both options are terrible and he chose the least worst. Except. Except. At that very same time another FBI investigation was going on. This one was into alleged links between Trump and Russia. Why, I ask, did he not make *that* one public? I find a phrase which I know will shock him, but it's too good not to use.

'People are looking at this and saying, "Weren't you guilty of double standards here? You were playing God!"'

'Definitely not playing God,' he fires back. He is a lawyer and a Christian and I can't work out which has quickened his response more. 'Trying to be an effective FBI director. And I understand totally why people are confused by that.'

He goes on to explain that the Russian investigation was in its very early stages; it was never going to be revealed as so little was known at that stage. The Clinton investigation, however, had already been public knowledge. The two were not comparable.

The trouble for me is that he is concerned how it would all 'look', whether Clinton would go on to seem compromised, illegitimate, if things were not revealed. I am struck suddenly by this contradiction. Either he is above politics, acting solely according to the parameters of the law, or else he's being swayed by public perception. To me, this is the crux of the whole interview.

'Why didn't you have on the noise-cancelling headphones that said, "No punditry, no polls, no press. I am the Director of the FBI and that is how I make decisions."'

For a moment I imagine he looks almost crestfallen.

'Yup, and I actually tried to live with those noise-cancelling headphones on. But here's the problem. I did not consider the polls in making this decision. But you must consider the public trust in the institutions of justice. Despite what our mothers may have taught us about not caring what people say about us, when you lead [this] institution you have to care that people have faith and confidence.'

And of course I understand why he's gone round and round in circles in his head on this very case. He must sometimes makes decisions that feel wrong, even if the perception is that they are right. It is a deeply unenviable position to be in.

Hillary Clinton, I remind him, believes that second opening of the investigation cost her the election. Has he spoken to either her or President Bill Clinton since she lost? Will he apologize to them?

He hasn't spoken, and he urges them, he says, to read the chapters in his book where he tries to explain it all.

'I would have been happy if Anthony Weiner had never, ever purchased a laptop in his entire life, but we were stuck. And so what we did was not done to help

Trump, or hurt Clinton, or the reverse . . . If she and others would read that part [of the book], I think they'd see that.'

I move on – fast forward to January 2017. One of the most sensationalized chapters in the book involves a description of Comey going to Trump Tower, just before Trump is inaugurated, to tell him about a dossier that involves allegations of conspiracy between Trump's campaign team and the Russian government. Did the president elect seem worried by that?

'He seemed focused on it in one respect, which was to try to confirm that it had no impact on the actual vote.'

Did that strike him as odd?

'Yes. Well, that's a legitimate question for a candidate to ask. What struck me was what wasn't asked. [The obvious question was:] "So, what's next, how do we protect the American democracy from this Russian threat?" I don't remember any questions about that.'

Now it's my turn to gulp. I am wondering how to word my next question. There is a part of the dossier that alleges Donald Trump paid Russian prostitutes to urinate on each other in a Moscow hotel-room bed once slept in by the Obamas. Comey chose not to raise this with the president and I'm wondering why. But as I wonder I catch myself thinking, Am I going to use the word 'urinate' . . . or 'piss' . . . or 'pee' . . . or 'wee' . . . Caught somewhere between English and Americanisms, vernacular or the clinically formal. Eventually, I just go for it ('urinate', since you ask).

'You held back from telling him that detail. Why?'

He grimaces. It is a wonderful moment of humanity and unsheathed honesty.

'Because it's hard enough to talk to the president elect and use the words "prostitutes" and "Moscow hotel room" in the same sentence, and my goal was to do as little as I needed to do to put him on notice that this was out there. It wasn't something the FBI was interested in . . . We knew it was going to become public and wanted him to know.'

'So it wasn't embarrassment on your part?' I venture.

'Just discomfort. The whole thing created an out-of-body experience for me, but just discomfort. What am I doing, as the FBI director, talking about something like this with the future president? I thought.'

I want to talk to Comey about his time alone with the president. The moves he says Trump made to muddy the waters – erode or at least cloud the non-partisan nature of the FBI and ask instead for his direct support. The occasions when he came under pressure from Trump to offer his 'loyalty'. And, by his own accounts, said nothing.

'Why didn't you just say, "You don't, Mr President, understand my job."'

He nods. 'Look, in hindsight, I think that's fair. I might have done it differently. But I don't want to be too tough on myself . . . I think a fair-minded president would understand.'

Was he intimidated by him? I wonder.

'Not intimidated by him personally. I have a tremendous respect for the American presidency and the White House [where they dined together] obviously is a central physical place in the life of my country . . . It just brings a sense of respect.'

At the time of their dinners and their meetings, Director Comey was investigating Mike Flynn, Trump's security adviser, and his Russian connections. In the book, Comey alleges that Trump tried to get him to drop the investigation. Something Trump denies. So was he trying to obstruct justice? Would Comey be investigating him for it now if he were in the job?

'Yes.' Blunt answer. 'And I expect the special prosecutor *is* investigating him.'

'And then,' I continue, 'he did fire you . . . Steve Bannon [his strategist] has called [it] Trump's worst mistake in history. You kept memos of the meetings.' And he made them public. 'Special Counsel Robert Mueller was brought in to investigate. Do you think if he hadn't fired you that the Mueller investigation would not be going on?'

'I don't know. It's possible there would still be a special prosecutor . . . But it's hard to answer a hypothetical . . .'

'Do you suspect now, from what you know, that there was coordination between Russia and Trump's team?'

'We don't know for sure. There certainly was ample basis to open an investigation . . .'

I check my watch. I've had a good twenty minutes with him. I can feel the sands slipping through the hourglass. I've covered Clinton, Trump, Russia. Now I need a bit of the human. I quote him.

'You talk of President Trump staining those around him. What did you mean by that?'

'I think the way in which he acts, and especially his corrosive effect on norms, truth-telling being the most important of them, has that staining effect on institutions and people who are close to him. He has a habit of – and even people who support him would agree with this, I think – of telling lies, sometimes big, sometimes casual, and then insisting that the people around him repeat them and believe them. And that stains any human.'

'Does he listen to those around him?' I ask. 'Are you convinced there are now enough sensible, reasonable people around him to stop impulsive behaviour?'

'I am not.' It is the most direct, stark answer of his entire interview. It's what he has come to say.

'So . . . you don't sleep easy at night?'

'I wake up some mornings and read the president is demanding the jailing of private citizens. Occasionally me. And so that's one of the reasons I'm confident the answer is there are not adequate people around him to stop impulsive behaviour. We've actually become numb to it in the United States, our president calling for the imprisonment of private citizens. That is not OK. That is not normal in the United States of America, or in the UK. It's not acceptable.'

My head starts thinking of the convention floor chanting, 'Lock her up! Lock her up!' I realize by the end of the campaign I myself had become immune to it. It was background noise. A soundtrack.

'He will stain everyone around him,' I repeat, almost to myself.

And I wonder if that's true even for the former Director of the FBI. Here's a man who has gone from heading one of the most powerful institutions on earth to lambasting the President of the United States on a book tour. He trolls him a bit on Twitter. He describes in detail his observations of the president's fake-tan marks, of the size of his hands.

'Do you feel stained?' I ask.

It feels dangerous. Even a little rude. What right do I, a British journalist, have to ask a man who has seen so much of American politics at its very epicentre? And for whom respect is such an important quality. And yet it speaks to what we have been discussing. *When they go low, we go lower . . .*

His pause is meaningful but his answer when it comes is phlegmatic.

'I don't. And I hope not. And I'm never angry on Twitter. I try not to be, I try to be occasionally funny and artistic and ambiguous . . . I hope people will read the book and see that I am actually trying to be an author and describe in a detailed way my boss . . . It isn't about picking on him, it's about describing a scene. So I don't think so. Again, it's hard to judge . . . but I don't think it's stained me.'

There's a rap on the door and I'm given a three-minute

warning. Our time is pretty much up. And I have most of what I need. He stays a bit longer, signing books, doing selfies with our make-up artist, Mayvis, shaking hands and posing for team photos where we all look ridiculously stunted at his side.

We shake hands and we are done. My job now is to rush away with my producers and stitch the interview together for the night's show – we will be live from Times Square and the interview will run almost to time: the whole show depends upon us getting our act together fast.

I leave the room wondering if an interview earns me the right to ask for us to stay in touch. I decide it doesn't. Quite. But two months later our paths will cross again. He will come to London, to speak to a packed concert hall: two thousand people at the Barbican Centre. And once again I will be at his side, asking the questions – and this time, he will tell me to call him Jim.

This time, there will be no holding back: no worrying about the tone or the edit or the timing or the TV. I will simply turn to him and say:

'Let's start with a nice gentle one, James Comey: do you feel responsible for bringing Donald Trump to power?'

And he will laugh, and wince, and begin to tell his story one more time.

#MeToo and the Chippendales

I am watching a man simulate masturbation in the shower. He has his back to me, so all I can see are taut buttocks and toned thighs. He is lathering his back with water – or possibly oil, it's hard to tell from where I'm sitting – in time to the aching, persistent beat of Prince's 'Purple Rain'.

Others join him. The shower disappears. There are workmen. There are policemen. There is a bare, heavily tattooed chest of a man straddling a motorbike and revving the engine. I sit still, sipping a dirty vodka Martini, trying not to let my face betray a single expression. I do not want to be caught *emoting*. Around me women are standing on their chairs. Trying to get a better peek – as if the visuals were not already graphic enough.

Every once in a blue moon an idea hits you that is so good you can't believe no one's had it before. In this case, it was actually my husband, Mark, who sent me off to see the Chippendales in Las Vegas.

I had decided to take my best friend, Bridget, and son Milo away for the cold February half-term. It was meant to be a week of desert sunshine, great food, endless chat and the odd show. But it was only when I started scrolling through the entertainment listings that something started to germinate. What would it be like to be a Chippendale, a male striptease dancer, in a climate where the rules are being redrawn. I was recalling the very question Piers Morgan had put to me several months earlier: his bombastic, imperious indignation about the fate of these poor men at the hands of horny women (see page 158). It was more of a ponder out loud, laughing, as we were in the car.

'You should go and ask them,' Mark said. Dead serious. And so the idea was born.

In the middle of a *Newsnight* shift, the Friday night before I flew, when our lead story was the predatory behaviour of certain Oxfam staff in Haiti, I was sending an email to the Chippendales' agent in Vegas, Michael Caprio. Perhaps because I was up against it, perhaps because I never expected a response, my request that day was blunt and honest: 'I'd like to interview the Chippendales about the Me Too movement,' I said. The sentence itself stared back at me. Ludicrous and inconceivable.

Then, minutes before we went on air, an email pinged back. 'We'd love to help with the piece,' said Michael. 'We should talk.'

Americans are always polite. Americans in public relations are scrupulously polite. Even when they mean '*No*, absolutely *not*.' So I couldn't really decide how seriously to take it. Did 'help' mean yes to an interview? Did it mean 'Thanks for reaching out but no way'? I was flying the next day and I didn't know whether to ready a

crew, alert the desk. TV tries its hardest to look spontaneous, but it can't be. You need camera people and
lights and set-up time. You need someone with a clear
diary to get to Vegas at a moment's notice. You need a
producer to check you're actually making sense. You
need the flexibility to know that, if the interview is pulled
at the last minute, you haven't committed to the endeavour a ridiculous amount of money and time and
goodwill. I send a tentative message to the co-editors.
Would they fancy it if I could make it work?

Truth be told, I still couldn't tell if it was ridiculous.
Was there real journalistic merit to it or would it feel
indulgent? I remember a late-night exchange with Stewart, the output editor, about whether you'd want the
Chippendale in traditional cuffs and collar or whether
you'd have to make him keep his shirt on for an interview so it didn't look like a hen-night gag. Stewart's
insistent that in this hypothetical situation we play it
straight. Clothes on.

For a long weekend, Michael the agent goes quiet. I
am starting to think it was PR niceness after all. Then
Monday morning dawns and he's back on the radar.
What exactly did we want to ask, he enquires. And I tell
him. About the interviews I've conducted with Emma
Thompson and Zelda Perkins over Harvey Weinstein.
About our current fascination with Formula One Grid
Girls doing their job. About my exchange with Piers
Morgan, who asked me what I thought about women
pawing men at these shows. I hide nothing; I embellish

nothing. But I say, 'There are no right answers. If your Chippendale feels he is being exploited, that's fine, and if he feels he isn't, that's fine too. If he enjoys it, great; if he feels uncomfortable but calls it a job, that's great.' I am trying to impress upon him that I have no preconceived ideas because, genuinely, just to hear a Chippendale say *anything* seems to me quite good telly and a useful contribution to the debate.

Finally, Michael comes back to me with the unforgettable phrase: 'I've found you one Chipp. Do you need more?' We settle on one for the interview, as long as we can get set-up shots with more of them: B-roll of the guys getting ready backstage and of course the show itself. How big is your crew? he asks. I describe bestie Bridget Fallon as my producer, since she coincidentally also happens to be an award-winning producer for RTÉ. I cannot quite bring myself at that point to mention that my thirteen-year-old son will also be with us, wondering to himself quite what he is doing hanging out with his mother and his godmother in a strip club.

It is arranged for Thursday night at the Chippendales' own theatre in Vegas. Peter, our DC-based cameraman, has flown into Vegas, avoiding a send to Florida to cover yet another school shooting. Pete and I have both covered many – too many – American shooting stories. There is between us an unspoken guilt about doing a story that feels so flippant by comparison. But it is outweighed by the uncontainable relief at not being at the scene of so much grief, at not having to ask, again and again, if anything will change when history has told us it won't. And that is how Pete, Pete's camera, Bridget-the-best-friend, my-son-Milo and I find ourselves on stage at the Rio Theatre, awaiting a man whom I've just had to ask to appear with his top on.

The Chippendales describe their show as entertainment but admit 'we reveal a little more'. Their T-shirts rip down the middle; their trousers come off in their hands. They simulate sex – both doggy style and reverse cowgirl – with their audience members, whom they call upon to do extraordinary things with bananas. This is Las Vegas at its most, well, *Vegas*. And it is here that I will finally get to ask the million-dollar question: do these men feel objectified by the work they do?

We have come far enough in the Me Too movement to recognize the questions we would ask of women in this profession. We would wonder about coercion and abuse. We would ask whether the simulated sex dance was a precursor – foreplay, if you like – to prostitution. We would think about the emphasis on the way they looked, whether they starved themselves to reach a perfect weight, whether they ended their work shift feeling bullied and degraded. Or scared as they wrapped their coats tightly round them and left the theatre after dark. So now I'm sitting here wondering if the time has come to ask the same questions of the men who strip for a living. Is there any kind of parity between what they do and the women hostesses at the Presidents Club? Or the

Formula One Grid Girls? The Me Too movement has mainly – rightly – focused on women's voices. But are we, as Piers Morgan suggested to me earlier this month, storing up resentment from men when we just single out *their* bad behaviour. At the time, I dismissed it, citing a million socio-historical reasons why he was wrong. But now I'm here, and I get the chance to ask.

'We want it to feel like a party,' Ryan Kelsey, the Chippendales' dance captain, tells me. 'A lot of times we do bring women up on stage to interact with us. They're usually given pretty clear instructions.'

There is no rulebook but, broadly, Ryan tells me, touching is encouraged on the upper body. Full-frontal nudity is prohibited under Vegas laws, so what they euphemistically call 'a sock' is worn at all times. The show is slick enough for the audience never to realize.

'On an average night,' I ask Ryan, 'how many hands touch you?'

He laughs. 'About forty to fifty.' He tells me about the 'crowd run': the men dive into the audience of screaming fans with the explicit intention of allowing the women to 'get handsy'. As he's said, interaction is a big thing here, as well as the muscular dancing.

And does he enjoy that? The touching?

'I love it. I do enjoy the touching. But it's mostly because – it's not so much the touching itself, it's . . . people are having fun, you know, you see the brightness in their eyes, and you see they're smiling, laughing; you walk away and they giggle with their friends.'

So does he feel belittled or empowered? I ask.

'The big difference here is that I know what this job is. I willingly show up to work every day, so it's not a surprise. It's not getting cat-called on the street . . . It's not belittling to me because it's voluntary, you know what I mean? I willingly show up every day. If I was uncomfortable, then it would behove me to find other work.'

It is an oddly archaic phrase. But it is a useful reminder that my initial prejudices about brawn over brains may need to be rethought. As if on cue, I meet Jack, another Chippendale, who tells me the job has paid him through university – a finance degree – and is now setting him on his way to his post-grad at law school. The new Chipps start earning around the $45k mark; it increases with experience. He does the show six nights a week: arriving at the theatre at 8 p.m., home by eleven. It's easy money, he says.

I ask Ryan if he's ever feared for his dignity in the job. I've heard tales of over-excitable fans leaving teeth marks in their calves, drawing blood with their nails. Have there been incidents where the fans got a little too physical?

He acknowledges there have – very occasionally. 'It's the nails, usually, if something happens, which is very rare . . . It's usually not from a place of malice or weird intent. It's just not knowing quite where the line is.'

So would he see himself as having the same job as female strippers, strip dancers?

He shakes his head. 'We have no tipping at our show.

So there's no dollars, there's no interaction based on how much money you have that day or that moment.'

For a second I don't understand the significance of tipping. I actually thought everyone in America tipped everyone all the time so I am slightly startled. He spells it out to me:

'You can't influence *attention*.' If someone in the audience is well off, he says, the cast might notice: '"Oh my God, this lady's loaded, she's throwing out twenties, she's throwing out hundreds [dollar bills]," and if you gravitate there, someone else that maybe saved up their whole allowance, had barely scraped by to see our show, could get ignored.'

He thinks of it as audience equality. But I am thinking of it differently. Without tipping there is, perhaps, no *ownership*, no expectation of favours – ultimately, sex – being owed or bought.

Who holds the power in the theatre? I want to know. Is it the dancers, or is it the women who pay?

'I don't think it's a clear line,' Ryan tells me. 'Obviously we have a little bit of power because they don't know what's coming. But ... they've also got the control because they're dictating my relationship with them, my interaction. We never want to make anyone feel uncomfortable. We want everyone feeling empowered here.'

The audience is mostly women, but there are men too; they make up around 15 per cent of the crowd. Most gay, but some who aren't. The Chippendales' agent, Michael Caprio, tells me of one husband who admitted after the first show he'd had the best sex with his wife for ten years. 'They came to see us six times in three days that week.'

The Me Too movement, I say to Ryan, has raised awareness of the way women have been abused or objectified. Does the question also need to be asked about men in these kinds of roles?

Ryan is a big fan of the Me Too movement. It shouldn't surprise me, but it does. 'I love what the movement is doing. And I love the amount of awareness it's created, including in myself. I theoretically knew some of my friends' stories, but watching them actually type them out on Facebook and actually hearing them just made it tangible . . . something I hadn't experienced, so I think the movement is very important. As far as it relates to our show, I think it's a little different because we are voluntary participants . . . I know that I'm going to be looked at just strictly for my muscles, but I've engaged in that agreement by working here.'

'Do you feel objectified?' I press.

'No, because I'm participating. I feel like I'm being admired for my physicality. Objectification means someone's reducing you against your will. This is not against my will. You could have guys with great physiques and great personalities that would have a hard time with this or would feel minimalized or objectified by this, and I'd say, "Then this is not the job for you."'

I catch myself wondering then why women feel now

that they can't say the same thing. Why would it *not* be acceptable for a woman to say, 'I work out and have a great body and don't mind flaunting it massively in front of adoring fans.' I paraphrase, but not by much. Are women now being told that their work as a Formula One Grid Girl, or a Walk On Girl, is demeaning, even if they don't particularly feel it?

Ryan pulls me up. And I am slightly shocked it is he who has to explain it to me. If he's not OK with it, he can get a different job. 'Which is what's different from the Me Too thing where everyone trying to crack into Hollywood has to go through Harvey Weinstein. That's a bit of a tougher situation.'

There are many people (I've seen them on my own Twitter responses – admittedly, not always the most useful marker of sanity), who tell me we have lost any sense of fun between the sexes. Does he agree?

'Maybe,' Ryan concedes. 'But I think this is an important step. I think we've got to lose our fun for a second. Take a step back. Because I think a lot of guys were having all the fun. It can't be at the expense of anyone. Maybe we've got to take a step back and allow the stories to be told and these people to heal so that a gesture that may be harmless but misguided won't cut so deep or hurt so bad. I think it's a necessary step. Now that we're finding out about all these stories and all these things that women went through, we might need to acknowledge it for a minute.'

Are we moving into a more puritanical age, though? Surely that will, ultimately, hit his own industry?

He shakes his head. Tells me ticket sales have been steady. Does he think it good or bad that roles for women as Grid Girls or Ring Girls and the like may disappear?

'It's complicated.' He pauses, searches for words. Finds them. 'Because, say, if any one of those girls was proud to do that. Proud to be there – maybe proud of their body. They enjoyed the money, thought it easy, thought it was a fun job – if they were there a hundred per cent voluntarily, then it's hard to argue against it. With that said, though, things have been wrong for so long that we might need to overcorrect for a while, before we find the middle ground that we all want to live at . . . Things that personify that old guard might need to drop off for a second. So socially, I feel one way, and then towards individual rights, I feel another. It's tricky.'

And his thoughtfulness has raised so many more questions I want to press on, and on. But I see him subtly check his watch, a reminder that he is due to perform in less than half an hour. And we are sitting on the very stage they need to set and dress.

We clear the stage and head to the entrance to film the women coming in. There is a bride-to-be wearing a tiara and veil. There is a trio of large twenty-year-olds proudly bursting out of the tiniest of culottes worn over fishnets; there is a slim thirty-something in brilliant vermilion who admits she's a Chippendales regular and has caught fifteen crowd-flung T-shirts in the times she's been.

As the queues grow in the bar – they call it 'the flirt lounge' – I am wondering why the theatre doors have still not opened. Suddenly over a loud, theatre-wide tannoy I understand why:

'Will Milo please leave the theatre? Doors cannot open until Milo has left the theatre.'

Under Nevada gambling laws – and hopefully every other law – a thirteen-year-old is not allowed to be present in the theatre once the strip show is under way. I abandon mic and camera and run inside to find Milo, beaming from ear to ear that he has somehow temporarily become a showstopper. I hustle him out to the burger bar opposite. 'Order a milkshake!' I hiss, before running back in to take my seat, my drink, and wait for the curtain to rise.

The next time I see Ryan, the casual tee will be gone, replaced with cuffs and collars, the Chippendales' trademark uniform. He will be centre stage of the whole line-up: pummelling the floor with his press-ups, gyrating his hips into the pelvis of a woman who's volunteered herself on to the stage. He will be a construction worker, bench-pressing the building-site scaffolding. I will feel his gaze fix on me as if I'm the only woman in the room. We all will.

And I will have to pinch myself that this force of pectoral nature is the same bloke who's candidly told me that we are due for a societal correction, that we need – culturally and socially – to reconstruct, because things simply couldn't keep going on the way they were.

And I will leave Vegas heady and delighted with the full Chippendale experience.

But for very different reasons than I expected.

Double Deaf Disco

Adam Cumiskey, the editor of tonight's programme, is unusually bouncy. He has come into my office with Jasmin Dyer, our producer, to run an idea past me for a last item on the show.

He has seen a story of a finalist, Mandy, in *America's Got Talent*. She has made it on to the shortlist as a singer even though she is profoundly deaf. She keeps in time with the music by using vibrations from the floor to pick up the beat although she can hear nothing. It is fascinating in its own right, and a topic we know little about, but the reason Adam is so intrigued is because she revealed, on reaching the finals, that she had received hate mail – even death threats – in the US from a minority of deaf people. They accused her of betraying her deafness by espousing 'oralism': the system of teaching profoundly deaf people to communicate by the use of speech and lip-reading. The hate mail, as I say, came from a tiny handful of extremists, but the discussion is a live one, shared by many within the deaf community. Their argument is that deaf people who join the 'hearing world' are limiting their own fully deaf world. Instead of using sign language, a language in its own right that covers everything between deaf people, 'oralists' place themselves in a world where they are only ever going to understand a limited amount. They live, the argument goes, a narrower version of communication.

'Let's have a disco!' declares Adam, hugely excited. Disco is our shorthand for 'discussion'. But somewhere deep in the *Newsnight* subconscious we also hope it will entail flashing lights and sweating bodies. 'We're going to have a double deaf disco.'

Adam's idea is that we will invite two guests into the studio to debate the merits of oralism. Does it enlarge the deaf person's experience by giving them speech *and* lip-reading *and* signing? Or does it limit by placing deaf people essentially in a 'hearing person's world they will never fully be a part of'. It is very much *Newsnight* territory, allowing us to put on television something we are pretty sure has not been done on a mainstream current-affairs programmes anywhere else.

So the disco is booked. Not easily, not simply, but eventually we find two deaf women who happen to be flatmates but have a very different understanding of what it means to be deaf. Honesty Willoughby and Zoe McWhinney come into the studio and will be signing throughout the interview; their words will go through an interpreter. I begin the discussion asking about the death threats to the singer, Mandy. Zoe tells me that although death threats can never be a good thing, it shows the frustration people are feeling. There is a pressure group in the US, she explains, who promote oralism: hearing people are always told it's the way forward, and deaf people are fed up. Honesty explains that when she was born, the medical profession told her family she should learn to speak through oralism, but her mother had looked into it and refused. Sign language, Honesty tells me, is like Spanish or French. It's a whole language, a birthright, which anyone can learn and which can be truly and fully communicative in a way that, for deaf people, speaking often can't.

I ask if the argument is one of political choice. 'Yes and no,' says Zoe. 'It's not an issue of saying I *can't* speak, it's saying I *don't* speak.' A way of establishing your right. And so it goes on.

The chat is interesting. But it is only when I come off air that I understand what really happened – and how near we came to having both guests walk out on us moments before going on air.

The women were very unhappy with the interpreter we had found. Not fully trained, they said; they couldn't believe we were making them use her. I don't think we had thought for a moment about quality control. We had just booked the person the BBC provided.

Your mind, perhaps, will now be ticking faster than I write. And you will be working out that the only way we learnt this was through the interpreter herself, whose job it was to translate the complaints the two deaf women were making about her. Whilst I had been on air, oblivious, doing the lead story, my producer had faced the sublimely meta moment of having an interpreter complaining about herself in the first person whilst the deaf debaters signed.

There we were, thinking we had conquered the world, stretched out into new pastures, opened our viewers' eyes, and all we had done was piss off a couple of deaf guests.

I cannot, of course, tell you whether she was good or bad. Whether she caught the nuances of their argument with sensitivity and clarity. She seemed great to me. But really, what do I know? What I can tell you is that things then got worse. Our camera crew – sensitive and vigilant to the last – are trained in the art of capturing the faces of our guests: the full range of emotions, the essence of the expressions behind their words. And that night was no different. They captured the guests' faces beautifully.

What they cut out of the shots, however, were their hands. The hands which were signing their words.

We ended the night realizing we had just performed the impossible: a double deaf disco, live on telly, that no deaf person could actually understand.

Sean Spicer: Corrupting Discourse for the Entire World

It should be a lazy, wintry Saturday afternoon – a 'day after' sort of day.

President Trump has just been inaugurated as America's forty-fifth president. He has told the world it's going to be America First. Melania has been at his side, regal, icy and impeccable in her blue Ralph Lauren outfit. We have been broadcasting live from Washington with an extended *Newsnight* special.

And, frankly, I'm hoping for the day off to mooch around and find a legendary all-day brunch.

Instead, I look down to see my entire fist creeping into my mouth. I am watching, transfixed, the new White House press guy – Sean Spicer – at the podium in the West Wing briefing room. He's telling assembled journalists why they're all wrong. Not just wrong, but irresponsible and reckless. He is angry at a tweet accusing Trump of removing the bust of Martin Luther King from his office. The bust was merely behind a door. He expects the journalist to apologize.

Then he explains why they're wrong about the inaugural crowd size. Photographs, he tells them, were intentionally framed in a way to minimize the enormous support that gathered on the National Mall. It was the floor coverings, he explains, used for the first time to protect the grass, that had the effect of highlighting areas where people were not. He is firm and fired up and (if I'm honest) a bit shouty, but he has an important job to do. His job is to stop journalists from saying Obama's inauguration crowd was bigger than Donald Trump's inauguration crowd.

And we know it is an important job because Donald Trump, in what is almost his first act, on the first day of his presidency, has woken his press secretary that Saturday morning and asked him to correct the narrative.

What happens next has become the stuff of Beltway legend.

First Spicer challenges the media directly. Then his colleague Kellyanne Conway pops up on TV to suggest Spicer was merely providing 'alternative facts'. No one quite knows if she's trying to support him or stuff him. But the die is cast.

We will enter a new era of dystopian doublethink where there can be more than one version of the truth. Sales of Orwell's *Nineteen Eighty-Four* will hit record highs within three days of her utterance. Melissa McCarthy will parody the hapless press secretary for *Saturday Night Live*, a super-soaker in her hand spraying reporters.

And Spicer will realize – with luminous Sophoclean clarity – that this beginning has already presaged his end. Which will not formally come for another six months.

*

It is July when I am next in Washington. The president has told Spicer he is getting 'killed in the press' and brought in his old mate from Queen's, a New York street fighter by the name of Anthony Scaramucci. They loathe each other; Spicer resigns and I intercept Scaramucci on the White House lawn just three days into his job, dragging him live on to *Newsnight*.

Scaramucci – the Mooch – tries to convince me Trump is a man of the people because he likes eating pizza and cheeseburgers. It's a bold, almost chivalrous call. I burst out laughing. By the end of the week, Scaramucci will be gone too.

The president, it seems, both loves and fears his alpha males. But anyone who burns too brightly cannot last. Even arch-ideologue Steve Bannon, the man credited with salvaging Trump after 'Pussygate', will be out of the White House a month later.

He does for them all with his plan of attack.

For a year Spicer is gone if not forgotten. Then he is back with his memoir: *The Briefing*. In it he describes the president as 'a unicorn, riding a unicorn over a rainbow'. No one has any idea what it means. But it suggests there's going to be more kissing and less telling. Nevertheless, we land – with the easy charm and hard graft of booker extraordinaire Sam McAlister – the first international interview since the book emerges, on the very day of its publication.

I will speak to Sean Spicer live from New York City. Originally I had planned to fly out. An interview in the flesh is a much warmer thing. You have eye contact, small talk; you learn gestures and looks, twitches and laughs. My bag is packed – miniature hair straighteners my only armour against one hundred per cent Washington humidity, and my passport is in my pocket – when I hear the timings have been switched around. After a raft of tense transatlantic phone calls, I realize it will make more sense for me to stay put.

I will head to the BBC studio instead and pray he turns up in his.

At 10 p.m., our line to Times Square is up. I can see him and I can hear him but the delay on the line suggests our chat will have all the conversational fluidity of a walkie-talkie. There is so much I want to hear from Sean Spicer. I want to know, if he had his time again, whether he'd do things differently: stand up to his president or call him out more readily. I want to ask him if he accepts he lied for a living.

And I need to check on that crowd size.

At ten thirty the link-up is working and we're live on air. It is a just over a week since Trump stood in Helsinki and appeared to side with Russia over his own FBI by telling a watching world he doesn't see any reason why Russia would have meddled with the election. Within twenty-four hours he is correcting himself. The 'would' it seems was meant to be a 'wouldn't'.

It's not Sean Spicer's problem any more, but I am curious. What would he have told the president if it had been?

Spicer is grinning broadly but it's more of a TV clench than a happy smile. He tells me he thinks Trump did the right thing in the end, attempts to explain that you don't always realize how a statement has gone down until later, then he reminds me how we often rush to judgement.

It makes perfect sense – in normal circumstances. But in a situation where Trump has just favoured America's strategic enemy over his own intelligence agencies it sounds ridiculous.

Was Spicer horrified to hear those words come out of his president's mouth?

'I've been rather busy the last couple of weeks – I got – I saw it happen – I saw them clean it up and I thought, Great.'

Or, in a parallel world: 'My overriding feeling was relief I no longer have to deal with this crazy shit.'

Which is essentially what he's said but more tactfully.

I remind him of the time when it *was* his problem: having to justify that inaugural crowd to a packed press room. This time I get Spicer at his most frank.

'If there's a day that I think I would love a do-over on, it's that one. I set the die on that day for a lot of what was to come. I think what I was trying to do – and clearly not well – was change the focus from the number of people attending [the inauguration] . . . Nobody, Emily, was happy with me that day.'

It's the first real admission he got it wrong. The press found him combative and the president himself was furious. Does he wish he'd stood up to him that first morning? Set a precedent for frankness?

'What people miss is they look at that one day in isolation . . . without understanding the mindset and the mentality that was going into that day. We had faced a press corps that was constantly undermining our ability in the campaign to run an effective ground game . . . If you constantly feel under attack, then you feel at some point [the] need to respond.'

I hear what he's saying. A hostile press made it impossible for him to get good coverage. Ever. Except, I remind him, that the Trump lies started long before he was even a candidate. Back in 2012 he was making false claims about Obama's birth certificate or spewing confections about global warming being a Chinese conspiracy. Is it any wonder the press were sceptical?

He has not mentioned 'alternative facts' in his book. An act of judgement in itself. Does he accept it was a game-changing moment – an admission 'the truth' could now be played with as opinion?

We have seen glints of Agitated Spice, angry Nerf-gun Spice, but at this point I once again get Contrite Spice. 'There are things that I absolutely would love to do over or that I could have done better. I had to do them in front of millions of people and I wish I could have done a better job . . . I am not sitting here saying I'm not without fault. There were days that were extremely lonely in that job because I screwed up.'

With each utterance I am more seduced. I know what it is to humiliate yourself live on TV in front of millions. I know how tough it is to be judged on one stupid, thoughtless phrase – so why, I wonder, am I holding back my pity?

Then it hits me: he has treated it all like some big joke. He played up to it when he presented the Emmys. It was never meant to be funny, I remind him, it was the start of a corrosive culture. By going along with the president's lies he corrupted discourse for the entire world.

I pause. Wonder if I've gone a little too far. He certainly thinks so.

'With all due . . . I'm sorry, Emily, you act as though everything began and ended with that. You're taking no accountability for the many false narratives and false stories that the media perpetrated . . . For you to lay that kind of claim and make everything sound like it started and ended with Donald Trump is just absolutely ridiculous.'

But I'm curious. How does it feel for a man who came to Trump through the Republican party machine, who calls himself a patriot, who believes in the freedoms and institutions and democracy on which his country was built, to have to stand there defending the inexplicable? Will he carry on telling me it's all the fault of media bias? Will he roll over?

In the end he reaches, almost wearily, for the only explanation he can.

'My job wasn't to interpret for him. I gave him the best advice and counsel that I could in private – but at the end of the day he is President of the United States. Whether you like them or not, those were his thoughts and his feelings. And it was my job to communicate them.'

He's sketched me the Platonic ideal of what a press secretary should look like. Bold in private, loyal in public, and in truth we will never know what went on between the two of them behind closed doors. That bit – spoiler alert – isn't in the book.

Would he ever go back and work for Trump? His answer sounds oddly, inexorably, tragic.

'I knew the beginning of the end was coming. No. I loved being able to do it. But I'll let somebody else do that now.'

It is the shortest answer of the night. And this time no one is going to doubt he's telling the truth.

After Twenty-Seven Years . . .

When I first decided to write a book – that is, write down some of the extraordinary encounters I'd had over the years and pray to God it would actually start to feel like a book – I went to chat to my publishers, Penguin. 'The one thing I *don't* want to write about,' I explained, 'is stalking.' I was terrified that the end product would turn into a whinge about 'my stalking horrors': a sensationalized account of 'life as a victim'. I couldn't think of anything worse.

They were instantly sympathetic, they got it, and we agreed that a red line had been drawn.

This book was never meant to be fully autobiographical. It was just a snapshot of the ludicrous things that happen at odd moments, the stories that the finished television programme never reveals.

I'd decided the three-decade-long history of my stalking was too intrusive. I didn't want to be defined by it or excused by it or even, quite simply, made to relay it.

So how then has it earned a place right here, within a book which is meant to be all about broadcasting? I'll tell you how. It happened by accident.

First: a (very potted) history. Read carefully: one fat paragraph is all you're getting.

The perpetrator was a man whom I had befriended at university, in Freshers' Week. He was unusual, kept odd hours, looked at the world differently. That's what college life was about. I thought nothing of it until we stopped being close friends in the second term and I was resented. Made to feel I hadn't explained 'why or what happened' (in truth, there were just more exciting and more interesting people I wanted to have as my friends). I was never forgiven. More than that I was plagued by letters, phone calls, visits; I was forced to 'talk about what had happened to us', 'explain why I'd changed'. Now I see it for what it is, so clearly. A desperate, manipulative, abusive form of behaviour which takes over when the aggressor has nothing left. But as a nineteen-year-old I didn't understand that. I felt it was all my fault. That I had caused him trouble. Somehow, it was of my own making.

A classic, classic response to a bully.

Three decades on it was still happening. Despite police intervention, a restraining order, prison sentences, warnings, mental-health medication – despite me even having moved continent for six years in the middle of it all – it was still happening. I was at my wits' end. Somewhere, if this doesn't sound impossible, between resigned and despairing.

So that's the background. This story really begins twenty-seven years later.

It begins, bizarrely, in August 2017, when I am on holiday in France. Sitting in the garden, in bright sunshine, in a deck chair beneath the walnut tree, idly scrolling through emails. I see one from Thames Valley Police. Over the years, I have had dozens and dozens of emails from the police. Emails asking me for statements, emails telling me he's been arrested, emails detailing when he will appear in court. Normally they require a deep breath, or a lot of procrastination, because I'm going to read something I won't like or that will require a heavy response.

This time the email began:

I bear good news. CPS have authorized charges against the perpetrator for breaching the restraining order . . . He will be summonsed to court. To that end please send me some thoughts on how this breach has affected you if you wish me to submit a Victim Personal Statement for you.

And because the sun is shining, and the kids are in the pool, and the dog is at my feet and I am sitting under a walnut tree at my most relaxed, I just do it. I write a statement which is short and to the point. I write in my own words so it doesn't sound like police-speak. But I try to give a sense of the impact it keeps having – especially most recently, when his letters managed to reach me from behind prison bars. This is the statement I send.

When I heard he had breached his restraining order I felt scared and let down. Scared because it meant that even from within the prison system the perpetrator was able to reach me; let down because the system had been unable to stop him getting in touch even though the crime he is serving time for is harassment for unwanted and ongoing contact. It has affected the relationship with my husband, who is frustrated that we cannot get to the bottom of this problem even though we have been tackling it through the Crown Prosecution Service and the courts for over twenty years, and it has scared my children who thought the threat had gone away – albeit temporarily – whilst he was behind bars. It has affected my ability to do my work. And it affects everyday decisions like how I leave the house and how I get to work and what time I feel able to come home at night. It also makes me jumpy around strangers for no reason. Altogether the breach has been a reminder for me that this man remains a constant threat in my life and my family's life.

I send the statement off without much more thought. I don't show it to anyone else. I assume it will be submitted as evidence to the judge as a document.

What I fail to realize is that five months later this rant from the heart will be read out loud in court. That the tabloids will splash the two or three lines about my marriage on their front pages with a picture of us both in what they might refer to as 'happier times' – a picture from the *GQ* awards, one of the rare occasions when husband Mark agreed to face the snappers. (His caution, it transpires, was well placed.)

I have blanked the impact statement from my mind – perhaps subconsciously – so it comes as a complete shock when, on 16 January 2018, my phone pings with another message from the police. It tells me that the stalker has been sentenced to forty-five months in prison and informs me my victim statement has been read out in court 'so the press will undoubtedly report on this statement for your information'. My stomach churns. I have never quite got used to hearing 'the press' used as if to describe an 'other'. I am the press too. That's what makes this quite so weird. I watch my own news organization report the story – including my full statement – as if I have nothing to do with it, and don't work there, entering the building every day. My face is splashed all over our website.

First call, then, is to my husband to warn him. I remember now, woefully late, that I never even showed him the original statement, just sent it off into the ether that long summer's day in August. Mercifully, he's laughing when he picks up the phone. A sign that I am already too late.

'Ahh, wife!' he says in a faux patrician tone. 'Have you come to reassure me my marriage is still OK? My brother has already called to check.' I grovel. Explain it was never meant to be made public. Then in my mind run through everything else I could have said in the statement, my heart racing and my head cowering. The words I might have used, unguarded, could have been far, far worse. I am chewing a hole in the side of my mouth, just imagining what could now be etched in print.

But I have little time to reflect; messages are already pinging through on my phone.

The BBC website is a wonderful thing. Until you're on it, as a headline, and you just want to hide. I hear from friends and neighbours, I hear from my poor son; I feel for my colleagues, who become this hybrid mythical beast: wanting, dovelike, to show friendly support, but also prodded by their own editors to ask hawkishly if I will speak out on it. I shudder.

I was once given an excellent piece of advice by Mark Austin, an old friend at ITN News, who said, 'When you enter a room thinking about all your own bad publicity just remember everyone else in it is only thinking about their own.' It's always been a comfort to me, and is mainly true. Most people are too busy worrying about how *they* will be perceived to even notice your own discomfort. Nevertheless, there is something about becoming a story, particularly on something as intensely personal as this, which just makes you want to hide under the bedclothes. It wasn't that it was bad publicity per se; it was just too public.

And amongst the kind messages of support there was one recurrent theme: people telling me, 'Hurrah, it's all over, he's in jail at last, you must feel great.' How to explain to them that this wasn't a victory, it was a reprieve? That the same man had been to jail for the same crime over a twenty-year period and each time he got out, some twelve months later, the cycle just started all over again?

I didn't want to explain this in response to each individual message, written out of kindness and support. But it told me I hadn't really done my job in conveying what was happening each time, and how the system was failing.

I wasn't working that Tuesday. It was a night for red wine and box sets and burying my head in my son's *Star Wars* robot project whilst occasionally glancing slyly down at the phone. And amidst all the texts and emails was one from a radio presenter at 5 Live, Emma Barnett, who explained that she was about to interview Conservative MP and GP Sarah Wollaston on her stalking bill. Dr Wollaston was, that very week, trying to get a private members' bill through the Houses of Parliament that would give victims of stalking more protection whilst they awaited the police procedure. She worried that between the reporting of a stalker and any prosecution there was a gap into which the victim fell – sometimes one of mortal danger. Emma wanted to know if I would join Sarah in the radio studio early the following morning to illustrate the problem first hand before we talked about the legislative changes needed. It was the only request that I looked at closely because, as I say, it seemed so time-sensitive and I had always admired the work of Dr Wollaston and found her – without party allegiance – a thoroughly decent MP. I didn't think at that stage I would necessarily do the interview, but I said I was happy to chat about what I thought. We talked on the phone; the next day was Wednesday and I was presenting *Newsnight* that night: did I really want to do an interview early in the day that would inevitably 'give legs' to a story I would then have to cover on my own programme? Would we then ignore it? What if we had the justice minister live on set? Would I find myself compromised because I couldn't do the interview without bringing my own experience into it? Would that be a good thing or a terrible thing?

I explained all this on the phone: I felt tomorrow was too early, I hadn't gathered my thoughts, I didn't want to make the news on a day I needed to cover the news. Emma suggested we do it as a 'pre-record' on Wednesday afternoon, to run the following day. Sarah Wollaston's bill would have its first reading in the Commons on Wednesday, the second in the Lords on Friday, so Thursday would be perfectly timed.

I went into the office the next day around two. The interview would be at four. I also had my own interviews with Labour's business spokeswoman and with the Foreign Office on Macron's visit to the UK, down at Millbank, so I was rushing around, and felt I had no time to overthink my own words. At least it's radio, I thought. Thank God. I hadn't bothered with make-up; I kept my eleven-year-old son's fleece on for the entire recording.

Emma Barnett was very considerate and very professional. I had explained I didn't want to go over and over how the stalking relationship had begun and what had happened. I just wanted to explain where the system had got things so wrong. I didn't want to hear his name or see a picture. That felt like a form of abuse itself. I didn't want to sound self-pitying; I just wanted to be useful. She supported me in just letting me do that.

At 4 p.m. on the dot, we started recording. Her first question was very open: 'What's gone wrong, in your mind, with this whole process?'

And then I talked and talked and talked.

It's not individuals, I explained (I'm précising my words slightly). 'Individuals in the police, in the Crown Prosecution Service, have been caring and helpful, but there is nothing that joins up the dots. We have an injunction – a restraining order against him contacting me and all the members of my family. But he's turned up at the house, at my mum's house in Sheffield, and at my places of work. Even though there is an injunction in place that is meant to be ongoing, each time it's breached you have to go back to the beginning. It's like snakes and ladders, where you think you're making progress – you've given a statement, an impact statement, a witness statement, you've told your story and a prosecution is given and a custodial sentence meted out – and then around twelve months later you're back at the bottom of the pile going through the whole thing again. The restraining order has been breached and you have a choice: do you just leave it – which is tempting but then it looks like you're not taking it seriously and don't believe in the law and aren't bothered by it. Or do you start the whole process all over again?

'People move jobs. There is a new detective, a different police officer, and someone you've never met comes along and turns up at your door just as you're trying to get the kids to bed and they say, "So tell me what happened." And actually, for a stalking victim, just being made to relive that stuff over and over again is punishing and debilitating and humiliating. We shouldn't be making *any* victim continually have to replay the events over and over again – and that's what happens.'

It is all tumbling out now; I am trying to keep my voice steady and unemotional but there have been twenty-seven years of frustration. I have never done this before. I keep trying to say it is not the fault of any one person. Then I suddenly remember the cop who called me at three in the morning to demand a statement because they were going to make a dawn raid and I think: "Bugger that, you really were an utter idiot who didn't understand the first thing about the crime or the perpetrator." I talk of the calls I was getting – sometimes twenty a day – from all the different agencies, different branches of police, investigations teams, welfare support, victim support, Thames Valley Police, the Met. All trying to do their best; none in touch with the other. So I end up feeling I don't even have time to do my day job, which is also a night job, as I'm too busy answering the same questions many times over. I talk of seeing a custodial sentence meted out but knowing all too well that it will be immediately chopped in half and that we will be back here all over again within eighteen months, arresting the same man for the same crime and watching the same sentence being doled out.

And I explain that this pattern of systemic failure exposes a more profound issue: whatever sentence he's being given isn't working as a deterrent and whatever treatment he's being given isn't working as a cure. He is also a victim in this, I remind myself. Stalking is a weirdo-glamourized way of describing unhinged behaviour. He's mentally unwell. He's wasted his life on this and I'm sure that would never have been his intention if he'd been of sound mind. Somewhere along the line we have to change the mechanism: the broken record of endless prosecutions and short custodial sentences and repetitions of the same crime, and the prolonging of the victims' discomfort because nothing ever changes or goes away. I know I am repeating myself but I need to hear myself say it, to make sure I've said what I wanted to say.

I say that the fact he was able to write to me from prison was a pretty serious breach. How it makes a complete mockery of the institution. That he was still able to contact me whilst serving time for the crime of contacting me puts one beyond despair. And I concede that I have been well sheltered from much of this – kind, generous colleagues and the BBC investigations team who've tried to protect me from it. That's because I'm really privileged to work somewhere it's taken seriously and I've had excellent pastoral care and I've been able to raise my voice because I'm quite well known. But what happens, I ask, when those protections aren't in place, when there isn't a place of work that can check you're OK or deal with the nasty letters or talk to police on your behalf? There are many, many more people who don't have that, and this interview is about trying to change a system so that it covers everyone – including people who are coming across stalking for the first time and have the chance to stop it being something that will dominate their lives.

We have covered a lot of the legal ground, the systemic problems, and Emma is keen, gently, to nudge me towards the more personal stuff, which she has left until the end. Exactly as I would have done, I remember thinking. Don't start with the hard stuff. Weave it all into the fabric.

She mentions Mark, my husband, and reminds me of the impact statement that I had so carelessly sent off into cyberspace without ever thinking it would be front-page news.

Mark, I say, has been my voice of humour and reason. The person who's helped me not to take it all so seriously, the person who's quietly, jokingly, offered to hire a variety of hitmen, or pick up and move continent.

But he's also been incredibly practical: calling police when I'd had enough, sitting with me through every detective visit, offering them wine as if it were some neat social occasion he was delighted to be hosting, and cataloguing the date of every call, visit and letter.

And I tell the story of the very first visit the police

made to the house in the early days of our marriage, when they pulled Mark aside and told him, 'You're the one we're really worried about.' How they warned us both that night of what they've seen happen so often before: a frustrated husband takes the law into his own hands, goes out, decks the guy, and you end up with the wrong person in prison.

We speak for half an hour. It has been easier than I thought. An entire reservoir of previously unuttered thoughts emerge with a coolness and a clarity of which I am actually proud.

And then Emma says, by way of winding things up, 'Is there anything you'd like to tell others out there going through the same thing?'

And for some reason I freeze. There is nothing like an invitation to be eloquent and profound to make you stop feeling like Gandhi and start sounding like Homer Simpson. I want immediately to say 'no'. As if I am scared to universalize what I've been through: a thoroughly female trait, I now realize, never to want to 'speak for other women's experiences'. Except if not now, then when?

I remember thinking, I do not want to end the interview on Facebook-post cliché ('Be brave' or 'You're not alone') and in fact I barely remember the words I actually used. I am already in post-interview mode, my head churning through everything I feel I haven't said properly and all the other things I fear I've over-laboured. It is as though I'm trying to be both interviewer and interviewee, thinking through every possible ramification of my words, working out almost as I speak which lines will become headlines, which phrases will be picked up in the papers the next day.

When we do finally end, I thank Emma and run along to my own interview in Westminster with Labour frontbencher Rebecca Long-Bailey. Ten minutes later I remember what I should have said as an answer to Emma's final question. *L'esprit d'escalier*, they call it: the thought that hits you on the staircase moments after you've left the room. The clarity of the perfect answer that it's just too late to give. But I ask Emma if she can add it into the back announcement. 'Tell people,' I say 'that you're not being stupid to report it or say it out loud. Just tell someone.' In truth, it will be the most important thing I learn from the day. That people will write to me about their own experiences – more men than women, curiously – and nearly everyone will start by saying, 'It sounds a bit silly, but . . .' That is the first thing we have to end.

That evening the programme is difficult. Some days work; others are an uphill struggle.

I fail to recognize the impact just downloading my own thoughts will have had on my ability to concentrate on anything else. I've also been running, geographically, between Westminster and Broadcasting House and it feels as if precious time has been used up in traffic.

By the time I get back to the office, one of our producers has had to leave for hospital and our editor has kindly gone with her, so we are two brains down and we have interviews to prep – and that's when things start going wrong. I am more fraught than usual, yet more desperate than usual to be brilliant on air as I don't want to be defined by the stuff I've been talking about. I want to be a Broadcaster again, not a Moany Victim.

On the programme that night I have two gymnasts who were victims of abuse by the former US Olympic team doctor Larry Nassar. But the poor woman who's booked them is the one who's had to rush to hospital, so I never get to hear from her first hand any of her concerns. Plus, they are down the line, on an outside source, from Michigan, which has a terrible time delay.

They come at the end of the programme, with no report beforehand, no pictures, just a straight interview. The British press has not covered the story that fully by this point, so I need to explain to my viewers who they are, why they're here. Before I know it I have made the cardinal error I have so despised others for making. I ask the women in Michigan 'what happened' to them. As soon as the words are out I want to claw them in. I don't want to make these women relive and repeat their own abuse. Goddammit, I've just spent an hour explaining in my *own* terms how unhealthy that can feel to victims. So what made me do it? I start beating myself up for the question even whilst the interview is going on. One of the gymnasts starts to explain. She gets quite graphic, discussing the form the abuse took, how she was routinely fingered during medical examinations, describing where the doctor put his hands.

I am trapped. I don't want her to feel she has to relive

all this, to tell me everything, but neither do I want to cut her off. When I interrupt her, thinking she is getting upset and trying to tell her it's OK not to go on, there is a bad jump on the line: she carries on speaking and it sounds as if I'm shouting over her.

I look rude and heartless, the confluence of bad timing and an unpredictable satellite connection, and I am just mortified. I say often that television interviewing is more about tone than anything else. Ask whatever you like but get the tone right. On the occasions when I misjudge, or mistime, I want to sink into the ground. This was one of them.

I leave the studio that night without going to the usual post-programme briefing as I am too fraught and too upset. I barely sleep – my dreams are full of accusations of hypocrisy: why would I not repeat my own history of abuse on air but ask others to do just that? In reality, I was probably just winding myself up ahead of the interview, which was due to air the following day.

I had given the interview to 5 Live but I normally wake up to Radio 4. Suddenly shattered and confused, I couldn't remember BBC protocol. What if 5 Live shared the interview with Radio 4? What if I had to wake up to my own voice, being replayed as soundbites, on the radio the next day? I was in a cold sweat just imagining it.

Thankfully, as twenty years at the organization should have taught me, there is still a fair amount of BBC silo mentality. An interview for one station doesn't just slip on to another. Or not immediately, at least. I woke but heard nothing, luxuriating in the sound of familiar parliamentary banter. My first shock, though, would come on my morning run, from Alice Thomson, soulmate and fellow journalist, who tells me she's 'seen the interview'. You can't have, I say, it's radio. She shows me her phone.

And then I pause, mid-run, to realize how ridiculously naïve I have been. Nothing is ever 'radio' any more. Everything is being filmed. But no one thought to mention it. And sure enough, I will return to find pictures of me with my sniffling nose and my son's bright blue hoody and my slightly bloodshot eyes and I won't know whether to laugh or cry. That after a career in television, an – clears throat, pompously puffs out chest – *award-winning* career in television spanning two decades, I was idiotic enough not to realize that the private little radio interview I had given – slouched down in my chair, manky tissue clutched in hand – was pasted all over the rolling news channels and social media sites of every UK daily.

And I am laughing because what I am now regretting more than anything is not the intimate detail of what I said, or what I left out, or even how badly my own programme had gone the night before. No. What I am regretting is that I didn't put eyeliner on. That if I was going to be pasted around the media for twenty-four hours as a victim, then, honestly, I just wanted to be a pretty victim. All my principles, all my sound advice, my wise words offered up to the world, crumble with recognition that what I needed most was a vital bit of superficiality and a dab of under-eye concealer.

*

The interview itself is well received. People are kind. Colleagues at *Newsnight* are always lovely but never more so than then, understanding perhaps why I've seemed like such a stressy bag of nerves for the past few days. There are curious invitations to do 'more' interviews from Belfast and the US, and the UK papers. *The Times* asks me if I'd like to do the Saturday interview to discuss both the BBC pay gap and the stalking. I laugh and say you only get to moan about one thing at a time. Anyway, I'm thinking, Never again. I need a duvet day.

But the next few days will remind me why I did it. MP Sarah Wollaston gets her stalking victim protection bill through both the Commons and the Lords, and pays tribute to my case in Parliament. I am thrilled to feel a part of that. And letters start to come in. From friends saying they have experienced the same thing but have 'never spoken about it before'. From a high-profile male presenter who wants to discuss it for the first time. From women who tell me their own experiences match mine, word for word. And for a while I will carry on fearing I have said too much, somehow created a new role for myself, opened myself up a little bit too deeply.

But it is what I ask our guests on *Newsnight* to do every single night. Many with far, far more painful experiences than my own. Sometimes, I think, it pays to be the interviewee for a day just to remind yourself what a terrifying experience it can be.

Anthony Scaramucci on the
White House Lawn

Television interviews come in all shapes and sizes. There are the ones you plan for weeks and weeks. You chat on the phone first; you send samples of your work to show that's what you do. You listen to their concerns, you sympathize, you encourage. You work towards something that you hope you will both be happy with. Those are the interviews we put heart and soul into getting on the show. People like Zelda Perkins, Bill Clinton.

And then there are the interviews that are so seat of your pants you can't actually believe they've happened. Anthony 'the Mooch' Scaramucci, on 26 July 2017, was one of those. I still think of it as one of our greatest broadcasting triumphs. Not because of anything he actually said, but simply because we got him to agree to it in the space of about four minutes. Whilst we were already on air in London.

Let me put it in context then. It was a Wednesday in Washington DC, a frustrating sort of end-of-the-trip day when nothing had really come together. The story of the week was about a UK–US trade deal and whether our poultry import standards would be compromised post-Brexit. The UK media had dubbed the problem 'chlorinated chicken' (or my personal favourite: 'swimming poulet', a reference to the system American poultry processing uses to disinfect the meat).

The morning starts at the National Chicken Council of Washington DC in the office of a man called Tom Super. It is a lacklustre interview, to be brutally honest. But I use it to ask everything I've ever wanted to know about the poultry chlorination process. So it is quite short. It is all meant to be part of a wider piece, and we are hoping to drive out to Delaware to find real chickens on a real farm. And, for good measure, we also have a bid in with the White House to cover the afternoon press conference with Sarah Huckabee Sanders, who's just taken over from the beleaguered and fired White House communications spokesman, Sean Spicer.

Sartorially, the day presents something of a challenge. I do not want to appear on a chicken farm in the Broiler Belt counties out east dressed in something that looks chicly tailored for the White House. I also do not want to appear in the West Wing wearing wellies and a processing-plant hairnet. It is one of those days where anything or nothing could happen so, in the end, I go smart and pack trainers, leggings and a fleece into my overstuffed handbag.

It is whilst we are interviewing the perfectly named and indeed unflappable Mr Super that confirmation pings through that we have gained access to the afternoon's White House press conference. I have covered the extreme oddities of America throughout the last three election cycles but, unbelievably, I've never actually been inside the White House grounds. I am almost too embarrassed to admit this to the colleagues I'm with, Maya Rostowska and Jack Garland (my producer and cameraman), also first-timers. Like a bunch of shaggy sixth-formers behind an imaginary presidential bike shed, we are all quietly determined to play it cool.

Access to the White House involves all the worst elements of American immigration with an extra layer of security and media distrust thrown in. It involves sitting around on the ground in 30-degree Washington July heat for nearly an hour hoping for an escort. It involves forms and waiting and X-rays and waiting and equipment checks and waiting and passports and then suddenly we're in and extraordinarily free to roam wherever we want, as if once the job of the front-gate guard is done, we're no longer their problem. We head to the press briefing room – the James S. Brady Room of the West Wing, to be precise, a place elevated to galactic magnitude in Hollywood but which is in reality a minute theatre the size of a large greenhouse. We are there early to set up and the place is empty. It gives us the delusional sense we are free to sit anywhere. In reality, every single seat is accounted for: paid for and engraved with each news organization's title, the stamp of custody and history. I crouch temporarily in the seat marked *Time* magazine, waiting to be moved. My camera crew position themselves across the room at an angle, a way to catch both the press conference and any question

I might be lucky enough to ask. And then we just have to wait.

My colleague Cordelia Lynch at Sky News has advised me where to stand. The out-of-towners, she explains, never get to ask the questions. Even the foreign media 'in-towners' rarely do. 'You have to intercept the spokes-woman's gaze – cut into someone else's question.' It sounds an excellent way to make yourself deeply unpopular in DC and get chucked out of the briefing in seconds. But I am drinking it all in. After an hour or so of empty room, there is a manic rush just before 2 p.m. The pass-holders come charging through the door and every seat is suddenly full.

There has always been a hierarchy of importance here: American network TV, American cable TV, papers, periodicals – foreign news distinctly last. The Trump administration has scrambled the traditional pecking order, inserting his personal favourites: Christian radio networks, One America News Network, papers with a sympathetic leaning – but the bottom half still remains: foreign news distinctly last. Sarah Huckabee Sanders enters the room ten minutes late, then spends the next ten minutes showing us a cute kid video to illustrate a philanthropic story no one will really remember. It's eat-ing into question time and my palms are burning up with the fever of impatience and fear. Then she points to the journalists and the theatre starts. First up, the front row. John Roberts at Fox, by Trump tradition; Major Garrett at CBS; Peter Alexander at NBC. It is a shield of impenetrable shouty front-row maleness. I don't stand a chance.

Then Sanders's eyes start to throw further out to the crowd. I am holding on to the wall with my left arm and leaning my right arm high up and way out in the hope of commanding attention. I am also conscious that everyone in the room that day is asking if Jeff Sessions, Trump's attorney general, will be fired. Unlike in UK press gatherings, where the media work as a pack to move the story on, here the same question appears to be asked over and over again. It is, I will realize later, so that each correspondent can be seen to be asking it in the camera cutaway for their own bulletin piece. In other words, the story doesn't move.

My own question is not so concise. It will contain the phrase 'chlorinated chicken', make reference to the UK environment secretary Michael Gove, whom no one has heard of, and will ask about a trade deal with the UK that no one else in the room cares about. It is, in other words, a long shot. Huckabee Sanders hops from one correspondent to another. Each time someone near me or around me is pointed to, I launch my impossibly long and unintelligible question. There begins a kind of media filibuster; I am trying to speak longer and louder than the bloke in front whom she may really be pointing at. It is a stand-off and I keep going until his question gets even louder and he is closer and so he wins. It happens a couple of times. Each go, I think I'm nearly there. And then suddenly, just when I'm in my stride, seizing the media ground, the whole thing abruptly ends. Trump's spokeswoman goes back through the wings and we are dispatched.

I join the rest of the team with a sinking feeling. We have nothing to give London. We were in the West Wing but we have nothing to show for it except some general footage of the inside of a briefing room. A heaviness descends. We call London and tell them not to bother leading on us. And so they put us second in the running order to offer a quick wrap: a view from Washington and an interview with a White House insider, Sebastian Gorka, a prickly guest but a loyal friend to Donald Trump, whose contributions mainly entail telling us the BBC is all fake news. Our camera is set up on a stretch of grass called Pebble Beach; it offers a view of the White House in the background and the sweeping curve of the drive through the ground just behind us. We are readying the shot in the changing light of a summer evening. Sebastian Gorka has appeared once and dispatched himself, angry not to be the top story. We have asked him to return in fifteen minutes.

It is as my cameraman is lining up the shot, correcting the focus through the lens, that he suddenly says, 'I think that's the Mooch, isn't it?'

Now let me explain. The Mooch is a mythical creature. Larger than life Italian-American New Yorker, financier, entrepreneur and, for one long week only, White House Director of Communications. It is he who has seen off the beleaguered Sean Spicer from his job just five days earlier. He is the man of the moment. Dashing in a sort of 1980s Bond-villain way with his extravagantly shiny hair and white teeth. Maybe a hint of the Fonz thrown in. He is walking along the path behind us with visitors who are clearly being given the tour of the White House. They are taking selfies. No one lasts long in the Trump administration: they've learnt to take those selfies whilst they can.

So back to Jack, the cameraman and his spot: 'I think that's the Mooch, isn't it?'

Jack is not required to know by sight each and every member of the White House administration. He has enough to worry about with lenses and lines and satellite feeds and the ever-rushed edits of pieces. Yet it is Jack who sees him and, thankfully, has the nous to say it out loud. I have my back to the Mooch as I am facing Jack, ready to go on air. I am wired up: a mic running down my back and an earpiece that connects to London gluing me to the spot. From the depths of my inner prima donna I do something I will never live down and just stand there imperiously shouting, 'GET HIM!' Maya, the wonderful producer at my side, leaps off, long Pre-Raphaelite hair streaming behind her; she will try to track him down and intercept him on the lawn. Then I realize the ridiculousness of my own command. I have to make a call. Do I run after Maya and see if we can somehow tease the Mooch into coming live on the programme? Or will we actually miss our live broadcasting slot when they throw to us in Washington and we are nowhere to be found, already out of sight, halfway up the White House drive? I make the most bonkers decision of my career to date, pull out the earpiece, unhook the lapel mic and dart off after Maya. Two panting and rather over-enthusiastic women arrive at his side, one with a microphone lead trailing behind her like a stray dog, just as a rather purse-lipped Chinese woman is asking for a selfie with him.

I cannot remember our opening gambit word for word, but the essence of it is: 'We are from BBC *Newsnight*, we know who you are, come over to our camera, we're live on air in four minutes, it'll be fun.' It sounds slightly odd when I see it written down but, broadly, I think that's what we said.

He looks at Maya. Looks at me. Looks at the Chinese woman trying to take the selfie. Then looks past us to Sebastian Gorka, who is at the end of the line-up. Gorka, to his utter and endless credit, doesn't hesitate. He pushes Scaramucci towards us and says, 'Go and do it. They're BBC *Newsnight*.'

What I remember most about these fleeting seconds is how little he asks. He doesn't know our questions, our format, our intent or even how long he'll be speaking for. But he gets that we are credible and he says yes.

The handholding during that encounter which endless commentators will write about actually starts there. And it is not him manhandling me, it is me grabbing his arm so tightly that he is unable to change his mind or escape. I lead him towards Jack, who has initiated the whole process but still can't quite believe Scaramucci has ended up in front of the camera. And we mic him up quickly – the audio equivalent of handcuffs – so that he can't suddenly change his mind. We do a sound check; my heart is racing so hard I find it hard to keep my voice steady as I try and tell London, sotto voce, who we have for them in Washington. That night's programme editor, Stewart Maclean, looks up at his screen and cannot quite believe his luck. He makes an instant decision that he will 'float' out anything that is not essential in the back half of the programme to give us as long as we need. And I am listening to the programme through the earpiece. They are having a debate on UK trade deals which seems, at that precise moment, interminable.

Then it is our turn. They throw down the line to me, and I suddenly realize I have not even had a chance to think about what I will say, or how to explain who he is to our British audience. They all know Sean Spicer, so I open by saying he is the man who has led to his resignation. And then off we go. I begin by asking about the story of the day, whether Trump is going to fire his attorney general, Jeff Sessions. Scaramucci cannot possibly know. (No one knows. Not even Trump himself.) But he uses it to launch his loyal defence of his president and what he calls a 'more open approach'.

'One of the things I cannot stand about this town is the backstabbing that goes on here, OK. Where I grew up, in the neighbourhood I'm from, we're front-stabbers, who like to tell you exactly where we're from and what we're doing. And so, to me, if you can handle the president's personality, you can handle his temperament – which I happen to love – then you're going to do great with the president.'

Without a breath, he turns from his defence of DJT straight to me.

'Do you live here in Washington?'

I am caught off guard – his tone is halfway between flirtation and emphasis. 'No,' I reply, waiting for the sucker punch.

'OK, see, you're lucky for you that you don't live here in Washington because what happens here in Washington is people say one thing to your face but they don't really mean it. And they say something else behind your back. OK, so what I like about the president, it's actually good leadership to say the things to people's faces, what he actually means, and then let's resolve it or not resolve it. We're either going to reconcile or we're going to go in different directions. But at least now everybody knows how they feel. What I love about the president – you don't think I've had tough conversations with the president, him and I? Of course we have, we've known each other for a long period of time – what I love is that he's a remarkably loyal guy. The loyalty, though, has to be symmetrical, and good loyalty is always symmetrical. You don't want asymmetrical loyalty. But he's here for a reason. The American people are fed up with this city, and so I'm calling on my friends in the city, a lot of these guys I like in the House and the Senate, to dial it back, support the president's agenda. Because it's your long-term agenda and it's in your long-term best interests.'

He's a cross between a New York bruiser and a motivational sports coach. It just flows out of him but I need to get him to answer on specific subjects – like Russia and the meeting that was alleged to have taken place between Donald Trump Junior and a Russian lawyer during the 2016 campaign. So I step in and say:

'Let me ask you something. If you were running a campaign and somebody called you up and said, "We've got serious dirt on your opponent; it comes from Russia," would you take that meeting?

He barely pauses for breath. 'Most people would take that meeting. I think what I have issue with is that all of us, myself included, are political neophytes – and so [is] Donald J. Trump Junior, who's a dear personal friend of mine, and I can attest to all of your viewers I know he's done absolutely nothing wrong, and he will be completely and totally exonerated.'

'Neophytes'. Wow. There's a word I wasn't expecting to come tumbling forth from the Scaramucci faucet. Calling his boss naïve?

'I didn't say he was naïve, I said he was inexperienced. There's a difference between naivety, which is simplicity and some level of stupidity, and inexperience, which is, "OK this is something I have some curiosity about and I'm going to take the meeting."'

This is threatening to undermine every other thing that the president is trying to get done, I point out.

'I don't believe that.'

'You don't think it's damaging?'

'Absolutely not. I think it's damaging short term because there's a lot of nonsensical things that are going on because we live in a town that manufactures scandals. This is Scandals Incorporated down here, so what we do is we manufacture fake scandals so that we can disrupt people, we can hit them personally.'

He has unwittingly dismantled Trump's entire modus operandi against the Democrats in his own election campaign, but for now I let that pass.

Then Scaramucci plays his killer line. The one we've now heard frequently and forcefully from so many millionaires in power. That they are somehow 'the people' and the people (like me) asking questions are out of touch. This time, something snaps and I cannot let it go.

'What part of Donald Trump is not elite?' I say. 'The business side? Or the politics side? Or the inheritance side? What part of Donald Trump is not? Many people in the UK don't understand that.'

'Oh my God, there's sooo many things about the president,' says the Mooch, like a man desperate to think of just one.

'He's a celebrity,' I push, exasperated. 'He's a billionaire.'

'How about the cheeseburgers?' he says. 'How about the pizza?'

It will become the most famous line of the entire encounter. Anthony Scaramucci trying to defend President Trump from accusations of elitism because he eats

burgers. I burst out laughing. I am delighted. I recognize
it for what it is: a moment of rare, unadulterated television gold.

'Everyone eats cheeseburgers and pizzas!' I cry. 'What
are you talking about?' It's a question I wish I were brave
enough to ask more of our guests more of the time.
Sometimes it just says it all. But Scaramucci turns his
firepower on me.

'You're coming across a little bit elitist, so let me
just say something to you, OK. I grew up in a middle-
class family, OK. We had a tight budget and little to no
money. I spent thirty years of my life trying to get into
the global elite so I could stand here and serve the president, and I missed the movement. Do you know why
I missed the movement? 'Cause I tunnelled myself into
elites and we had this circular conversation about what
was going on, which was completely wrong.'

As I write this down verbatim, the message he's trying to get across becomes clearer to me. He's referring
not only to his time as a Goldman Sachs banker on
Wall Street but also perhaps to the fact that his past
has been politically ecumenical: supporting the Obamas (he was at Harvard Law School with Michelle),
then Wisconsin governor Scott Walker for Republican
president. Then Jeb Bush, one-time heir to a political
dynasty. He is working hard to convince me – in the
spirit of a man who's blurted out his ex-girlfriend's name
in the middle of sex – that Trump is in fact the one
for him.

So, I persist, he's telling me Donald Trump is not elite, then?

And he is sweetly confounded and looks like a puppy trying to hold two bones at the same time. 'Oh, very much so. He's both. He knows how to operate in an elitist world and he has unbelievable empathy for the common struggle that's going on with the middle-class people and the lower middle-class people. He has something that, frankly, I don't have, and it's embarrassing to me to admit it to you on a live television show, but I missed the movement. I grew up in a middle-class family and I didn't size the economic desperation that was taking place in my home town.'

The interview tumbles on; he is engaging and spontaneous and, frankly, unstoppable. We talk local Washington politics and global politics and then I hear the urgent voice of Stewart in my ear reminding me that we started the night in London talking about trade deals and he wants to know Scaramucci's views on chloronation chicken. Dear reader, it will not surprise you to learn that poor Scaramucci, five days into the job, financier, New Yorker, friend of Donald Trump, does not *have* views on chicken. He is disarmingly honest and says to me:

'You and I are meeting each other for the first time. I have no idea what's going on with the chlorine-rinsed chicken. And so even to pretend and make something up to you, I'm just not going to do that, OK. But if you want to interview me in a week or two, I'll figure out what's going on with chlorine-rinsed chicken and I bet I'll have a clever answer for you.'

It is the perfect response because it gives me the excuse to go back, in a week, a month, a year and pick up where we left off.

We have been on air nearly fifteen minutes. It is time to wrap things up but, before I let him go, I say, 'Last question to you. You've been in the job less than a week. Give us a sense of how it feels, what is it like being right in the centre of the White House.'

'I'm super-excited to be here. I had lunch with the president today . . . He looked over and he says, "Doesn't Anthony look like he's having a good time?" and the answer is yes.'

'You're here to stay?'

'We'll see. I'm here to serve at the discretion of the president. If he wants me to leave tomorrow, then I'm not going to be here to stay.'

'Great to talk to you,' I say. And he takes my hand, half shaking, half holding:

'Emily, sorry I called you an elitist.' He turns to talk to the camera directly. 'She's probably not an elitist but she was hitting me very hard . . . I didn't mean to call you that. I apologize to your viewers.'

It is only once the camera is off us and London has moved on that I look down and realize he has actually been holding my arm or my hand or my elbow for the best part of ten minutes. Twitter commentary has gone wild with the interview and all the touchiness. I have barely noticed. He is Italian-American and I am Jewish. That's culturally the same thing in terms of personal space.

I walk him back to the now shell-shocked Chinese guest. He cannot stop apologizing for calling me elitist. With something like pain in his eyes and a now even broader New York twang, he turns and says, 'Emily, my dad worked in construction for decades. He went *deaf* from the sound of the machines. And now I'm a millionaire and a banker and I know the White House. You know what that makes me feel?'

'Lucky?' I supply.

'Guilty!' he shouts back definitively. 'I have' – he gestures across the White House tax-payer-funded lawn – 'ALL THIS.'

And then from nowhere I produce one of the most bizarre reassurances and attempts at empathy I have ever heard. I start to tell him that I, too, grew up in a different place. In Sheffield, during the miners' strike.

Has he heard of the miners' strike? I ask tentatively, grasping for fictional references that might fill the knowledge gap. '*The Full Monty* was filmed in my town,' I say. 'Or perhaps you've seen *Billy Elliot*?'

He has seen *Billy Elliot*. He loved the musical. Together we clutch at that. Our shared reminder of former, poorer worlds.

Even though, truth be told, I have never been down a Sheffield mine or even known a miner, and *Billy Elliot* was actually set in County Durham. I think it was the adrenalin of the moment. But it still comes under the category of strangest things I've ever uttered. We say goodbye (another selfie, this time with the patient Chinese woman in the middle). My job is done.

The first thing I see when I check my phone is a text from my editor, Ian Katz.

It just says: Holy Shit.

Somehow, after the verbal jousting and the verbosity, the hot air, the hand-holding and the hand-wringing apologies of the past half-hour, those two words seem to be the only possible response.

Five days later, the Mooch will be gone. Fired from his job after accusing White House strategist Steve Bannon of self-fellating, and calling the chief of staff, Reince Priebus, a 'fucking paranoid schizophrenic' to a journalist whom he says he didn't realize was putting every word he said on record. It is the only possible ending to the ball of fire that was Antony Scaramucci: White House comms director. For ten and a half days.

But, as he predicted, it is not the last time we meet. In fact, we keep meeting. And each time I forget to ask him for his updated response to chlorinated chicken.

Stuck in a Lift with Alan Partridge

I am sitting in Make-up. My hair is in in Velcro rollers, tissues are tucked into my collar to protect my clothes, and my eyes are shut. I'm aesthetically vulnerable, in other words. As I perch there mouthing words to myself, I feel the presence of someone by my chair. I open my eyes and see a mint-green shirt, a navy blazer, stay-press beige trousers and a slicked-back gel combover.

It is the embodiment of sports casual. It is unmistakable. It is Alan Partridge.

He greets me with an awkward hello. Bends down to kiss either cheek tentatively around the make-up, and asks if we're all right.

We are. We just very much are. I can hardly speak.

The invitation, five weeks earlier, had been an unusual one. Would you like to come into the BBC on a May bank holiday to film a scene where you go up and down in a lift for five hours, being yourself. On every level that would be a no. Except the scene is with Alan Partridge. And my love for him knows no bounds. Alan has been the third person in my marriage from the early years of *The Day Today* series when, more than a decade earlier, I realized that my daily job as a TV journalist was being satirized to perfection by Chris Morris, to the long car journeys where we played the audio book of *I, Partridge* for the kids and their admiration for him blossomed as we looked on (via the rear-view mirror) with fulsome parental pride.

This is the moment, then, when I realize I have made it: I, Maitlis, have been chosen to star (yes, let's leave it at star) in the new BBC series where Alan Partridge is finally allowed back on telly.

I, Maitlis, have interviewed presidents without losing my cool. Prime ministers without breaking a sweat. I've met David Beckham across a signed Real Madrid strip and chatted to Usain Bolt about the speed of my whippet.

But this is the moment. My professional coming of age: I get to rehearse going up and down in a lift for five hours with Alan. And my enthusiasm is verging on indecent.

And because it is a bank holiday, the family have decided they are coming too. I don't remember inviting them, actually. They shadow my steps as if they are my personal security detail, holding open doors, carrying bags, cleverly making themselves indispensable so no one will ask awkward questions. Thus it is that on a baking-hot Monday we head into New Broadcasting House laden with a suitcase of 'things that make me look like Emily Maitlis'. Which, for some bizarre reason, is harder to find than it should have been.

I am shown through to the costume department.

They tell me that what I'm wearing is fine and I look just like Emily Maitlis. Then I am hurried into Make-up, where I am given a script. (A script! The Maitlis character has real lines!) I am practising them under my breath with varying indistinguishable intonations when Alan himself hovers for the aforementioned two-peck. He is already Alan; he is definitely not, in other words, Steve Coogan. And for the entire day I shall call him Alan because my big scene with real lines surely warrants method acting.

My *Newsnight* deputy editor, Adam Cumiskey, a besotted fan himself, had been coaching me earlier. 'Remember, when you meet him in the lift, he's not Alan Partridge, he's the bloke in the BBC canteen you spend your days and nights trying to avoid. He's the person you didn't realize still worked here. The one you sort of thought was dead.'

I can tell Adam is nervous that I will let the *Newsnight* side down by being a bit girly and star-struck. It is very important to Adam that we, as a programme, get this right.

I am so determined to play it cool – despite the rollers and the collar tissues and the scrunchy-eyed mad mouthing moment – that I come across as deathly serious and Alan looks a little scared by the intensity with which I have adopted my role. 'I don't think I would say "Cheers",' I explain, flapping the pages I have been given. 'It's not what Emily Maitlis would do.'

'No, that's OK, then. No.' He sighs quietly and draws a line through the script. 'You say whatever comes naturally.'

My son, Max, aged eleven, is hovering outside Make-up. Max's claim to fame is that he once had to call the school IT administrator to unlock his computer and explain that his password was 'Anal dirge prat' – adopted from a chapter in *I, Partridge* and which highlights the unfortunate anagrams associated with our eponymous hero. I am unsure whether to reveal this. It seems to paint me as a terrible mother who has little idea about her son's cyber life. But then I am. And I don't. And once I have accepted this we decide to tell Alan. He looks quite chuffed but sympathizes with the schoolboy awkwardness. 'Did your teacher get the reference?' he asks Max. And Max says, fortunately, he did, yes, and they both enact a mock wiping of relieved brows and the moment is made. Max tells Alan he is, in fact, Simon Fisher: the small precocious child (played by Doon Mackichan) on the original radio show *Knowing Me Knowing You*. The scene ends, from memory, with Alan threatening to push Simon Fisher into a disused canal, Alan hitting Simon, and Simon weeing with fear down his own leg in the studio. I am torn between nodding at Max's decent efforts to find cultural hinterland and fearing we might reawaken the Alan that doesn't like small children if we go too far down that track in the moments before we start filming.

I am led over to meet the scriptwriters and we all head off to what feels like the situation room; an all-white space with sofas in circles where we will practise our lines until we get the full feel.

In this scene Alan has accidentally become the host of *The One Show*. He is interviewing a hacktivist – who is wearing a giraffe mask for anonymity – but it's going so badly that the hacktivist storms off air, leaving Alan running after him. Alan jumps into the lift in hot pursuit and that's where he finds me. Original script as follows:

ALAN

Why don't you finish the interview? I know
you can hear me under there. Why?

WOMAN IN LIFT

Can you press floor 2?

ALAN

Why won't you finish the inter— Oh my God,
Emily Maitlis. Pleased to meet you — Alan
Partridge. Just wanted to say I'm a huge
admirer of your whole technique. You really
strike the right note.

HACKTIVIST

Yeah. Tenacious without being aggressive.

ALAN

Exactly. Thank you. I like the way you ask
questions with a biro between your first two
fingers. It just works.

EMILY MAITLIS

Cheers.

ALAN

And if I'm allowed in the current gender
climate, can I just say you bring a welcome
bit of class to Newsnight and leave it at
that.

EMILY MAITLIS

Very kind. Thank you.

ALAN

I'm sort of doing the same thing you do.
Just been interviewing this chap. A
hacktivist, trying to wriggle off the
hook.

EMILY MAITLIS

Have you put it to him how hypocritical
it is that they're being funded by
people with a totally different political
agenda?

ALAN

Yep.

HACKTIVIST

No, you haven't.

ALAN

Haven't I?

HACKTIVIST

No.

ALAN

Emily, I'm just going to roll the dice here.
Can I have your email address?

EMILY MAITLIS

No. I'm sorry.

ALAN
    (seeking instant recovery from
    humiliation)
I think this building is an architectural
triumph.

*Lift doors open. Hacktivist and Emily Maitlis
leave.*

We read through the whole scene with the writers, our scripts on our knees. We discuss Alan's response to celebrity (he is in awe of me! Ha ha); Alan's response to the Me Too movement ('He doesn't care about women but he cares about sounding as if he's at the forefront of a trend'); and then my response to Alan (you would *never* give him your email but don't want him to badmouth you around the building).

It is – and this is the funny bit – intensely serious. I sense myself trying *so hard* to get this right.

I ask if I would be horrified by Alan's presence. Would he be a huge, lumbering lift presence smelling of body odour? And Alan is quick to correct me. 'No, no, he would smell of many artificial things, like a car show-room, but definitely not have body odour. No, he'd be very conscious of that.'

We do not emerge until the lines have been learnt and the scene is flowing. Then it is time for the lift. Normally, the crew explain to Max, we would just remove the whole side of the lift so we could film straight through. But because it's actually a working BBC building we are not allowed to take a screwdriver to it. We must put the camera crew in the lift with us. It is a crowded affair. Alan and Gavin (the hacktivist) enter the lift as Gavin is fleeing the interview. Two extras are in the lift to give the scene texture. I am squashed into the far corner, only spied once the extras have exited.

Take 1: we roll.

The first attempt shows the difficulties of trying to

cram the length of the script into the time of the lift descent. We land at the bottom with way too many lines to go. A red marker pen goes through the script, and the lift journey is slowed down by pressing more buttons en route.

We try again. This time the extra ('Woman in Lift') forgets to mention her floor when she gets in.

Each time we end at the ground floor we must reset, recall the lift, and head back up to the seventh floor. By the fourth time everyone has a curious sort of claustrophobic vertigo. It is time for a break, KitKats and crisps.

Clearly, I catch myself thinking, there will be no Toblerone because of Alan's unfortunate Toblerone addiction, detailed with such raw honesty in his autobiography. There are bottles of water provided for each of us – mine has a straw to avoid lipstick smudging.

I am feeling more diva than Mariah Carey.

By now, they have Max 'on cans'. With headphones he can listen to the audio and correct me when my intonation is a bit off. He cannot be in the lift with us, but he manages to appear wherever we are each time it stops and we reset. I overhear him offering 'helpful tips' to the lead director and wonder if my own dear Simon Fisher might need to be gently gagged. But the crew reward his observations with kindly, encouraging noises. And his day is made when Alan tells him, one day, he's going to make an excellent director.

We pause to make a few script tweaks back in the situation room. This time Max sneaks in, promising not to talk. We are firming up the lines, the timing of delivery, when Max – his promise of four minutes ago now forgotten – instructs Alan calmly, fearlessly, not to rush into his last line about architectural triumph. Everything goes silent. I cower – anticipating an explosion. Alan manages a sideways glance but, mercifully, says nothing. I exhale. Max has won a reprieve from a disused canal. For now, at least.

Back in the lift for three more takes. I am getting confused now between the new extras joining us in the lift and the random BBC colleagues who seem to be in the lift anyway without realizing we are all being filmed. I start explaining that we are filming to people who already know that we are filming because they have been hired to be in that bit of the film. I am getting a bit hot and dizzy with all the up and down.

We have by now sorted the lift timing to fit the script, or perhaps the script to fit the lift timing. And even though Alan has the lines written down they tend to be delivered differently, fresh, every turn.

It is getting better and better. I am more relaxed, Alan is more funny, I have the performer's gut instinct that this time will be the perfect take. We come to it: the build-up, the stare, the reveal when, suddenly, I hear Alan fluff my name. Maitlis becomes Mailtiss, or Maylice, or Maiekeliss. Not dramatically wrong but just a little off. So much for the performer's gut instinct, I think. And start to climb to the seventh floor again for a brand-new take.

But no one else comes with me.

Suddenly, it's all over. There are kisses and hugs and thank-yous and a big round of applause as everyone gives everyone else a clap.

My face is blank. I do not understand what just happened. Surely we are redoing the scene so that my name is right? I am searching faces but I'm told it's a wrap, it's over. 'But my name,' I start explaining to anyone who will listen. 'You see, my name was . . . I think maybe we need . . . I heard the . . .' I am mumbling about the Maitlis. But the set (such as it was) has already been dismantled and everyone is delighted with that last take and indeed very happy on this bright bank holiday Monday to call it a day and go home.

And as I pick up my coat and my case of Emily Maitlis outfits, and the water bottle which still bears my Mariah Carey anti-smudge straw, I take Max's hand, which begins swinging gently at my side. He is not talking about the name, or the indignity of them getting it wrong, or the last take.

He is beaming from ear to ear. More worryingly, he is about to accost the nearest stranger to explain – in unforgiving detail – just how extraordinary and unforgettable our afternoon has been.

How to Interview through
a Balaclava

In the three years from March 2016 the epidemic of knife crime in UK cities had risen by 52 per cent. And in the first six months of 2019 in London alone it led to ninety attempted murders and some eighty killings.

As I write I can see how shocking those numbers are. But what shames me is that we at *Newsnight* were in danger of missing how bad things had got. We had made documentary films about County Lines, the drug running and the gang violence the summer before, but recently we had become obsessed with Brexit, the psychodrama that sucked the lifeblood out of virtually every other news story. The serial boxed set with an increasingly implausible plot was strangling our ability to see real things happening around us; we'd all become hypnotized by 'no deal' hypotheses and parliamentary poker.

The stabbings and deaths had something of a pattern. The victims were often but not always young men; often but not always black. The crimes took place predominantly but not exclusively in the less affluent parts of the cities. And the danger, we began to realize, was that we would begin, subconsciously, to normalize this extraordinary and horrific rise in violent crime. When organized crime gangs were blamed, or when it involved County

Lines drug running, when it was the same neighbour-
hoods and the same names, there was a danger we'd
assume it was somehow all the same murky story, rather
than an individual, unimaginable murder of our young
each time.

Three months into this year the trend had become
impossible to ignore. And on one weekend in March two
fatal stabbings were announced which broke the mould.
One was of a young woman, Jodie Chesney, stabbed in
the back in the playground of a Romford park. She was
seventeen years old, a scout leader and a self-confessed
'proud geek'.

The next day, Yousef Makki, a teenager of the same age
who attended Manchester Grammar School on a scholar-
ship and dreamed of becoming a heart surgeon, was killed
by a 'friend' in a row over cannabis.

No homicide is any worse than any other homicide and
no teenage life is more important than any other. I mention these details just because it marked a turning point
in the mainstream British media coverage. It was as if
we had all collectively sat up and realized that we could
no longer pretend it was a trend that was somehow
self-contained within a criminal underworld. It could
be everywhere and it could be anyone. There is something deeply uncomfortable about acknowledging that
it was the deaths of a beautiful young white woman and
another smart academic kid from a well-to-do neighbourhood that forced the story on to the front pages and the
top of news bulletins. But news is – at its crudest and

rawest – about novelty. That's how it works. And this time was no different.

The Wednesday after these deaths we had our usual *Newsnight* meeting. We were now less than a month away from our exit date from the European Union, parliament was in pieces, compromise had failed and no one had a clue what would be happening in four weeks' time. But the progressive accumulation of knife killings and the circumstances of the latest teenage deaths made us realize the domestic agenda had been pretty much obliterated in the concentration on parliamentary amendments and the world's worst-named piece of legislation in history: 'the Meaningful Vote'. We chose to lead on knife crime that evening. But we would approach it from a policy perspective. Had the ten years of austerity contributed to what was happening on our streets today, or was the prime minister right when she said there was no correlation between cuts to police numbers and certain crimes? Was Stop and Search a valuable tool in identifying criminal behaviour before it had happened, or a policy too often driven by prejudice that drove communities to distrust local police with disastrous consequences? We sought to bring together a panel that could speak from the left and from the right. That would give us Whitehall theory and street-smart reality. That would bring together gut instinct and hard data.

In the end we chose the Walthamstow Labour MP Stella Creasy, whose constituents had included some of the youngest victims of knife crime. She'd attended their funerals. We had Shaun Bailey, the Conservative candidate for Mayor of London. He'd been a youth worker for over two decades and an adviser to David Cameron as PM. A black man raised by a single mum in a council house, he shattered the stereotype of what a traditional Conservative looked like. But he was an advocate of the 'hand up not a handout' school of welfare reform, and hated the idea of benefit dependency. Dame Louise Casey had advised four prime ministers on social welfare and crime. Our last panellist was a drill musician, a Chicago-originated style of trap music: dark, nihilistic and often violent in its lyrics. He went by the name of DrillMinister – he never appeared in public without a balaclava; and he would, we hoped, widen the parameters of the debate away from political partisanship.

It is a *Newsnight* practice to record our opening menu some ten minutes before we go on air. It allows us to bring in and showcase all the contributors that will be in the programme and to rehearse any of the more technically complicated bits of the opening sequence. This time was no different. We would have around ten guests through the course of the evening, and wanted the top panel to be there in our headlines menu. Four chairs had been laid out around a coffee table, with glasses of water for each guest, on what we call the 'soft set'. This is where we hold discussions. Three seats are filled: Stella, Shaun and Louise have made it there on time. The last is empty. I am looking nervously over at the fourth chair, not wanting to start before all our guests are in place, but not wishing to leave it so late we miss our chance to record it properly. I have an earpiece which allows me to hear the gallery and a microphone which allows me to talk to the producer and director, but, as is also custom, they have turned me down so they can concentrate on getting things straight without having to listen to me mithering. Five minutes to on air I start to mime, waving my hands at the camera to get their attention. Have they realized we are missing our fourth guest? There has been no sign of DrillMinister and it is almost 10.30 p.m. My phone pings. It's the assistant to the editor telling me that DrillMinister has arrived at the BBC but they won't let him in. 'What?' I text back. It sounds astonishing but there's no time to be astonished. Another text. 'Security won't allow in a man wearing a balaclava and he won't remove the balaclava. I think they're having a stand-off.'

In this late panic I suddenly recall Caitlin Hanrahan, a youngish, very bright producer who had raised this prospect hours earlier. How we had all laughed insouciantly at her youth and then gone back to making tea for our biscuits. I am slightly regretting that now. I hear myself asking if they can get security on the phone. 'I'll talk to them!' I say, as if expecting a Red Sea parting of the waves at the very mention of my name. They ignore me. The tussle between our man in the balaclava and BBC security is going on at the main entrance. They say he can't enter the building without having his photo taken by the ID unit. He won't remove his balaclava for the photo. They won't do the ID without the photo. They are locked in administrative wrangling whilst I am three floors below nervously counting down the seconds to our broadcast. Finally, they reach a compromise. They will allow him down, but only if he agrees to be escorted the entire time. Caitlin is happy to oblige.

She has battled him through the frontline security, but now encounters another wall of defence and more demands for a photo. It seems DrillMinister is a folk hero to the BBC doormen. They are star struck and invite him to stop for selfies.

Caitlin is now tugging in what she hopes will be an urgent but non-aggressive way at DrillMinister's sleeve. She is metaphorically holding his hand and her tongue until finally, she is able to deliver him with the tender care of an obstetrician, right into our arms.

There is a commotion in the studio and in walks DrillMinister, large, layered and behooded. He wears smart grey sweatpants. Grey top, black coat, black bala-clava. And, oddly and incongruously, on top of the balaclava but beneath the grey pulled-up hood he wears steel-framed glasses: the one identifiable bit of the musician's entire head. Scampering two paces beside him is his flunky. He waits until DrillMinister is sitting in his chair before saying in a semi-conspiratorial whisper that only I pick up: 'I checked out the room, boss. There is no evil eye.'

I can't quite believe what I'm hearing. It was anthro-pologist David Graeber who first coined the term 'bullshit jobs' to describe the existence and societal harm of utterly meaningless work. It was a phrase perhaps born for this moment alone: a music manager type whose role is to tell his diva employer that our *Newsnight* studio *is not cursed*. And – I find myself thinking with something curiously approaching indignation – he has arrived too bloody late to even know if that's true. How *dare* he write off our putative preternatural dealings with so little due diligence?

I do not, however, dwell on the spiritual dimensions of Studio B, Basement 3, New Broadcasting House for long because we are suddenly on air. We open with the comments made by the former Met police commissioner Lord John Stevens, who accused Prime Minister Theresa May of not listening to police advice. She was warned as home secretary, he explains, of the ramifications her cuts to police numbers would have on crime. Nick Watt, our political editor, has done our top piece: part reflection on the horrendous legacy these crimes have on families and communities, part analysis of how much policy was to blame. And then we are into the panel discussion. Shaun Bailey says he's with the PM. That the scene has changed and that you can't blame gang violence each time there's a stabbing. Stella goes straight for the government's jugular; she remembers a time when she could help build relationships with the police and the local kids but things are too tight now – they've lost two hundred officers in her borough alone, as well as mental health workers. The fourteen-year-old whose funeral she just attended was the sixth little boy buried in the last eighteen months. Don't tell me – she turns her fury on Shaun – that resources don't make a difference.

The argument is real, heated and based on the experiences of both. But I need to widen it to include the other panellists. I bring in DrillMinister. My editor has made it clear that we must not just ignore the balaclava as if we are at some peculiarly English tea party of upper-middle-class in-laws. We must confront it, and explain to our audience that we recognize it's not entirely normal to see an unidentifiable panellist.

'We don't know anything about you,' I begin gently, 'and you wear a balaclava. Explain to us what that's about and why we should be listening to you.'

DrillMinister responds, 'I wear a mask because it's about my message for my music. That's the first thing I'd put out there. The prime minister is talking about something she doesn't actually understand. It's not for me to chastise her or diss the woman or whatever, but she's not in these areas, she doesn't walk those streets, she doesn't see those incidents, she's not in those school lessons where the teachers are kicking out the youths at fourteen . . .'

At first I think he's making a point about class. But it's actually more subtle than that. It's about character. It raises an issue that has arguably tailgated Theresa May ever since the fire at Grenfell. Do we want her to be a street empathizer? Or a practical doer? Do we have to see her grieve, cry, wring her hands? Or do we just want a pragmatic, financial response to a crisis?

I am about to step in and ask but DrillMinister is already on a roll. Lyrical. Visceral. Unstoppable.

'You want to talk about this and cuts and all these fancy words. But when I see the woman selling her body on the street to feed her kids I don't see no Theresa May there.'

I am half hypnotized by the image he's rattled off, imagining Theresa May sizing up a South London prostitute. But then I realize what he's just said. It's utter rubbish.

'When you say "Cuts is a big word",' I suggest, 'it's not. It's a very small word . . . Does that have an impact on what's happening on the streets or not?'

I feel pedantic. But it also seems to me to be important. He is attempting to cast the discussion as one that out-of-touch liberals are having. 'Fancy words' is a way of gaining currency as the authentic voice when – truth be told – all the panellists know what they're talking about. Stella has seen it first hand; Shaun has *lived* it first hand, resorting to petty crime as a kid – by his own admission – to make ends meet; and Louise has been working with homeless people for decades. I wonder why the musician who wears a mask and lives in fear of the evil eye gets to cast himself as the true believer.

DrillMinister continues unabashed. 'Cuts is a word because people are surviving. They're not surviving easy, they're trying to adapt . . . We didn't ask for cuts, we didn't ask for bankers to be bailed out. This was You Man's job. You Man messed up. Now you're blaming youths. But what about the schools? What about the mums who ain't got no good leg . . . ?'

No one has blamed the youths themselves. Literally no one.

But I am trying to work out whether he's saying 'humans' or whether he's saying 'You, man' to Shaun, the government representative on the panel. The balaclava means it's all a bit blurred. There's too much wool to hear properly.

Louise Casey saves the pause. 'I'll put it in Whitehall language,' she says, 'but there's no doubt he's right. There's a dissonance between the political classes having views that ring hollow. We're not "left behind", we're "kept behind",' she tells us. She blames the concentration on Brexit that has seen knife crime and domestic violence and child poverty all rise. I feel myself redden as if I am partly to blame through our own journalistic priorities.

It's at this moment that it becomes a little surreal. Stella Creasy leans in to DrillMinister. I think for a moment she's about to take him on. Instead she says, 'This is what is so frustrating for me. And you're right, DrillM— if I can call you Drilly?'

I hear through my earpiece the gasp of a muffled laugh from my programme editor China Collins. It threatens to ignite my own squashed giggle but I know I cannot afford to lose it when the subject matter is so serious. Is Stella being ironic? Is she subtly marking territory as a fan of his music? Or is it just a gesture of friendliness?

Perhaps we will all now start calling him Drilly, as if the ice has been broken at our AA meeting.

Stella is still talking, and I am concentrating on what she is trying to explain. I am concentrating so hard that I miss the moment of the interview that will ultimately go viral. A moment that Twitter will not get over for several more days.

Because I am looking in her direction, I do not see DrillMinister lean forward. I do not see the moment he picks up his glass of water. I do not see the second he puts it to his lips – forgetting he is wearing a balaclava – and is unable to find the hole. I do not see the moment he spills water right down the front of his jacket. But our studio cameraman has not missed a beat. He has swooped in like a magnificent bird of prey and captured the whole movement. It is this – these twenty seconds of footage; this one gesture – that will come up whenever anyone searches for DrillMinister's *Newsnight* appearance amongst the press cuttings. It is the unforgettable vision of a bloke who's come to tell the politicians how life really is, unable to find his own mouth.

After we come off air I head to the gallery, one floor up, for my usual debrief with the team. It has felt like a long night. A night in which we had a stand-off with security over a guest, had to run the headline sequence live because of the subsequent delay, had to reassure said guest we had no malign studio spirits before he was happy to appear on the show, and had to mop a load of water off the studio floor.

China is really pleased with the show. The discussion has touched on so many things: the causes that lie behind the knife crime epidemic and the cost of not looking at more rounded solutions. All the guests have been worth listening to; all have been passionate and outspoken and thoughtful about their own experiences. China is the perfect editorial combination of upbeat and realistic. 'I think we got there,' she reflects, scrolling gently through her Twitter feed, which is now in overdrive. 'But perhaps it might all have been a little easier without the balaclava . . .'

Taking Back Control

During the long sweltering summer of 2019 the nation became obsessed with a group of contestants living in isolation from the outside world, constantly under video surveillance and given air time on prime-time television six nights out of seven. For normal people that meant *Love Island*. For political hacks it was the Conservative Party's leadership contest. It began the day that Theresa May formally stepped down as Tory leader. And it went on for six endless weeks. It was hailed as a chance to find our next prime minister but it involved the votes of just 160,000 people – the party members – or a mere 0.3 per cent of the British electorate.

Many sensed they knew how the contest would end before it had ever begun, with the crowning of the man who as a child had dreamed of becoming World King: Boris Johnson. But if the outcome was already written in the runes, the process itself was tortuously, perhaps deliberately, formalized. There were endless hustings and interviews, speeches and debates. From a crowded field of ten candidates it would be whittled down to just two by the parliamentary party: the MPs. Then, the members would be asked to make their choice. And our new prime minister would emerge, phoenix-like, from the ashes of those who had been cast out.

The BBC decided to produce a debate at the high watermark of the process. And I was asked to host it. The phone call I had with my producer was perhaps the first indication it was untrodden ground. 'We don't yet know when it is. And we won't know how many are in the debate. And of course we won't know the names of the candidates that are in it.' The date eventually chosen was 18 June, a Tuesday in the middle of the knock-out stages. It was, they reckoned, the day on which the number of candidates would be reduced to four – if we were lucky.

We just wouldn't know which four.

The morning of the debate I am up early, running and swimming the Serpentine. Trying to clear my head and prepare for an event which is still anything but clear. We will not know who's been knocked out and who's made the next round until 6 p.m. that evening. And we are due on air at 8 p.m. For that reason the briefing chats have been broad and open. The BBC has – controversially – decided against having a live audience. Live audiences, my producer explains, are fraught. You need to double-check everyone's background to ascertain there's no imbalance. No one trying to use the event as a platform for politicking. Put like that, it sounds sensible. Instead, we have invited questions from across the country via email. The people who have written in will go to their local BBC studio on the night and pose their question to the candidates from there. It has not – at this point – even occurred to me to ask why this should be any different from a live audience. We have a good idea of what the questions will be, but nothing will be nailed down until we know the actual identities of the panellists. And by the time we know the panellists it will, in any case, be impossible to ask new questioners to get themselves to a BBC studio in time for the live debate. In other words, we have contrived to make this whole feat as logistically difficult as possible.

The other thing that's controversial this time around is the furniture. Where once we would have placed each speaker behind a podium, it has been decided to ditch the traditional debate prop and instead use something that is a cross between a chair and a stool. Large white space age buckets. But high up with steel legs. The birth of the chool. The director thinks it gives a more modern feel to the set. In any case, he explains, if they're not sitting down their heads will be chopped off by the large screen behind them. I nod as he explains all this, assuming it's not quite as literal as it sounds.

Just before six o'clock we gather in the green room to watch the results come through and work out which of the six men left standing have gained enough votes to go on to the next round. All the women have already disappeared from the process, which will make the optics of the debate look rather lopsided. I cannot ignore the fleeting thought that this is why I've been asked to do it.

There needs to be at least one woman on stage amidst the man wall.

The elimination process is less glossy than the *Love Island* one and takes place in the committee room of the 1922 Conservative backbenchers in parliament.

Exactly 313 ballots have been submitted and this is the moment that Dominic Raab – our former Brexit secretary and arguably the hardest Brexiteer of the lot – is knocked out. Extraordinarily, the maths means that all the other candidates have made it through. There is a heart-sinking moment when we realize we must have five candidates on set instead of the hoped-for four: the recognition that everything will feel a bit more rushed, too crowded. We have been given just an hour for the debate, and there are to be ten questions from members of the public. What had seemed doable with four candidates is in danger of feeling cumbersome with five. We head back to the stage to rearrange the space age chairs. The one that had been earmarked for Dominic Raab is now pulled from its place, and tumbled sideways into a corner behind a big black curtain. A cull that is somewhere between brutal and comic.

The remaining chairs are arranged on stage in a horseshoe like an orchestra. But instead of placing me in the centre as the conductor, I am positioned at one side so that the large screen showing the questions from members of the public is not hidden from the candidates' view. They have had their advisers pick lots to choose the order of seating. Dominic Raab had been directly at my side, but now he's out I see I have Boris Johnson at my elbow. Next to him is Jeremy Hunt, the foreign secretary, who will eventually go on to fight the contest with him. Michael Gove, the environment minister, is after that; Sajid Javid next; and at the end the maverick of the competition: Rory Stewart, International Development Secretary, an insurgent who has energized the race from the left by not playing to the same tub-thumping Conservative base that the others have.

Fifteen minutes before the show begins I head on to the set to record the opening trail. One by one the candidates troop in to try out the chairs. It is like watching newlyweds in a bed showroom as they gingerly lower themselves down and bounce up and down. The stool format has caused consternation. And the worst bit is, it is directed at me, as if I am the bed showroom facilitator who can explain to them pocket spring numbers and the two-year warranty process. They ask me how they should sit, where they should look. I don't feel qualified. I don't want the responsibility. I only met the chairs an hour ago myself. And I am trying to get us on air.

At 8 p.m. we are launched and we open with a question from Lee, in Norwich.

Which of them, he asks, will commit to leaving the EU by 31 October.

Some have explained that if they need more time they will ask for it. Johnson has pitched his campaign on a 'Deal or No Deal We Leave' rallying cry. Yet this time he appears to row back – talking about it being eminently feasible rather than imperative. I have to check I've heard him correctly. But he won't actually stop talking.

The second question comes from a woman in Southampton, Carmella. She's worried about No Deal, her husband's job and her children's future. Can any of them reassure her? This time, the moment is held by Michael Gove. None of them can entirely calm her concern, no, but he turns directly to the screen and without irony, but with an ultra-large Govian blink, declares, 'Well, Britain is a very great country.' She doesn't seem entirely convinced.

We hop between studios around the country, questioners and my own unruly panel of five. We have ditched the conventionality of the opening statement to give us more flexibility, but this means that everyone is fighting for airtime. The volume goes up and the clarity goes down.

There are more questions on Brexit and the Irish border, on austerity and climate change.

And the news lines are coming thick and fast. There will be plenty for the bulletins to work with tomorrow. Jeremy Hunt admits that cuts to social care via the austerity programme went too far. Boris Johnson decides he'd no longer stop the Heathrow expansion he once said he'd lie before bulldozers to prevent. Rory Stewart confirms no early tax cuts or spending sprees.

We take our next question. It comes from Abdullah, an imam. Rory Stewart – famously once deputy governor of two provinces in Iraq – greets him with an as-salam alaikum, as if he's just encountered him on an eighteenth-century Silk Road. The imam explains he's from Gloucester. His question is about the effect on his community that he's perceived from the language that gets thrown around. 'Words', he says, 'have consequences.' It is such a profound phrase and it comes just after Katie Hopkins has been writing angrily and provocatively about 'Londonistan' and Donald Trump has been retweeting her to consolidate his good kicking of Sadiq Khan, London's mayor, two weeks earlier.

The response to Donald Trump has been interesting. From some, forthright condemnation. From others, a reminder of the need for diplomacy. When I get to Boris Johnson – a man renowned for his colourful and occasionally corrosive language – I ask him if he agrees words have consequences. Does he recognize that his depiction of Muslim women as letterboxes has had an impact on how people in Abdullah's community feel? He starts on what is possibly the oddest rant of the night. About his Muslim great-grandfather coming to Britain from Turkey. The force of his xenophilia is slightly lost, however, by his repeated inability to remember the name of the questioner. 'Abdullah' is the one name of the whole night that he forgets. And to those watching on TV, it speaks volumes. He is ignoring the phrasing of the question itself, choosing his own anecdotal, familial response.

It is a tactic I have been warned of by none other than former prime minister David Cameron, who had told me over dinner at a friend's that they will each attempt to 'not debate' with each other. They will not engage with the interlocutor, he warns me, and they will try and speak down the barrel of the camera.

Now I am watching it in action. It looks bizarre. Boris Johnson is steadfastly refusing to acknowledge my questioning. I actually have to ask him if he can hear me, and I am close to laughter, realizing how odd it must look to viewers, the effort being put into shutting me out. I repeat the words Abdullah has used: 'Words have consequences', and this time I bring in Johnson's own words to MPs in a select committee about the imprisonment in Iran of the British woman Nazanin Zaghari-Ratcliffe: a phrase he used to them – 'When I look at what Nazanin Zaghari-Ratcliffe was doing, she was simply teaching people journalism, as I understand it.'

It was a statement that was not only incorrect but one that her husband and many others believe significantly increased her prison sentence. So I ask him there, finally, whether he recognizes his own words have had consequences. Does he accept, in other words, that his did for her? He does not stop talking to respond.

Sajid Javid, the home secretary, has previously called for an independent inquiry into Islamophobia in the party. Would he like to take this opportunity now, I ask, to see if the other candidates will join him? He does, seizing the bait and emerging triumphant as they all fulsomely agree to his inquiry. It is Javid's finest moment of the hour.

The last question comes from Aman, a lawyer from London, who asks about mandate. Do they recognize how little authority they have been given to govern by this contest? A nod to the 0.3 per cent of the electorate who will be calling the shots. Will any of the candidates call an immediate general election?

They won't. And on that note of party unity we end; the show comes to a close. Stewart and Javid attempt a group hug – the two of them anyway; the others head off the stage wondering what's just happened. It has been a shouty, irascible affair of undeliverable promises and little concession to the intransigent realities of Brexit. It has been awkward in parts, but it has yielded plenty of breaking-news lines – on Brexit promises and GATT tariffs, on austerity and tax – but without an audience in the room there has been no sense for us of how any of it has landed. Jeremy Hunt gets the audience vote that night. He has certainly seemed the most gracious of those on the stage. The one most at ease with the format – answering directly, without interruption, and then just shutting up. He is the only one who thanks me and the team for the event as he leaves the stage. It is something I do not clock until much later.

In the green room I and the rest of the BBC team try to catch our breath. The programme editor has heard from the Johnson team. They are angry about the Abdullah question because they believe it was pointed at Boris

Johnson. Perhaps they are worried that he emerged from the segment poorly. Certainly, it suggests a deeper concern about his presentation. But each question was relevant to all the candidates, and was meticulously put to each one of them – we have stuck to the rules of engagement.

I cannot dwell for long on the post-show reaction because I must go straight on to do *Newsnight*, where we have two full panels of supporters and agitators lined up to help us make sense of the hour we have just produced, including Boris Johnson's own father, Stanley, who will try and interpret what we have all heard with paternal insight. Never before will I have been in a position of having to analyse an hour of television in which I have been centre stage.

It is too meta. Too fast. Too bloody odd.

I leave the studio before midnight, having agreed to do the *Today* programme the next day. More post-match analysis. I have set my alarm for eight-thirty to do the eight-fifty slot on the phone. I'll wing it, I think. But my subconscious knows better. I wake, as I should have predicted I would, at 4 a.m. Winging it is for the men, perhaps. I cannot do insouciance as readily as I pretend I can.

I need my notes. My collected thoughts. My felt-tip *highlighter pens.*

The interview goes without incident. For an hour afterwards there is calm. I run the dog, swim, clear my head of the night before. Then the calm is shattered by a text from the show's producer. They have discovered controversial tweets on the imam's own social media pages. He has made ugly claims about Israel and has said extraordinary things about women and rape.

The team is utterly confused. They had asked him if he had a Twitter profile. He had told them no, that it had been deactivated. Now it's back, clearly visible, and makes it look like we haven't done our homework even though the team has been irreproachable and thorough. I know instantly the next twenty-four hours will be brutal. The very phrase Abdullah uttered in the debate – 'Words have consequences' – will come back to bite him – and by implication us. Words *will* have 'consequences'. It will be grim all round.

Within half an hour my suspicions are confirmed. A text from Lynton Crosby, the Australian election strategist who is running the Johnson campaign from the shadows. He has sent me three tweets from the Guido Fawkes website: two are write-ups of Abdullah, the now infamous imam; one about Aman, who asked the general election question. Aman works – it now transpires – for a law firm Labour had used in the past, something the BBC did not make explicit.

'This is why', the text from Crosby reads, 'I don't engage with the BBC. Sorry.'

It is the 'sorry' that gives the tone away. Turns it from indignation to triumph. It reads like a man delighted that he's found a distraction. He is the one who made famous the 'dead cat' strategy: when something is going wrong on a campaign (an answer, a debate, a candidate's performance) you look for the 'dead cat': throw into the mix the thing that has the power to divert attention, to make the public look elsewhere. I wonder what we should all be looking at now.

I cannot pretend that the revelation of Abdullah's tweets has been anything other than a massive and horrendous own goal for the BBC. But right now, it's also the greatest thing that could have happened to the Johnson team. It's their dead cat, as it allows them to shut down any further access to Johnson from a position of hastily acquired moral authority. They will push it out to all the newspapers, exploiting it for all it's worth.

At a Murdoch summer drinks party – to which I have accidentally tailgated Piers Morgan – later that week, I find *Sunday Times* columnist Rod Liddle, who offers me a sip of his extremely good martini. He is keen to debate the debate with me. And there is certainly plenty to discuss. He wants to know why Islamophobia was even a question from the public. 'Why didn't you choose one on immigration?' he asks. 'Because,' I explain, 'of the hundreds of emails we received from the public virtually none discussed immigration. They think Brexit has fixed it all.' It goes to the heart of a bigger issue: should the debate try and harness the real questions people have written to us about? Or the bigger, fundamental questions they didn't actually ask? We have gone for the former. There will no doubt be a review.

'Why didn't you have a live studio audience?' Liddle asks next. And I explain to him and the Murdoch editors gathered around that the vetting process needed for a BBC audience is complicated and costly and often results in accusations, fair or unfair, of imbalance. And then I have to laugh at my own painstaking and rather BBC corporate clarification as I realize that is where we have ended up anyway, in an absolute shocker of a political hijacking mess. And I wonder how I have become the one trying to explain debate process and protocol to a roomful of Murdoch guests when I didn't even want to have responsibility for the darn stools.

As ever after a big event I will spend the next couple of days wondering what I personally could have done differently. Half my critics will berate me for my interruptions. And the other half are telling me I should have gone in harder. Perhaps I should have conducted from the middle. Perhaps the whole thing would have been better with more time and fewer people. Or maybe the very nature of the beast – at that fraught stage of the leadership contest – was that you inevitably get more heat than light. And the results are rarely edifying.

Unusually for me, I cannot point to one specific thing I could have done differently. No question I should have asked. No question I wish I hadn't. There is no thunderclap middle-of-the-night moment of clarity and regret.

I turn to Hannah, a friend, for her honest opinion.

'Chairs,' she says idiosyncratically, as if we've walked into an Ionesco script. 'You should never have allowed the chairs. Chairs are for heated discussions. Podiums are for debates.' I raise an eyebrow of thanks and go off to contemplate the vastly overlooked feng shui element of the evening. She is probably right.

In the end, after a seemingly endless six weeks of debates and discussions, interviews and hustings, Boris Johnson will become prime minister on 24 July. Jeremy Hunt, who has fought a tough campaign alongside him, will be fired as foreign secretary and take to the back benches. Michael Gove will be back in as Boris's cabinet enforcer, Sajid Javid as his chancellor. Rory Stewart, who swore he could never work under a Johnson premiership, will resign. Indeed, a stunning seventeen members of Theresa May's cabinet will quit or face the sack. Less a reshuffle, more a purge. Inside Number 10 Downing Street we will see the key strategist and advisers from the 2016 Vote Leave campaign. The band, it seems, is back together. They have done what they always promised and Taken Back Control. As if the three years in between – the Theresa May years – had never even existed.

It is the outcome, in other words, so many had predicted the moment the Brexit referendum vote was over. And it will make me – a journalist, not a fatalist – consider whether this moment was already set in stone. The Sophoclean ebb and flow of a narrative already written long before it comes to pass.

And a contest that began with a dozen contestants isolated from the outside world? By the time we'd looked up from the Tory Contest, *Love Island* was already finished.

We still don't know which of the two will have a longer shelf-life in the public imagination.

Moody Takes the Train

The dog has a limp. I discover this when I return from my *Newsnight* shift at midnight on Tuesday as I'm helping myself to a medicinal vodka. He still manages to make it over to the fridge, but it is a three-legged kangaroo sort of hop. He looks slightly deranged. First thing next morning we're at the vet's. We can't find the source of the limp but the back foot is infected and he's clearly running a temperature. 'On antibiotics. And off games for a week,' declares Johnny the vet. The dog looks miserable. Whippets do generally look soulful but this one looks positively suicidal when he hears the orders.

He barely moves from the sofa for ten days. Finally the kangaroo hop subsides and the antibiotics are done. 'I think', I announce, 'he needs a change of scene: fresh sea air and a bracing cliff walk.'

The dog looks at me witheringly. 'Don't anthropomorphize me,' he tuts. 'I'm a dog not a sodding Victorian orphan.' His language is terrible but I put it down to stress and let it pass.

It's been a busy week. Full of lots of shouty men shouting. I'd thought the BBC leadership debate was loud but they literally had nothing on the next night. Piers Morgan and Anthony Scaramucci battling it out in a Mayfair pub.

Piers is going on and on about Obama's deportation strategy just because no one else is. 'You liberals,' he rails, 'none of you either know or care that he was a deporting machine.' It seems an odd accusation to level at Scaramucci; then again, the Mooch definitely seems more liberal than Piers. We head from the pub to a Murdoch party, losing Scaramucci to a barrage of selfies along the way.

By Friday I am planning the seaside break. I want to combine a restorative dog trip with a belated birthday voucher I've been given for goat – yes, goat – yoga. The dog is sceptical. He genuinely can't see the point of yoga – he does the 'Downward Dog' naturally every time he gets off the sofa and thinks the whole thing sounds 'a bit liberal elite'. I threaten to send him to Piers for the weekend.

It is only when we arrive at our goat farm in Devon the next day, that his edginess makes sense. His reluctance is not to do with the yoga, but with the goats. It's jealousy. I should have guessed. They are incredibly sweet and tactile. They climb on your back whilst you stretch. They nibble your hoody as you try and balance. Clearly I will have to go into overdrive for the rest of the weekend to regain the love of my aloof and entitled dog. For twenty-four hours we do coastal runs and sea dips; we do midnight forays and bacon butties. Then it is time to go home.

And we time our train miraculously as the first raindrops start to fall.

*

The train is an overpriced and under-resourced affair. I have reserved a seat but my friends – who are getting on and off in different places – have not and we try and sit together. We land at a table that we share with a friendly young Spanish woman. The dog is squeezed on to the floor at the mercy of GWR sandwich wrappers, his head lying on her feet. I'm feeling guilty but she's delightful and reaches a hand down to absently pat his head as she reads.

An hour later she's left the train. Another man has got on. And put his bag on the seat next to him.

The dog is now sprawled between all of our feet, bony whippet limbs shooting off in every direction like antennae. At Reading, the chap leaves too. Taking his seat-bag with him. The dog has been remarkably still for three hours. But now he starts to stretch out (Down-ward Dog) and I remember the poor infected paw. There are two empty places at the table. The train is clearing out. The seat behind me has its own pair of feet on it.

The dog jumps up on to the seat next to me and instantly falls asleep.

And that, dear reader, is where the story ends.

Or should have done. But the next day, I see the dog everywhere. He has been photographed napping on the seat of the train. And I have been train-shamed by an outraged passenger who clearly didn't see his incrimi-nating photo also contained the feet of an elongated passenger on the row behind us.

'At least you weren't dribbling,' I say as we scroll through the photos. The dog is not amused. Whippets don't dribble. Ever.

He sulks off and I realize I have yet more work to do to win him back. He didn't like the antibiotics. He resented the goats. And he was squashed on the train.

An appalling thought occurs. One I can barely bring myself to commit to paper.

Has he set the whole 'pap snap' thing up to punish me? Teach me a lesson? Funny how those pictures just 'emerged' with such superb timing . . .

Clearly we are going to need to talk. This time, no goats. And I'll get him the bacon butty first . . .

Meeting a Prince

There is no easy way to ask a senior member of the royal family about their links to a prolific paedophile. There is no easy way to ask a senior member of the royal family if they had sex with a minor. I have been turning these formulations over in my mind on the way to the interview and, believe me, there just isn't.

I am heading across the courtyard of Buckingham Palace for the third time in as many weeks. I am lugging a huge silver Sweaty Betty bag bursting at the seams with shoes and jackets. It is so large and so bling that it looks as though I'm trying to move in. And I realize, as the armed police officers wave me across to the diagonal corner – 'look for the glint of red carpet' – past the sentry guards and the formal front gates, that once I leave I am unlikely ever to be invited back.

Where does the story of this interview begin? Perhaps with our formidable planning team, led by Sam McAlister, who a full year earlier had approached the Palace to ask Prince Andrew to sit down and talk. Perhaps it begins in May, when the Palace returned the interest, suggesting that he might want to discuss a whole range of things – trade after Brexit, his projects, and Britain's place in the world. His friendship with the convicted paedophile Jeffrey Epstein was the one area they did not want discussed.

This rings alarm bells with our deputy editor, Stewart Maclean. His news antennae – and discomfort with being told what can or cannot be addressed, will become instrumental to this whole process.

And so we decline – just out of principle. Red lines are never a good starting point for any interview.

But two months later – in a bizarre twist we never saw coming – Epstein is arrested on further charges of trafficking and exploitation of dozens of underage girls. And is found dead in his New York prison cell in August. It is only then that we begin to learn the scale and breadth of his exploitation, as his victims come forward to speak out – sometimes for the first time.

Prince Andrew had known Epstein and his girl-friend, Ghislaine Maxwell, for a decade. He had stayed with them, travelled with them, partied with them. What's more, he had been named in the legal deposition of one woman – Virginia Roberts – who claimed that she had been trafficked to him for sex on three occasions. What did the Duke of York actually know of Epstein's behaviour? And what had he himself done? Those questions were becoming harder to leave unanswered.

The Palace knew they had a problem. They had sent out statements vigorously denying the claims. But those perhaps lacked the conviction of a human voice behind them. And so we go to meet his team. They feel that a *Newsnight* interview is the only way to clear the air. To put across his side of the story. We feel we can afford no editorial interference. This cannot be a walk-round-the-garden chat – with a quick, euphemistic allusion to the scandal at the end. All the usual royal protocol will be out the window. This has to confront the issue head-on. Take the elephant in the room. Sit it down. And hear it speak.

Our talks are candid. All they demand from us is an open mind.

We discuss the now infamous photo that appears to show the prince's arm around the waist of a seventeen-year-old Roberts. Some of his friends had called it a fake. Were they suggesting the same thing, I ask. They shrug. 'We just ask you to consider everything.'

Our investigations unit had been sifting through the timelines, the court depositions, the photos, the money that's changed hands. We had tried to determine what had come from media interviews and what had come from legal documentation. We endeavoured to match up dates and places. Quotes and witnesses. Then, on Monday of last week, we return to Buckingham Palace. We propose a forty-minute extended interview – with a set-up piece to explain the background of all that had been said. This time, it will – fittingly – be Stewart's candour that will ultimately get the whole thing over the line.

We have finished laying out our pitch. An awkward moment of silence falls. And the duke tells us he must 'seek approval from higher up'. It dawns on us then that he means the Queen herself. At 8 a.m. the next day we have a message telling us to call his office. The Queen, it seems, is on board.

From that moment the week becomes a blur. We have set up the interview for Thursday, and for two days I must carry around the weight of what we're about to do without breathing a word. We draw up a list of far too many questions – every allegation, every twist in the narrative, everything we genuinely do not understand. We role-play the interview in an office the size of a kennel. The *Newsnight* editor, Esme Wren, takes the part of Prince Andrew and she bats away my putative questions by telling me – in assumed character – they're 'improper' or 'tasteless' – unbecoming of the BBC (she is, as it turns out, fiercer, more obfuscating and more threatening with me than the prince will be).

It is impossible ever to feel ready for an interview like this one. It will be one of a kind. But at 1 p.m. on Thursday I am bundled into the cab to the palace, with Jake Morris, the investigations producer, at my side. He has researched each question, cross-checked dates and quotes. 'What if I forget to ask about the photo?' I panic. 'What if I don't dare talk about sex in a bath?'

'I'll shout out anything you forget,' he says. It is too odd a thought even to contemplate. But at that moment I just believe he will.

This time, once we cross the courtyard of Buckingham Palace, we are taken into the Queen's own entrance. We will film in the south drawing room – in truth, a

modest ballroom – and we will reach it through a seemingly endless journey the length of the extraordinary
Marble Hall, where investiture ceremonies are performed. The walk is dazzling, stately and, frankly,
intimidating.

I am trying to understand the significance of the
Queen giving us her own formal quarters in which to
film, but it feels like a code I do not properly understand. Is she endorsing her son? The need for this
interview? Or am I reading way too much into every
step, merely because there are so many of them? The
door to the stateroom opens before me and all I can
focus on is the carpet, a swirling, blinding riot of reds
and yellows.

It is making me dizzy, but I can't take my eyes off it.
Which is why, as I trip into the room, Bag Lady Supremo,
I do not realize the duke is there before me. I have no
free hand to shake. And if I curtsy now I may not make
it back up again.

I quickly sidle off to the loo, see I have chocolate on
my teeth, and start to scrub with what I realize too late
is a palace hand towel.

This is the most disastrous start to any interview I
can imagine. And then I suddenly recognize it for what
it is: pure stomach-gripping nerves. And the recognition
of something so obvious relaxes me.

Back in the room, the duke and I begin the
preamble – small talk. He seems at ease, fascinated by

the mechanics of the whole process, laughing at the number of cameras Keith and Jonathan have set up. The sound engineer, Paul Cutler, comes to mike me up. The duke notices a trail of a wire from my jacket and is looking pained. His engineering brain has kicked in and it seems to him really obvious the wire should be on the other side, tucked around the opposite edge of the chair so it won't stick out. He starts directing the mike placement until the cameraman and the sound engineer are following his orders. He finally sits back, satisfied that he has solved a technical conundrum for the team. He does not seem particularly nervous. He doesn't seem like a man who's about to decide his own fate in an on-camera interview.

We start to roll. My opening question must be broad and encouraging. But it must also nod to how extraordinary this moment is. We are in the heart of Buckingham Palace and we are interviewing a senior member of the royal family about his paedophile friend Jeffrey Epstein and his own sexual conduct. The grandeur and splendour of the setting are thoroughly out of kilter with the seediness of the subject.

'Your Royal Highness,' I begin, 'we've come to Buckingham Palace in highly unusual circumstances. Normally we would be discussing your work and duty. Today you've chosen to speak up for the first time. Why have you decided to talk now?'

I'm expecting him to embark on a long ramble about his work and his royal duty. But he doesn't. He does something that stops me in my tracks. He just answers the question directly. 'Because there is no good time to talk about Mr Epstein and all things associated, and we've been talking to *Newsnight* for about six months . . .'

The elephant, it seems, has joined us. Right from the word go. And it is a relief to me to hear the name said out loud, an acknowledgment we are both here to discuss the thing we knew we must. And thus begins the most extraordinary encounter of my professional life. A man who has not talked publicly on this subject for a decade has now been permitted to do so and won't stop.

He tells of their friendship, and what he got from it. Tells of Ghislaine Maxwell, and how she had been the initial link. And he is vehement in the denials of his own wrongdoing. He cannot ever remember meeting Roberts, he tells me. I am trying to understand if he knows he didn't or if he just can't remember. It seems a vital difference. And I need to hear which he believes.

He pauses, thinks briefly, and tells me: 'No, I have . . . I don't know if I've met her, but no, I have no recollection of meeting her.'

Other things bring more clarity. He has come prepared to admit that he made a grave error of judgement – staying with Epstein after his conviction. He let the side down. 'The side' being Buckingham Palace and all it stands for. But when I ask if he regrets the Epstein friendship I get a breathtakingly candid 'no'.

He talks about the 'opportunities that I was given to learn by him' and he tells me he's guided by honourable behaviour, by which I think he means that you can't break up with a mate (who is a convicted paedophile) without doing it in person. He must have known what Epstein was like, I press. Roberts's legal team has said that you 'could not be around Epstein and not know'. The duke reminds me that he was a patron of the NSPCC. He would recognize 'what the things were to look for'. He swears he never saw them.

By now his words will have been pounced on and pored over. Bitten off, spat out. Chewed and, maybe, swallowed. People will make their own minds up about what they heard and saw. And some minds will have been made up long before they even saw him speak to me.

In person he is courteous, affable and eager to please. There is no question that he shies away from, no issue with which he refuses to engage. Indeed, I reflect afterwards that there have been more riders and red lines drawn in the interviews I've done with C-list celebrities and backbench politicians than with the Queen's reportedly favourite son.

From an interviewer's perspective he has been everything you could ask. Approachable and expansive, polite and generous with his time. He has given me fresh detail, new thoughts and told me things I had certainly never heard before. It is what we want from every encounter. It is what we long to hear.

Our news world is so often full of bland figures trying wilfully to be more bland. Say nothing. Avoid scrutiny. Dodge and deviate from every question asked. And whatever comes of this, I must admit to respecting an interviewee who is prepared to approach head-on every single thing that he is asked.

As we part, he walks me back down the Marble Hall until we stop at a statue of Prince Albert. 'The first royal entrepreneur,' he tells me proudly. 'Next time you come, we will talk about [his entrepreneurs' initiative] Pitch@ Palace.' It nods to the fact he feels he can now get on with the work he loves. But I probably shouldn't wait by the phone.

Back in the south drawing room I collect my bags. The floor is being transformed by palace workmen. It looks for a minute as if railway tracks are going down. The kind young woman who has shown us in sees my confusion. 'It's for the Buckingham Palace cinema,' she tells me. 'All the people who work here come along. It's *Judy* tonight if you want to stay.' But my day has already hit peak surreal and I think I need to disappear.

'Perhaps you want to get everyone along for Sunday,' I say. 'It's the new series of *The Crown*.' She looks moment- arily apologetic. 'We had *Downton Abbey* last week. But we don't do *The Crown* here.' With that, finally, it feels time for me to leave.

And Then They Died (End Thought)

When I was about six years old I kept a notebook of short animal stories I'd written. A year or so later, at the grand old age of seven and a half, I rediscovered it in a cluttered drawer and went through it with a critical eye. I remember thinking, in my new-found maturity, that the endings all seemed a bit twee, conventional and cheerful. Happy endings, I knew now, were 'for babies'. I corrected every one with a more sober, world-weary view. This time, the story about the puppy or the donkey or the kitten would end uniformly, with the same ominous phrase: 'AND THEN THEY DIED.'

It was perhaps my first encounter with revisionism, although that was not a word I'd come across for another two decades. The sense that the ending you understand — or even want — at the time is not the ending you'll think of as the right one in later years.

To some extent, this just involves an ability to let go, to offer up your version of the narrative at the point of going to print. But even in the time I've taken to write this book some things have changed.

Donald Trump is perhaps the most obvious example. How do you tell a comical tale of a New York businessman's beauty pageant when his presidential contribution to history is still being formed? How do you write about Bill Clinton in the age of Me Too, a movement that has the power to change – or perhaps we will see it as overcorrect – all our responses to the men of his era?

Some people in this book – James Comey or Steve Bannon or the Chinese student protestors or the Dalai Lama – have played their parts at a unique time and place in history. Others will disappear altogether from the narrative. And some we may choose to revise and rejudge. A friend was bemoaning the fact she'd made a film of Burma's Aung San Suu Kyi in her glory days as a Nobel Prize-winning human rights activist. It emerged from the cutting room at the height of the Rohingya massacre, when the world would come to see Suu Kyi very differently.

There is no solution to this except to ask for your indulgence. If World War Three is in fact started by Steve Bannon, I'll put up my (charred) hand and admit I got it wrong. If Sheryl Sandberg becomes the visionary behind the solution to Russian interference and fake news, I will accept I misjudged her response in the patter of her answers to me that day.

If people are allowed to administratively self-define not only their gender but their age and race, perhaps we will reopen the Dolezal chapter of history as a woman out of step with her time rather than her skin. Perhaps, who knows, this will be read when democracy is a staple of the Hong Kong political system and the European migrant crisis is a thing of the past.

My need to recount what happened here is partly a recognition of how much I've loved working in the centre of things. It's also by way of explanation to my kids, who understand better now than perhaps they did at the time why once again I'd failed to make the carol concert, or why the class bake-sale lemon cake looked as if the dog had got to it first (it had).

On a bigger note, it's also my attempt to recognize what Peter Morgan's character James Reston Junior in *Frost/Nixon* calls 'the deception of television', how 'it diminishes great, complex ideas, stretches of time, whole careers . . . to a single snapshot'.

A huge amount of thought goes into what we do. Interpreting moments of history whilst they are still unfolding is both deeply rewarding and endlessly challenging. Television news is messy. It gets things wrong. It is imperfect – sometimes laughably so – and sometimes you just nail it.

There is a concept in philosophy called 'the principle of charity' (introduced to me by the author Jonathan Haidt in his book *The Coddling of the American Mind*), which I have come to embrace more and more strongly the older I get. It requires interpreting a statement in the most rational way possible. Perhaps I would add to that: in the most benevolent way possible.

It doesn't mean we as broadcasters shouldn't correct our mistakes, apologize, seek to do better. That is an essential part of my job and always will be. But it presumes that an audience will try and reach for the most likely explanation first (a last minute let-down with guests, a traffic jam, a brain freeze or a totally human error). In other words, assume – as I stated much earlier – cock-up, not conspiracy.

This is becoming harder and harder to do in the age of social media and the hyper-rapid shared response. Some people use any perceived error wilfully to their advantage, to disseminate misinformation that matches their particular proselytizing propaganda. They are very few, and my message here will have little impact on what they choose to say and do.

My attempts to explain the backstories, then, are for everyone else. Anyone who has ever wondered how an interview came to be. Why it ended suddenly. How it came to ask some things and omitted others. Why a broadcast went wrong or why, against all the odds, it actually worked. Why some bits never make it to air. Why others get picked up around the world. How these chapters and characters of recent history were shaped.

This book, I hope, illuminates that combination of careful thought and utter chaos: the big deep breath that comes when you've lost contact with the gallery, the guest has walked out, the riot police are at your back and all you hear is the sole instruction to keep talking.

Airhead is homage to the jumble of noise, the whistle of silence, the blind panic and the ecstasy of adrenalin when the camera starts rolling – and it's all falling apart.

Acknowledgements

To my parents, Marion and Peter, for their endless love, wisdom and advice just in the places it was needed.

Hannah MacInnes, who became my voice of sanity on our infinite long runs, for her boundless encouragement and acute perceptions, without which *Airhead* would be floundering in a drawer.

Bridget Fallon, Alice Thomson, Simon Page, Lou Mitchell, Kavita Puri and Joanna George, for their invaluable friendship and perspective on all the things that matter and all the things that don't.

Nicky and Sally Maitlis, my brilliant sisters, for making me cry with laughter at deeply inappropriate moments throughout our childhood and long after.

Vilma and Garry Martinez for their exquisite care and kindness.

Joanna Thomaj, who helps me face the world.

Adam Cumiskey, for the brutal editing of the really pretentious bits.

Verity, her dad, and Banjo, who has a habit of sneaking into unusual credits.

My *Newsnight* colleagues, who have, sometimes inadvertently, helped write virtually every page of this book. I could not dream of working with a lovelier bunch of people.

ACKNOWLEDGEMENTS

David Miller, who told me I should write this book long before I believed him.

Ariel Pakier, my editor, who has worked so skilfully and thoughtfully to bring it to fruition, and Rowland White who was kind enough to publish it.

Richenda Todd, for her meticulous observations (and extraordinary patience making sense of my rather catholic spelling). Your work has been breathtaking.

Nicola Jeal at *The Times*, Terry Payne at *Radio Times*, and the *Sunday Times* for kind permission to reprint.

My teachers at King Edward VII School, Sheffield, for the best possible start in life.